WORLD WAR ONE, AMERICAN LITERATURE, AND THE FEDERAL STATE

In this book, Mark Whalan argues that World War One's major impact on US culture was not the experience of combat trauma, but rather the effects of the expanded federal state bequeathed by US mobilization. Writers bristled at the state's new intrusions and coercions, but were also intrigued by its creation of new social ties and political identities. This excitement informed early American modernism, whose literary experiments often engaged the political innovations of the Progressive state at war. Writers such as Wallace Stevens, John Dos Passos, Willa Cather, Zane Grey, and Edith Wharton were fascinated by wartime discussions over the nature of US citizenship, and also crafted new forms of writing that could represent a state now so complex it seemed to defy representation at all. And many looked to ordinary activities transformed by the war – such as sending mail, receiving health care, and driving a car – to explore the state's everyday presence in American lives.

MARK WHALAN is Robert and Eve Horn Professor of English at the University of Oregon. His previous books include *American Literature in the 1910s* (2010), *The Great War and the Culture of the New Negro* (2008), and *Race, Manhood and Modernism in America: The Short Story Cycles of Sherwood Anderson and Jean Toomer* (2007). He has published in *American Literary History, Modernism/Modernity, Modern Fiction Studies*, the *Journal of American Studies, Twentieth Century Literature*, and *African American Review*, and is coeditor, with Martin Halliwell, of the Modern American Literature and the New Twentieth Century series with Edinburgh University Press.

WORLD WAR ONE, AMERICAN LITERATURE, AND THE FEDERAL STATE

MARK WHALAN

University of Oregon

CAMBRIDGE
UNIVERSITY PRESS

CAMBRIDGE
UNIVERSITY PRESS

University Printing House, Cambridge CB2 8BS, United Kingdom

One Liberty Plaza, 20th Floor, New York, NY 10006, USA

477 Williamstown Road, Port Melbourne, VIC 3207, Australia

314–321, 3rd Floor, Plot 3, Splendor Forum, Jasola District Centre,
New Delhi – 110025, India

79 Anson Road, #06–04/06, Singapore 079906

Cambridge University Press is part of the University of Cambridge.

It furthers the University's mission by disseminating knowledge in the pursuit of
education, learning, and research at the highest international levels of excellence.

www.cambridge.org
Information on this title: www.cambridge.org/9781108473835
DOI: 10.1017/9781108563611

First published 2018

Printed in the United States of America by Sheridan Books, Inc.

A catalogue record for this publication is available from the British Library.

Library of Congress Cataloging-in-Publication Data
NAMES: Whalan, Mark, 1974– author.
TITLE: World War One, American literature, and the federal state / Mark Whalan.
DESCRIPTION: Cambridge, United Kingdom ; New York, NY : Cambridge University Press,
2018. | Includes bibliographical references.
IDENTIFIERS: LCCN 2018011148 | ISBN 9781108473835
SUBJECTS: LCSH: American literature – 20th century – History and criticism. | World War,
1914–1918 – United States – Literature and the war. | War and society – United States –
History – 20th century. | Modernism (Literature) – United States.
CLASSIFICATION: LCC PS228.W37 W43 2018 | DDC 810.9/3587391–dc23
LC record available at https://lccn.loc.gov/2018011148

ISBN 978-1-108-47383-5 Hardback

Contents

Figures

Acknowledgments

This book has been a long time in the writing, and so the list of people and institutions to which I owe various forms of intellectual and material debt is long, and doubtless incomplete. It gives me great pleasure to reflect on the various communities and relationships that helped shape this book, and I hope those listed here will also take some satisfaction at seeing their fingerprints on what follows.

I am grateful to the University of Exeter for providing a sabbatical that helped me conceive the beginnings of the project, and for supporting the work of my excellent research assistant, Rebecca Welshman. The majority of this book, however, was produced at the University of Oregon, and particular thanks are due to Harry Wonham, Paul Peppis, and Mark Quigley, both for bringing me here and for providing such enriching intellectual community once I arrived. I have benefited especially from Paul's tireless work in support of modernist studies in particular and the humanities in general at the University of Oregon, and have learned a great deal from his wide erudition in early twentieth-century Anglophone culture. The resources of the Robert D. and Eve E. Horn Chair in English have been indispensable in allowing me to write the book, and I am very grateful to the Oregon Humanities Center for awarding me time for writing and research in early 2017 through the Ernest G. Moll Fellowship. The heads of the English Department, Karen Ford and David Vazquez, have also been wonderful colleagues and unfailing in their support of this project; and the book gained considerably from Karen's mentorship and her enviable wisdom on how to read American modernist poetry. I have been fortunate indeed to work in two such friendly and impressive English departments, and Regenia Gagnier, Jo Gill, Jason Hall, Helen Hanson, Tim Kendall, James Lyons, Alex Murray, Sinéad Moynihan, Vike Plock, Helen Taylor, and Paul Young at Exeter, and Kirby Brown, Bill Rossi, Helen Southworth, Courtney Thorsson, Molly Westling, Betsy Wheeler, George Wickes, and Mary Wood at

Oregon deserve special thanks. One of the greatest pleasures of my career has been to work with the graduate students at the University of Oregon, and I have drawn many lessons from their scholarship, particularly that of Paul Bellew, Liz Curry, Hannah Godwin, Matthew Hannah, C. Parker Krieg, Stephen Summers, Avinnash Tiwari, Ramona Tougas, and Rachel Tanner. The Modernist Reading Group has also been a very stimulating and enjoyable forum for thinking about the relation between American modernism and war, and acknowledgment is due to its regulars and its occasionals alike. Thanks also to Beth Linker, Lesli Larson, and Mandi Garcia for their expert help in preparing the images for the book.

I am also grateful to the scholars who took the time to read portions of the manuscript, labor that considerably improved the final version. I benefited from the insights of Laura Doyle, Betsy Wheeler, Harry Wonham, and Paul Young in this regard, and also from anonymous readers at *Modernism/Modernity*, *American Literary History*, and Cambridge University Press. Feedback from colleagues at conferences has also been wonderfully helpful, including at meetings of the British Association for American Studies, the Modernist Studies Association, the American Literature Association, the European Association for American Studies, the Willa Cather Spring Conference, and at specially convened conferences to mark the World War One centennial held at the United States Military Academy, the University of Oregon, and at the British Academy. Claire Buck, Christopher Capozzola, Santanu Das, David A. Davis, Alice Kelly, Pearl James, Jennifer Keene, Hazel Hutchison, Patrick Joyce, David Lubin, Patricia Rae, Lisi Schoenbach, Vincent Sherry, Matthew Stratton, Stephen Trout, and Mark Van Wienen have all been important interlocutors for me in thinking through the issues of this book, and I am grateful for the conversations and friendships this book has occasioned with many of them. Ray Ryan at Cambridge University Press deserves special thanks for his unfailing and long-standing interest in this project, and for his encouragement that I stop tinkering and get it finished.

Finally, it would have been impossible for me to write this without the love and support of my family. Brian, Lou, Rachael, Dan, Dylan, and Haydn in England, and Linda, Henry, and Catherine in Texas, unfailingly provided those things. My daughter Lily has given us so much joy, and I will always associate the years of writing this book with our happiness at her arrival and the delights and adorable mishaps of her early childhood. I dedicate this book to Lee, whose unwavering faith in this book and whose day in, day out support of what it took to get it written were as important as the myriad ways her insight and discernment made its language and major claims so much better. I couldn't wish for a more loving and supportive partner, or a better reader.

I am grateful to *American Literary History* and *Modernism/Modernity* for granting permission to reproduce work that first appeared on their pages.

Introduction

In his 1937 autobiography, *A Long Way From Home*, Jamaican-born writer Claude McKay reflected on working as a railroad waiter in the Northeastern United States during World War One. McKay would write some of the Harlem Renaissance's most scathing criticism of US war policy – decrying the war's imperial and capitalist foundations, its devastating effects on workers and peoples of color worldwide, and the brutal violence enacted by newly empowered state and vigilante actors alike in reasserting the economic and racial status quo at the war's end.[1] *A Long Way From Home* begins with one of the most notorious actions of this security state, the "slacker raids" of 1918. These saw the American Protective League (APL) – a citizens' group 250,000 strong in that year – essentially become deputized by the Justice Department to conduct dragnet raids to root out draft dodgers in cities across America, assisted by local police and soldiers on furlough. Able-bodied men of draft age without their registration or classification cards were detained; in the largest raid, in New York City, historians estimate up to 500,000 men were interrogated and some 60,000 held, in some cases for several weeks.[2] Having lost his registration card, and away from home in Pittsburgh on a railroad run, McKay was swept up in one of the earliest raids. He was arrested and detained overnight; so overcrowded were the city jails from the APL's actions that he was held in a fetid toilet, locked in with two other men. The next morning the judge overseeing his case reminisced fondly with him about the beauties of Jamaica, admonished the police for arresting an essential worker, and provided McKay with paperwork he "was able to use ... for the duration of the war without worrying about a new registration card" before releasing him.[3]

The surprising thing about his recollection of this incident, though, is not McKay's scorn for the overbearing combination of eager and overempowered private citizens with expansive federal policing that typified the raids and indeed the entire home front during the war.[4] Instead, it was his

I

balancing of this feature of the wartime state with a sense of exhilaration at its scrambling of the prewar status quo, in a section worth citing at length:

> in those days of 1918, life was universally extraordinary and we railroad men were having our share of it. The government was operating the railroads, and Mr. McAdoo was Director-General. The lines were taxed to their capacity and the trains were running in a different way. Coaches and dining cars of one line were hitched up indiscriminately to the engines of another. Even we waiters were all mixed up on the same level! Seniority didn't count any more; efficiency was enough. There were no special crews for the crack trains; new men replaced the old-timers, expertly swinging trays to the rocking of the train and feeding lawmakers to the amazement of the old elite of the crews. The regular schedules were obsolete, for the dining cars were always getting out of line, there were so many special assignments … [And] under the new system we were getting better wages and pay for overtime.[5]

On the one hand, this section exhibits a leftist exhilaration at the nationalization of the railways, long the Holy Grail for Progressives keen to democratize a national economy dominated by oligarchic trusts. As Herbert Croly put it in his hugely influential 1909 Progressive manifesto *The Promise of American Life*, the railroad companies were "economic monsters" who would either "destroy the [American liberal democratic] system of ideas, institutions, and practices out of which they have issued or else be destroyed by them."[6] Figures like W.E.B. Du Bois could marvel in 1920 that railroad nationalization in the United States was a wartime consequence as miraculous as the fall of the Russian Czar or women's suffrage, Home Rule in Ireland or democracy in Germany.[7] Yet mixed with McKay's political delight – and inseparable from it – is his thrill at the changed socialities of this new venture in state control, the "indiscriminate" hitching of previously incongruous cars and engines and the newly heterogeneous clientele he was called on to meet and serve. This new "indiscrimination" not only forged exciting new personal contacts across social divides; it improved workers' wages, upended previous hierarchies of seniority and rank, and dissolved a well-ensconced "old elite." McKay was no fan of the American state, but here, at the zenith of progressive reform, its rapid transformation of social experience (including multiple forms of segregation), its improvement of labor conditions, and its jolt to hierarchical order in the bastion of monopoly-corporate America seemed to energize even his revolutionary spirit.

This book is a study of how the American writers of the era, often deploying the formal strategies we now associate with modernism, tried to render legible the changes in political subjectivity and social experience effected by the wartime transformations of the state, changes that often far outlasted the Armistice of 1918. Like McKay, most of the writers I consider were ambivalent about those changes – leery of the political rhetoric of security and its new laws and institutions, but also excited by the new patterns of social connection forged by the state, and by the prospect of how its expansion might effect social betterment. In tracing this account, I offer an alternative to scholars who identify the existential shock of attritional, industrial trench warfare as the war's primary influence on modernism, a shock that purportedly shaped a literature fascinated by trauma and suspicious of religious and political orthodoxy.[8] In the United States, this narrative is often linked to the literature produced by a "lost generation" of young men spiritually, politically, and sometimes physically debilitated by the war (even though many of those young men – John Dos Passos, Ernest Hemingway, F. Scott Fitzgerald, Malcolm Cowley, E.E. Cummings, William Faulkner – never served in the American Expeditionary Force [AEF]).[9] Yet this interpretation misses some of the specificities of the American cultural reaction to the conflict. The AEF saw serious casualties in helping repulse the threat to Paris from the German spring offensive in 1918, and suffered again in the bloody Meuse-Argonne campaign from September to November. Yet although Americans fought and died at staggering rates in the summer and early fall of 1918, they avoided the huge casualty lists experienced by other combatant nations.[10] American troops – present in force for only the last five months of the war – avoided the inconclusive and massive long-term engagements that delivered so many of the war's total casualties; and they were spared the extended, dreary, and attritional years of trench stalemate, both of which conditioned so much of the canonical European war literature.

At least as important an effect as combat experience on the national culture, therefore, was the establishment of a huge federal state within a country that before 1917 saw "little role for the federal government other than delivering the mail," in the words of one historian.[11] Progressivism had already transformed American citizenship in the previous decade – in widening the franchise, expanding practices of federal safety and financial regulation, initiating protocols of environmental protection, and introducing more direct forms of democracy. Wilson's first term, in particular, had delivered sweeping reforms that changed the basic relation of the federal government to the national economy – including the establishment of the Federal Trade Commission and the Federal Reserve, and the establishment of a federal income tax.[12] But nonetheless, the total federal budget in 1916 was a mere $0.75 billion, and the federal state had few administrative resources or reliable information on the size and distribution of American economic production and activity.[13] The US Army was ranked equal seventeenth in the world, alongside Chile, Denmark, and the Netherlands.[14] Within a year of entry, the war had transformed this situation. It made many peacetime Progressive ambitions a reality, from the nationalization of major industries to government arbitration of labor disputes and commodity prices. Twenty-four million men were registered for the draft, and 4 million men served in a military that conscripted 73 percent of its manpower.[15] Laws effecting the most drastic curtailments to free speech since the Alien and Sedition Acts of 1798 were enacted. The Food Administration's 500,000 workers distributed cards pledging families to practices of patriotic conservation in an effort that "literally reached into every kitchen in America."[16] The federal government enlisted 150,000 people – over half of these unpaid, and many of them writers and artists – in the Committee on Public Information, by far the largest government intervention into the arts before the Works Progress Administration's Federal Project Number One in the New Deal era and "the most overwrought and repressive propaganda agency in U.S. history to date," in the words of Jonathan Vincent.[17] The federal budget was $19 billion in 1919, and the war's costs lasted well beyond the Armistice: it cost over $10 billion in the 1920s alone to service the debts accrued from the war and to pay veterans' pensions and medical care.[18]

American literature in wartime and after was deeply engaged with these events. It participated in fierce contemporary debates around the nature of citizenship, and over what the extent of federal governance should be; it also assessed its own relationship to the tremendous technocratic energy then rapidly establishing new state-managerial structures. It often assumed the representational challenge of depicting a state now so vast and complex it threatened to defy representation altogether. Moreover, as new forms of connection and community emerged through the expansion of governmental networks of communication and organization, and as the government itself became a huge producer of culture, writers sought new ways to represent the novel forms of sociality these changes had initiated. Whether in the activities of sending mail, receiving health care, driving a car, writing in free verse, or thinking about one's "regional" experience, authors sought to craft forms capable of mediating the state's insinuation into the practices of everyday life, and to frame the new systems of power and political and social subjectivity this entailed. Often, they aimed to understand the new forms of freedom possible within this expanded liberal state, and how that state itself might be the producer of those freedoms. They strained to craft formal and thematic resources capable of mediating the gap between personal, local experience and the often abstract expanse of the state at war, or the disconnection between a federal government that often felt both geographically and conceptually remote and yet was so immediate and even intimate in its effects. In doing so, I contend, they laid the foundations for an imaginative culture hospitable to the new political, infrastructural, and social conditions of "liberal interdependence" that would soon underpin the birth of the welfare state proper in the 1930s.[19]

It will be obvious already that this analysis is unusual for prioritizing the state above the nation in its account of US literature's relation to World War One, and also because it departs from how the state is typically discussed in literary studies. In what follows, the state that emerged from the war is not solely a coercive force attenuating a prelapsarian, prewar political experience of greater individual sovereignty, where "what little military service there was in America was voluntary, that taxes were infinitesimal, that if you could scrape up the price of a ticket you could travel anywhere in the world except through Russia and Turkey, without saying boo to a bureaucrat," in the melancholy words of John Dos Passos, who built much of his career on that narrative.[20] Nor was the state that writers sought to represent always someone else – faceless, easily externalizable, and separate from the material practices, infrastructural flows, and affective investments of everyday life. My view of how American political formations were shaped by World War One therefore delivers a different literary history to familiar accounts of modernism as a literature unequivocally distanced from statist expansion, characterized by what Patricia Chu calls a "modernist affect" of alienation from the state produced by a "sense of limits created by jurisdiction, categorization and rational management."[21] Chu's location of such an affect in what Foucault called the encroaching "governmentalization" of the modern state is characteristic of many studies following his lead, which often overlook the nuance of his later views on the welfare state to deliver declensionist accounts of modernity as the increasing regimentation of people into subjectivities of "docility" within a proliferating series of governmental institutions and disciplines.[22] Moreover, such accounts are not restricted to modernist literary scholarship on the state, or to critics working in a Foucauldian tradition. As Matthew Hart and Jim Hansen observe, whether seen through Nietzsche's characterization of the state as the "cold monster," the New Left's skepticism over the possibility of liberation within a state apparatus, or more recent accounts theorized through Giorgio Agamben's work, literary studies has been particularly attracted to "an intellectual history in which artistic autonomy is opposed to institutionalized politics."[23]

In following a different path to such traditions, I am indebted to recent historical scholarship that has challenged the notion that America's dominant experience of World War One was the overreach of an enormous and coercive state, or that citizen-soldiers' shattering experiences led to widespread postwar disillusion with institutional politics. Instead, historians have recently argued that citizen-soldiers were crucial participants in determining wartime army policy, partly because their postwar political influence was anticipated by army brass and thus actively courted during the conflict. In assuming such political agency, as Jennifer Keene argues, this generation of citizen-soldiers helped shape the modern military and successfully defined their participation in the war as opening a lifelong contract of obligation between themselves and the federal state – a definition that led directly to the passage of the 1944 GI Bill of Rights in the next war.[24] Kimberly Jensen's scholarship has examined women's work within the wartime state, work that suffragists used as crucial political leverage to shape that state in arguing for the Nineteenth Amendment; as she notes, "many suffragists believed that it was women's wartime service that finally took them 'over the top' to victory."[25] In other work, Chad Williams has recast the long-standing narrative of African American service in World War One as a singular story of institutional racist abuse and state betrayal. While racist stratification and discrimination were a fact of life for black soldiers in all areas of the military, nonetheless they were empowered in their self-identification as citizens, and their service "presented a rare opportunity to infuse this essentially moribund political status with life and effective meaning." Moreover, for the most disadvantaged black recruits, Williams finds their service afforded tangible benefits "such as financial allotments and improvements in health and education, that tightened both the material and imaginative bonds between African Americans and the nation-state."[26] Steven Trout's fine account of memory culture in the postwar United States considers how actively the American Legion, especially through the fiction published in its periodicals, constructed a dominant narrative of doughboys' service in the war that stressed its role as invaluable training for civilian success and civic engagement.[27] Conversely, historians have examined how the wartime state's expansion into new areas of authority provoked not merely disillusion and disengagement but activist opposition, as many Americans saw uncomfortable parallels between this encroachment and the "Prussian" system they were fighting.[28] For example, the 1917 Espionage Act prompted fierce debates about the First Amendment that had long-term influence on American politics, culture, and jurisprudence, including the formation of organizations such as the American Civil Liberties Union.[29] Indeed, as Christopher Capozzola has observed, the war saw both the peak of a citizenship culture of "coercive voluntarism" that framed support of the war as a matter of unavoidable patriotic obligation and the seeds of the long-term erosion of that culture. This dynamic in the war prompted "one of the twentieth century's broadest, most vigorous, and most searching public discussions about the meanings of American citizenship," a discussion that gave new weight to citizens' rights before the state rather than their obligations to it.[30] The drift of all these studies, then, suggests that the American experience of war was one where both direct engagement in the future role of state institutions and the passionate negotiation of understandings of citizenship were a widespread phenomenon with significant long-term effects on US civic experience.

My book is also informed by recent work examining how American literature participated in the cultural work of making expansive federal governance – and, eventually, the mature welfare state of the New Deal – possible in the United States, no small task in a country with long and passionately defended political traditions of local autonomy and individualism. If such a political change required – and was sometimes shaped by – new imaginative and affective conceptions of mutuality and interconnectedness, scholars such as Michael Szalay, Sean McCann, Bruce Robbins, Lisi Schoenbach, Jason Puskar, and Jonathan Vincent have demonstrated how literary fictions had an important role in such innovations of consent.[31] Particularly salient among these accounts of the longue durée of a culture of acclimation to the welfare state is Vincent's recent, and brilliant, book *The Health of the State: Modern U.S. War Narrative and the American Political Imagination, 1890–1964*. This argues that war fiction in the Progressive Era helped provide statist Progressives with "the ideological thrust needed to overcome an ingrained resistance to bureaucratic growth and programs of public management," serving as a "symbolic register from which to challenge the older faith in liberal individualism and a readership recalcitrant to state power."[32] By depicting the "joys" of sublimating individual desires and wishes into a revitalizing military corporatism that served the common good in the face of ongoing external threats, American war writing of the 1910s offered a "steady revision of citizens' spatial and temporal optics and acclimation to permanent war readiness [that] helped organize and optimize, at least for some pockets of the nation, [a] culture of statit consent."[33] Indeed, war was the primary modality for effecting this political shift; as Vincent argues in his reading of William James, there simply *was* no moral equivalent to war – its prosecution, and the threat of its possibility, offered unrivaled political and psychological narratives for producing consent to the disciplinary exigencies of the modern liberal welfare state.

However, Vincent differs from Robbins, Schoenbach, and me by identifying the primary driver of social consent to statist expansion as what he calls an "ontology of permanent threat," wherein acquiescence to statist incorporation and regimentation flourished under widely held feelings of continually imperiled security. He also prioritizes the *means* of statist organization, its tendency to centralize, regiment, and incorporate, rather than its *ends*, in which case the difference between the Selective Service Act or sedition laws on one hand and Social Security or the Wagner Act on the other tends to be rather obscured. In contrast, I see those ends as crucial to how Americans both experienced the state and negotiated their own political agency within it. Often, that negotiation used singular institutions and infrastructures as synecdochic or allegorical forms for the state in its entirety, forms that authors turned to as they imagined new postwar sovereignties and models of citizenship. For example, the Post Office and the relationship of the US state to the oil industry were expansive organizational and infrastructural phenomena that underwent sizeable wartime transformation, and offered representational form to the state to modernist writers keen to overcome the state's sublime evasiveness to literary figuration and to negotiate the new civic conditions of American life. An important methodological feature of my approach, therefore, is the understanding that even in moments of statist extremity such as war, "far from being the source of all power, there were and are many 'authors' of the state," as Patrick Joyce puts it.[34]

Unsurprisingly, it is usually the macroscale of the powers of the wartime state that occupies critical attention, especially its new powers over bodies in the violent acts of conscription, incarceration, and waging warfare. Yet the extensions of what Joyce calls the "mundane state" are also key sites wherein considerable changes in political subjectivity and its relationship to cultural expression took place. It is often there, as Joyce explains, that we can locate a more supple, multidirectional way in which the state is formed and continually reproduced across multiple sites of agency, in "what has been called the 'co-production' of the state," a "co-production" "extended to those within and without the state proper: the humble 'engineer' of vitally important filing systems, say, but also the citizen him or herself, [who reproduces] the state in daily life." This approach disperses and multiplies the sources of the state, for "produced and reproduced in this way the state was returned to those in authority in new and often critical forms."[35] Authors exploring the wartime state were as engaged with its effects on the materiality of daily life as they were with its spectacular displays of disciplinary and coercive power, and in fact often found these mundane locations brought into sharper relief both the benefits and the abrogations that expanded federal power might bring. A major focus of this study, then, is how modernists' experimental approach to form often took pleasure and satisfaction as well as umbrage from accommodating the new infrastructures and institutions of the state, and returned an image of the state to those in authority in "new and often critical forms." This became a kind of "co-production" of the postwar state – as I explore in how veteran authors like Laurence Stallings critically considered the discourses of rehabilitation that informed the new Veterans' Bureau, or how John Dos Passos imagined the pleasures and the pitfalls of the new era of the private motor car that the war had done much to advance.

As will become obvious, this kind of approach to the state cuts across traditional political lines – covering the spectrum from the increasingly conservative Progressive regionalism of Willa Cather through to the left radicalism of John Dos Passos's most impactful writing of the 1920s. Of course, those political differences surface in very different approaches to aspects of the wartime state – Cather nowhere deployed the scathing accounts of the wartime state security apparatus that Dos Passos did, for example, even as she shared some of his views on its deleterious intervention into public rhetoric, or on its disturbingly close connections with America's large corporations. Similarly, as the political register where these authors explored new experiences of federal governance was often that of quotidian experience, or through the effects of a singular institution, there is an unavoidable diffuseness to the tradition this book seeks to outline. Yet the equivocal and transactional attitude toward the federal state that emerges across the texts I discuss offers more than an ideology of habituation or a politics of melancholia: there is a shared sense that the state's thoroughgoing presence in everyday life makes it malleable and even responsive to democratized agency.

To fully uncover the history of this legacy, however, requires some retracing of the relationship between American modernism and the Progressive Era state – from before the war to the aftermath of the failure of the US Senate to ratify the Treaty of Versailles. I begin by examining often-overlooked continuities between prewar Progressive ambitions for the state and the innovative literary cultures of the 1910s, a collaboration staked largely in a shared enthusiasm for a broad definition of democratic creativity. This history helps inform why so many American writers were keen to embrace the war as an opportunity for global progressive change in early 1917, but also why a modernist engagement with state innovation persisted into the 1920s. I then turn to some of the literature most critical of the domestic impacts of the American war state to indicate how writers critically responded to the new techniques of coercion and the control of public information unfurled in 1917–1919. Upton Sinclair's depiction of the work of the Justice Department's collaborations with private policing on the home front in World War One, and E.E. Cummings' writing on the Committee on Public Information, are important here, and exemplify a broader cultural rejection of the federal security apparatus developed under the Wilson administration. Yet while that political critique is an important feature of the postwar literary reaction to the war, it is far from the only one. In 1967, reflecting on his service in the AEF, Edmund Wilson concluded that his experience of military discipline, with its "many injustices and absurdities, had given me a sympathy with the victims of any sort of power machine that I was afterwards never to lose."[36] But he also saw his army experience as having a "liberating effect," jolting him from the "habits and standards" of his prewar life that subsequently felt "too narrowly limited by its governing principles and prejudices."[37] It is the literary culture of this balance – between a critique of the state's new disciplinary powers and the exhilarating expansion of socialities and even changes to "habits and standards" effected by its new forms of political association – that the remainder of the book will explore.

The Aesthetics of Progressivism: Literature and the Progressive Consensus to 1918

While American literary realism's frequent alliance with the Progressive political project has attracted a considerable amount of scholarship, similar approaches to the literary culture of the 1910s are much harder to find.[38] There are at least two reasons for this, the first being the sheer diffusion of interests, institutions, policies, and methods that passed under the Progressive label by the moment of its peak decade. It was nonpartisan; institutionalized through both major parties and a bewildering number of special-interest associations, single-issue political and voluntary groups, and welfare organizations and charities; both technocratic and grassroots; possessed of both a radical and a conservative wing; and associated with innovative techniques of governance at both the local and the federal level. Indeed, this heterogeneity has led some scholars to dismiss the label as too capacious to be of any definitional value.[39] The second reason is the incontestable fact that the avant-garde nature of much early American modernism often found the political extremes of anarchism or radical socialism better bedfellows for its aesthetic iconoclasm than the indelibly middle-class and gradualist stamp of reform. Consequently, the most celebrated and best-known aesthetic-political collaborations of the prewar period – such as the Paterson Silk Strike Pageant, the work of *The Masses* magazine, the *Little Review*'s fascination with Emma Goldman, or the Socialist Party of America's roster of writers (including Upton Sinclair, Carl Sandburg, and Jack London) – have been of this kind. Yet many writers – modernist and otherwise – were loosely aligned with what John A. Thompson has called the "progressive consensus" in the period.[40] This held in common a desire for wealth redistribution, and a belief in the social ethics rather than the institutional forms of Christianity. It also held a nationalist faith in expansive definitions of democracy, which saw democracy not merely as "a form of government nor a social expediency," but rather as a distinctively American "metaphysic of the relation of man and his experience in nature," as John Dewey influentially suggested.[41] This progressive consensus worried that such a metaphysic had been imperiled by the growth in wealth disparity seen during the Gilded Age, and the consequent rise of a "powerful but limited class," an "aristocracy of money," whose "chief object it is to hold and to increase the power which they have gained," in the words of Herbert Croly.[42] As Croly went on to suggest, replacing laissez-faire principles with a more interventionist state willing to "discriminate against all sorts of privilege" was necessary to restore the democratic vitality of the republic, which he idealized as a polity organized "for the joint benefit of individual distinction and social improvement."[43]

Such ideas were highly visible in key locations of early American modernism – in the writings of the Chicago renaissance, and especially *Poetry* magazine, for example, which as John Timberman Newcomb has discussed was largely responsible for reasserting the social and cultural relevance of the genre of poetry by printing numerous poems engaged with political ideas such as these.[44] They were firm beliefs of John Dewey, the thinker who, along with William James, had arguably the most significant philosophical impact on American literary modernism. They informed the cultural theory produced by the "young intellectuals" Randolph Bourne, Van Wyck Brooks, and Waldo Frank in the decade, and were evident in the magazine they produced, *The Seven Arts*. Progressive ideas informed the work of the major African American magazine of the period, *The Crisis*, published by the National Association for the Advancement of Colored People (NAACP); and Willa Cather worked for six years at the main Progressive muckraking journal *McClure's*, including four as managing editor (she also ghostwrote the autobiography of Samuel McClure). This is not to varnish over the fact that many avant-garde writers were hostile to progressivism's middle-class elitism and its moralizing exhortations, especially on issues of leisure, sexuality, and the obligations of service, which they often rightly saw as a drive toward class hegemony in the cultural sphere. But what Newcomb says about the New Verse held true for much early modernist American writing: it was "a dynamic discursive field committed to a synthesis of 'aesthetic and political points of view,'" much of which fell under the broad umbrella of the "progressive consensus."[45]

Moreover, this relationship was a two-way exchange. Progressive general interest magazines such as *The Nation*, the *New Republic*, and *The Outlook* regularly covered modernist writers, especially poets. In addition, influential Progressive political theorists of the era described their project in specifically cultural terms, and sought to blur or erase lines demarcating political and aesthetic innovation. Few were more influential than Walter Lippmann, who had called in 1913 for a new culture of "creative statecraft" in US policy-making. Lippmann's progressive manifesto *A Preface to Politics* (1913) called for such statecraft to deal with the formidable governmental challenges of global industrial modernity. For Lippmann, such statecraft would see the state evolving to deliver "productive" as well as "repressive" effects. He suggested that "the government is best that governs least [but] it is also true that that government is best which provides most," and predicted that parties would soon compete over who could deliver the better "program of services" rather than the most appealing "armory of platitudes or ... forecast of punishments."[46] And, rather than the overbearing technocrat he is sometimes described as, he identified a balance between Jeffersonian and Hamiltonian approaches to the state as crucial. For "Without the Jeffersonian distrust of the police we might easily grow into an impertinent and tyrannous collectivism; without a vivid sense of the possibilities of the state we abandon the supreme instrument of civilization."[47] As we shall see, that attitude to the state – mindful of its overreach and attracted to its productive potentialities – was in fact characteristic of many writers both during and after the war.

Moreover, Lippmann contended that progressive ambitions for the state were reliant on specifically aesthetic innovation, arguing that "the goal of action is in its final analysis aesthetic and not moral – a quality of feeling instead of conformity to rule."[48] A society of genuine political innovation and social welfare would only be possible, he concluded, amid "a culture practiced in seeking the inwardness of impulses, competent to ward off the idols of its own thought, hospitable to novelty and sufficiently inventive to harness power."[49] Lippmann, here, called for a cultural milieu attuned to iconoclasm, one that was aware of the irrational desires that propelled political realities (a prescription he drew from his keen reading of Freud), and was capable of empowering (and perpetual) innovation – a call, one might say, to make it new. A "lively artistic tradition," he explained, was not only "essential to the humanizing of politics"; it was "the soil in which invention flourishes."[50] Such a "tradition" was not antithetical to instrumental governance and its attendant institutions, as so many later commentators would claim, but was instead essential to its extension and perpetual responsiveness; as he said, "literature in particular elaborates our insight into human life, and, therefore, enables us to center our institutions more truly."[51] In later essays, he would go further in spelling out exactly what a progressive modernism would look like. He first decried the idealist, or even utopian, tendency of some modernist work. For Lippmann, this often evidenced "divine impatience with method in an inspired enthusiasm for the result" (he linked this political myopia to readers of the *Little Review*, in tacit contrast to the *New Republic*, the magazine he had co-founded with Croly in 1914 and which served as the Progressive bible in these years).[52] Yet a politics of the possible was not incompatible with the creative energies of modernism, he argued, praising what he called the "disciplined creator," who lived "in that fringe where reality and desire play against each other" and who was best suited to concocting the "state-making dream." Indeed, existence in that fringe was essentially an aesthetics of the politically possible; for the "test of a true culture" was whether such "disciplined creators" could possess the ability to "make the opaque world translucent, to see fact and dissolve it into hope, to know pinched things and see them grow wide, to feel throttled things shake themselves free, and know in all relevant life the longing which effort could realize."[53] This vision is close to what Lisi Schoenbach has recently identified as a significant political tradition in US modernism, that of a "pragmatic modernism" characterized by "a gradualist, mediating approach to social change and artistic innovation that was fundamentally different from the revolutionary ideology of the avant-garde" – a modernism that moves us beyond "the false choice between a purely adversarial avant-garde and the soul-deadening institutions against which it crusades."[54]

Lippmann's arguments about the importance of the aesthetic to a society supportive of "creative statecraft" enlisted some of modernism's most distinctive features as buttresses to a projected political culture of restless and permanent invention. Key features of how modernist artists defined their projects in the 1910s were aligned with the cultural work he felt would best support the perpetual and pragmatically responsive modernizations of an expanding service-state. His ideas about the aesthetic nature of political innovation, or that literary fiction held an important place in institution-building, or that certain forms of political imagination were as much representational problems as they were practical – shackled by the "foggy vocabulary" of Enlightenment-era political theory and in need of a new, modern language – in effect imagined a collaborative democratic project with American literary modernism.[55] As we shall see, elements of that sense of shared mission between Progressive politics and modernist literature run through much of the literary response to the war, and to the postwar state that emerged in the 1920s.

Nonetheless, the eager meliorism of *A Preface to Politics'* vision of institutional renewal, and the happy symbiosis it imagined between cultural innovation and political reform, was rarely seen from mid-1919 onward. As is well known, this is because of the inevitable postwar recoil from the pervasive rhetoric that war represented a generational opportunity for progressive social change deployed by many within the "progressive consensus" in early 1917, including by many modernist writers.[56] Even after having watched the unprecedented, industrial carnage of total war from afar for two and a half years, and despite the tenor of isolationist pacifism that typified much of the American intellectual reaction to the war in its earlier phases, by April 1917 many American intellectuals held a cautious optimism about the long-term political ramifications of American entry. This was a moment, Lippmann proclaimed, when "new sources of energy are tapped, when the impossible becomes possible, when events outrun our calculations," when one could "dare to hope for things which we never dared to hope for in the past."[57] Principal among these hopes was a "federation of the world," a "union of peoples determined to end forever that intriguing, adventurous nationalism which has torn the world for three centuries."[58] Moreover, such a democratic federation would ensure America turned "with fresh interests to our own tyrannies – to our Colorado mines, our autocratic steel industries, our sweatshops and our slums. We shall call that man un-American and no patriot who prates of liberty in Europe and resists it at home."[59] Such ideals were widely shared on the left, including in many of America's major modernist magazines. *Poetry*, for example, was particularly hospitable to the notion that the war presented a rare opportunity for global progressive reform. The month after the US declaration of war saw the poet Edgar Lee Masters, who had won *Poetry*'s prestigious Levinson Prize the previous year, express on *Poetry*'s pages a fervent hope that war would effect "a thorough house-cleaning abroad and at home. Let us have a world clean-up economically and spiritually ... Do You, O Mars, rout crookedness out of our business, social, and political life. It is time for every one to set about the business of abolishing poverty, along fundamental lines."[60]

As scholars such as Mark Van Wienen and Hazel Hutchison have shown, American writers' political and creative reactions to the war were as varied and complex as those of the population at large – reactions that often fractured along lines of ethnicity, class, gender, party affiliation, race, and region. Yet many writers wrote fiction and poetry that welcomed the war as an agent of progressive reform and national renewal. Willa Cather would later praise the "wave of generous idealism, of noble seriousness" that "swept over the state of Nebraska in 1917 and 1918," a wave that offered respite from a dominant culture of "materialism and showy extravagance" that sought "to buy everything ready-made: clothes, food, education, music, pleasure."[61] Prominent authors such as Arthur Train, Temple Bailey, Ellen Glasgow, and Booth Tarkington wrote novels welcoming the war as a revivifying force that would erase preexisting national political fault lines within a new politics of national incorporation and mutuality. Often, their fictions envisioned the war as occasioning an outbreak of selfless democratic renewal that rejected the indulgent and socially stratify-ing pleasures of a modern leisure and consumer economy. War's dangers, in this view, were preferable to the "dangers" of peace, as Bailey put it, dangers that "emasculated by ease of living."[62] Train's *The Earthquake* (1918) was one of the more successful examples of this popular trope; it forecast social renewal in the wartime moral rehabilitation of America's elite, who would not relinquish power but instead use it more beneficently; its protagonist was a Brahmin, WASP bond merchant who learns the value of thrift and service during the war. For Train, war's unifying imperative would enact the social reforms that socialism promised, but without a "bitter struggle between classes"; as a Wall Street colleague who has thrown up their lucrative job to enlist declares, "it's fine to drive the boches out of

Belgium, but it would be fine, too, to drive poverty and crime and disease out of America!"[63]

Subsumptions of the goals of progressive reform into a national project of unifying martial purpose and rejuvenated citizenship were made by popular and avant-garde writers alike. The most prominent serial in 1917 and 1918 in the *Ladies' Home Journal*, Grace S. Richmond's *Mrs. Redding Sees It Through*, adopted the title of H.G. Wells' British wartime bestseller to represent the wartime activities of a small-town family with a son in the service, and echoed Train's technique of showcasing the transformations in the daily life of each member of a nuclear family as the cipher for broader social change.[64] Gadfly sons become brave soldiers; young women forgo their spring shopping sprees to donate to a fund for Italian war refugees; and class divisions are smoothed over by practices of shared sacrifice. The *Ladies' Home Journal*'s wartime speculative fiction serial *Mildred Carver, USA* looked toward a time when all Americans, men and women alike, on reaching the age of eighteen, undertook a year of Universal Service – with their citizenship forfeit if they refused; in the same issue, the March revolution in Russia was praised for its liberation of women.[65] And as the discussion of Harriet Monroe and *Poetry*'s reaction to the war in Chapter 1 indicates, modernists were thinking about how the new, expansive forms of free verse might be the perfect representational vehicle for the global expansions of political community that informed the most utopian of Progressive hopes.

This Progressives' war was, then, often a "managerial dream" that promised "an opportunity for remaking both the polity and the self – erasing class differences, elevating women, eliminating selfishness, disciplining indolence and pleasure," a dream that captivated the political and literary imagination alike.[66] Yet the work of enacting this dream carried an empowering thrill that could easily mask the terrific violence such managerialism was designed to inflict, and could just as easily override democratic, ethical, and even legal constraint. Right from the outset critics saw the creative energy at the heart of statist expansion as one of its most dangerous features. Perhaps the best-remembered of those critics, Randolph Bourne, had been edged out at the *New Republic*, and in a series of articles in *The Seven Arts* in 1917 took aim at the composite program of political, philosophical, and aesthetic rationalizations underpinning the Progressive enthusiasm for the creative possibilities of war. He described a horrifying spectacle of a generation of Progressive technocrats like Lippmann thrilled by the opportunity the war afforded to exercise their expertise; indeed, it seemed "as if the war and they had been waiting for each other."[67] This was all the more calamitous because these young intellectuals were "liberal, enlightened, aware ... [and] touched with creative intelligence toward the solution of political and industrial problems," yet also devoid of any "clear philosophy of life except that of intelligent service."[68] This rendered their pragmatic creativity dangerously unhitched from any political or moral commitment: for their "burrowing into war-technique hides the void where a democratic philosophy should be."[69] Moreover, war's destructiveness could never really be an effective reformist opportunity, as "The luxuriant releases of explosive hatred for which peace apparently gives far too little scope" could never be "the raw material for the creation of rare liberal political structures."[70]

Bourne's critique of Deweyan pragmatism in these pieces is famous, but less well remarked is his insistence on the decoupling of political and aesthetic creativity – a union underpinning Lippmann's idea of the progressive consensus. Blasting this Progressive technocracy for having failed as "value creators," and for being void of "The allure of fresh and true ideas, of free speculation, of artistic vigor, of cultural styles, of intelligence suffused by feeling, and feeling given fiber and outline by intelligence," Bourne suggested that these things would only come from the war's "malcontents."[71] In predicting that these figures "will take institutions very lightly, indeed will never fail to be surprised at the seriousness with which good radicals take the stated offices and systems," he intuited that "their own contempt will be scarcely veiled."[72] In predicting that such malcontents would look to read – and perhaps write – an anti-institutional literature possessing "a tang, a bitterness, an intellectual fibre, a verve," he offered a good forecast of the literature of recoil from the wartime state that remains the best-known American writing to emerge from the war.[73] Produced by a new generation of authors who had often seen the war at first hand, such as E.E. Cummings, John Dos Passos, and Ernest Hemingway, this was a literature which often held a "contempt" for institutions, and a concomitant suspicion, in the words of James Dawes, of "creation exercised at the scale of the public."[74] (Or, as the "malcontent" H.L. Mencken put it, "we suffer most when the White House bursts with ideas.")[75] Moreover, many of the authors and intellectuals who had considered US entry in the war to be what John Dewey had called a "fair adventure" of global progressive opportunity, a fight replete with the "genuine possibilities" of "a world organization and the beginnings of a public control which crosses nationalistic boundaries and interests," recanted that view as hopes for such realignment dimmed in 1918 and 1919 and "the rainbowtinted future of reformed democracy went pop like a

pricked soap-bubble," in Dos Passos's acerbic terms.[76] Such writers also
often exhibited, as Hazel Hutchison notes, "a bad conscience about the
ways literature had been commandeered as a vehicle of governmental
policy in 1917–18."[77] Dewey and Lippmann lost faith as the Espionage
and Sedition Acts bit hard into the freedoms of the liberal press, and sent
journals like *The Masses* and *The Seven Arts* out of business.[78] For socialists
like Upton Sinclair who had reluctantly supported the war, the United
States taking up arms against the Bolsheviks in Russia in fall 1918 was the
breaking point. For Willa Cather, it was the extinguishing of the dream of a
globalized progressivism in the Treaty of Versailles and Wilson's failure to
ratify it at home that was the point of disillusion. As she wrote on Armistice
Day 1922, "why they celebrate that day with anything but fasts and sack-
cloth and ashes, I don't know."[79] In broader terms, much of the fertile and
mutually constitutive interplay between modernist aesthetic experimentation and reformist or radical politics that was characteristic of the early
1910s – and was so readily apparent in the era's little magazines, its salon
culture, and its bohemian enclaves – was dissipated by the war. This shift
has often been taken as the defining political feature of 1920s modernism,
so often seen as a literature in retreat from statist power and institutional
rationality. Yet, as we shall see, Lippmann's sense that literary experimentalism had a dual role in political reform – as the best interpreter of statist
possibility, but also serving as a crucial check on the state's coercive and
disciplinary tendencies – would be a significant feature of the literary
reaction to the war in the decade that followed the Armistice.

Literature and the Repressive War State

The genuinely typical American story of the war would probably not deal
with the fighting at all, but with the astounding and unparalleled phenomena that accompanied and supported that fighting at home. After all, very
few Americans actually saw any slaughter in the grand manner. By the time
the main army got into action, the Germans were already retiring. …
Among the Germans and the French, probably one adult male out of two
was under rifle, machine-gun and shell fire during the war; among
Americans not one in twenty had that experience. But practically every
American, male and female, had some hand, either as actor or as victim, in
the grotesque and inordinate monkey-shines that went on at home – the
loan drives, the cadging for the YMCA and the Red Cross, the looting of
enemy nationals, the spy-hunt, all the other patriotic whoop-las of the
period. In that period, there is abundant material for a penetrating and
ironical novel. It would be amusing as literature and valuable as history, and

it would let some needed light into the dark places of the American character.[80]

The literature of recoil from the state did not always retreat to the "diminutive ranges and more controllable outcomes of private creation," as Dawes has suggested.[81] Disillusion with Progressive statist ambitions was certainly an inescapable feature of public and literary life in the 1920s, and authors were now warier that the state was "the supreme instrument of civilization." Yet the war was an undeniable demonstration of its novel and supreme instrumentality, both at home and overseas. In just over two years, that state had silenced or jailed dissenters from the war, including the leadership of the Socialist Party of America and the Industrial Workers of the World (IWW). It had censored mail and shut down numerous publications critical of the war, and had targeted the nation's foreign-language press for particular harassment. It had thrown hundreds of conscientious objectors into military prisons. It had dominated the public sphere of information in a campaign that fueled long-standing social fears and prejudices and fed the resurgent nativism of the 1920s – a decade which saw drastic immigration restrictions drawn along racial lines and the rise of the Ku Klux Klan as a mainstream political movement. It developed a sizeable surveillance apparatus that harassed and targeted its own citizens, an apparatus which became a permanent feature of American civic life. And after establishing unprecedented levels of federal support and protection for workers' rights and remuneration during the war, in 1919 it largely abandoned those workers to a plutocratic order keen to reassert the status quo ante, a retreat that informed two years of bitter (and often violent) labor disputes that culminated in the crushing defeat of the Gary Steel Strike. As Mencken suggested, many authors agreed it was this – rather than the traumas of combat – that counted as the representative American experience of war, and that investigating the "dark places of the American character" that such state expansion had empowered was necessary cultural work. Accordingly, several influential writers sought to limn the dimensions and implications of Lippmann's "repressive" wartime state, particularly its innovative modalities of coercion and surveillance, its dramatic repression of leftist politics, and its reshaping of the entire cultural landscape of civic information and acceptable speech.

The Wilson administration's repressive actions were protested from the outset in lively cultures of political poetry, particularly in the publications of the Woman's Peace Party and the IWW. Publications with antiwar socialist messages such as *The Masses* and its successor, *The Liberator*, as well as African American radical magazines like *The Messenger* and *The Crusader* also protested as vociferously – and for as long – as they could. These magazines were often shut down either by direct judicial prosecution or by the withdrawal of financial support.[82] Yet arguably the first major novelist to critically depict the expansion of power of what Louis Althusser terms the Repressive State Apparatus of police, prisons, censorship boards, and intelligence agencies in the war was the most famous muckraker in American fiction, Upton Sinclair.[83] In 1919 and 1920, he produced two novels that were indeed "piercing and ironical," and explored the often-occluded concatenation of privately funded corporate security forces, paramilitary volunteer organizations, local police, and federal justice agents who collaborated in driving the ruthless crackdown on labor activists and socialists during the war period. His novels *Jimmie Higgins* (1919) and *100%: The Story of a Patriot* (1920), in fact, serve as parallel texts – the former following the life and career of an antiwar socialist who eventually enlists, in part, to help protect the nascent Bolshevik regime in Russia; and the latter following the wartime life of a spy and stool pigeon embedded in leftist circles in the hire of the security forces of an industrial trust. The novels track Sinclair's own views on the war; after leaving the Socialist Party due to their opposition to American entry, and hopeful that "the inevitable social dislocations of the war mobilization might exert a definite push towards socialism in the United States," he later recanted and became fiercely critical of the Wilson administration.[84] Indeed, he published an open letter to Wilson in 1917 expressing the futility of "helping to win democracy abroad, [while] we are losing it at home"; by 1926, he could declare that "if at the beginning of 1917 I had known what I know today, I would have opposed the war and gone to jail with the pacifist radicals."[85]

In both novels, Sinclair is keen to make visible the brutal, and informal, wartime coalition between private, state, and volunteer forces who collaborate to protect corporate interests under the name of national security – a coalition commonly withheld from public view. In this, Sinclair echoed growing concern in the period that the governing mechanisms of political power were hard to perceive, and in fact gained much of their power from this opacity. "Invisible government" was the term that crystallized those fears, first deployed in the Progressive Party's 1912 platform to describe a hidden and "unholy alliance between corrupt business and corrupt government" that they planned to dissolve.[86] In *A Preface to Politics*, Lippmann referred to "invisible government" as a "malign" force indicative of a "decaying political system done to death by an economic growth."[87] And

Randolph Bourne famously observed in his late, unfinished essay on the state that much of the state's power resided in its "mystical" nature; government was merely "the visible sign of the invisible grace."[88] Yet Sinclair identified a new force in this invisible governance in the rise of covert policing during the war. In *Jimmie Higgins*, agents from a secretive Justice Department agency interview Jimmie about a conspiracy to sabotage the local munitions factory, a conspiracy that they have spies placed to disrupt. The protagonist of *100%*, Peter Gudge, is a spy for the "Traction Trust" in the fictitious "American City" who has infiltrated local radical movements. Not only does he report on them to both his corporate paymasters and local and federal law enforcement but he helps to frame them and send them to jail – in ways clearly reminiscent of the Tom Mooney case.[89] Such moments gesture toward the Justice Department's huge covert operation to suppress and discourage wartime dissent – among immigrant communities, religious leaders, African Americans, socialists, union leaders, pacifists, and clubwomen – often through campaigns of harassment and intimidation. As the retiring Attorney General Thomas Watt Gregory boasted in August 1919,

> After the first six months of the War, it would have been difficult for fifty persons to have met for any purpose, in any place, from a Church to a dance hall in any part of the United States, without at least one representative of the Government being present. I doubt if any country was ever so thoroughly and intelligently policed in the history of the world.[90]

As Sinclair's novels laid bare the state's sub-rosa collusion with private or volunteer security forces, they also stressed the state's reliance on such forces to perform illegal actions it tacitly endorsed. At the close of *Jimmie Higgins*, for example, Jimmie is stationed in Archangel in Russia to help assist White forces in their fight against the Bolsheviks (the AEF would remain there until 1920) – an order that horrifies him and leads him to begin distributing pro-Bolshevik literature in his army base. He is arrested and tortured – in scenes which Mark Van Wienen notes are as "graphic as anything before written in American literature" – by an army sergeant who "had been an 'operative' for a private detective agency" where he did similar work in peacetime.[91] The most brutal moment in *100%* is when "younger members of the Chamber of Commerce and the Merchants' and Manufacturers' Association," led by the security forces of the "Traction Trust," raid an IWW meeting, take prisoners to the countryside, and whip several of them before lynching their Secretary, a parallel to the Frank Little murder in Montana.[92] (Indeed, so keen was Sinclair to stress the truthfulness of his accounts of extralegal violence, torture, and collusion between corporate security forces and state police agencies that he included a thirteen-page appendix to *100%*, including a bibliography, detailing the real incidents that informed his novel.) Moreover, Peter's impatience at the state police forces' nominal adherence to the "due and regular" form of legal statute – in contrast to the more direct and brutal methods of the "Traction Trust" – was in fact a common feature of cultures of "citizen policing" that had existed before the war, and which greatly expanded in scope and intensity once America joined.[93] As Christopher Capozzola has noted, many nonstate actors, committed to a long-standing citizenship culture of obligation that included the duty to enact patriotic social vigilance, felt the wartime state was failing to thoroughly suppress dissent at home, and stepped in to fill that perceived "gap" – sometimes through brutal acts of vigilante violence. Yet this "apparatus of [volunteer] surveillance would not have been constructed if Americans had not viewed vigilance as basic to good citizenship and had not officials at all levels of government tolerated and even encouraged that vision of political obligation."[94] It was the major political work of Sinclair's two novels to show how these various agencies worked in secretive concert, and to make the shadowy culture of domestic wartime policing visible. In addition, Peter's late turn into a respectable burgher suggests the normalization of such policing within cultures of American citizenship; his violent, duplicitous, and illegal work has, by 1919, attained not only the patina of anti-Bolshevik "heroism" but the sheen of the white-collar professional. Indeed, Peter comes to believe that "the secret agent was the real ruler of society … the trustee, as it were, for civilization" – he delivers public lectures for the Improve America League and he even contemplates running for president.[95] In such representations Sinclair registered the firm institutionalization of the twentieth-century US "surveillance state" of federal monitoring of purported political "radicals," and contributed to a nascent literary culture that both describes these new practices of surveillance and even imagines them as a key element of its own readership.[96] Sinclair certainly understood his novels would fall under the purview of the surveillance state, especially as the Sedition Act remained in effect until 1921. He worried over whether Boni and Liveright, who produced *Jimmie Higgins*, could publish it unaltered; and he printed *100%* himself.[97]

100%'s Peter Gudge is an avid reader of the newspapers, and the gap between their inflated patriotic rhetoric and what was actually happening also indicates another feature of the wartime state that widely conditioned American literary modernism and indeed all postwar public life: the government's unprecedented intervention into the management and production of public information. Indeed, this experience reshaped both the theory and the practice of how public information related to the participatory choices of citizens within American capitalist democracy.[98] It fueled the boom in the public relations and advertising industries in the 1920s, as corporations sought to emulate the stunningly effective techniques of shaping public preferences that had been developed during the war. As Edward Bernays, the leading figure of the public relations industry in the 1920s, put it, "it was ... the astounding success of propaganda during the war that opened the eyes of the intelligent few in all departments of life to the possibilities of regimenting the public mind." The government's innovations in public relations in the war, he explained, had "appealed to individuals by means of every approach – visual, graphic, and auditory"; and had manipulated the "mental clichés and the emotional habits" of the public – peddling stories of atrocities, tyrannies, and terror – in order to produce "mass reactions."[99] Perhaps most notable in his *Propaganda* of 1928 – part Machiavellian handbook, part sales pitch to corporate clients – was his claim that the shapers of public opinion were now the governing class in the United States, an "invisible government which is the true ruling power of our country," a claim devoid of the alarmist deployment of that term by Lippmann, the Progressive Party, and others. Rather than presenting such "invisible government" as a deplorable threat to republican, democratic popular sovereignty, *Propaganda* instead positioned it as unalterable fact, if not an exclusive club that his prospective corporate clients should consider joining.[100]

Bernays had learned his trade in the Committee on Public Information (CPI), where he served in the Latin American division. Established just one week after the US declaration of war, the CPI was headed by the pugnacious muckraker George Creel, a man Wilson praised as having a "passion for adjectives" and who proclaimed in May 1918 that "Democracy is a religion with me, and throughout my whole adult life I have preached America as the hope of the world."[101] This indivisibility between democratic idealism and American nationalism was one keynote of the output of the committee, the other being the brutality of German autocratic militarism; both informed its "dramatic record of vigor, effectiveness, and creative imagination," in the words of its first historians.[102] The United States forswore some of the compulsive tools of mobilization deployed by other belligerent nations – eschewing steep tax hikes by borrowing heavily to finance the war through the Liberty Bond Drives, and launching conservation rather than rationing efforts through the Food

Administration.[103] Both initiatives relied on mass voluntary support from the American public for their success. As David Kennedy notes, this plan had the "crowning appeal [of] the assurance that informed public opinion could substitute for radical institutional reordering or for the naked brandishing of state power as a solution to the problems of the day."[104] To generate support for such programs, the CPI sought to mobilize "the mind of the world so far as American participation in the war was concerned," in Newton Baker's words, a mobilization focused on promoting what Creel called the "American idea."[105]

As Bernays noted, the CPI marketed that idea with a media scope and saturation that astonished war planners, public relations men, politicians, and citizens alike. The Division of News issued press releases and appeared in around 20,000 newspaper columns per week. The Foreign Language Newspaper Division translated CPI publications into foreign languages, and monitored the foreign-language press in America; the Division of Work with the Foreign Born strove to promote patriotism in various immigrant communities. The Division of Industrial Relations and the Division of Labor Publications worked with unions and developed patriotic literature to appeal to the working class. The National School Service Bulletin sent a sixteen-page, bimonthly sheet to 600,000 school addresses, encouraging teachers to become "expert" on issues connected to the war, and to encourage "unswerving loyalty" among their students in their role as an honorary "officer of the state."[106] The Division of Films liaised with Hollywood, leaning heavily on filmmakers to produce the "correct" kinds of war films, and even entered into its own film production. The Bureau of War Expositions displayed trophies captured from the Germans, and even put on sham battles (Chicago's exposition alone was visited by two million people). The Division of Pictorial Publicity, headed by the popular visual artist Charles Dana Gibson (who himself produced several posters featuring his well-known "Gibson girls"), produced 700 poster designs for many of the wartime agencies and programs. The Division of Four Minute Men and the Speaking Division recruited an army of 75,000 volunteer speakers, who delivered, in total, nearly a million talks on the US war effort.[107] The CPI also ran huge foreign sections, which disseminated US news and propaganda overseas.[108] Although Creel would often claim the CPI's success never relied on censorship, he sat on the interagency Censorship Board alongside Postmaster Albert S. Burleson – whose denial of mailing privileges to periodicals critical of the war effort was arguably the most direct form of state control of permissible speech. As historian Jonathan Auerbach puts it, "the CPI was instrumental for the war effort, bringing the state to the doorsteps of ordinary Americans as never before, and arguably never since"; the draft went off relatively smoothly, and the four "Liberty Bond" drives were oversubscribed.[109]

Novelists and poets worked with the CPI from the outset. The organization briefed fiction writers about the stories they should write. Its Division of Syndicated Features recruited popular novelists such as Booth Tarkington, Rex Beach, and Samuel Hopkins Adams.[110] It liaised closely with the writers' group The Vigilantes, an organization that served as a patriotic writers' union and syndicate for the distribution of their war art and writing. In 1917, this counted 328 writers pledged to it, including Edward Arlington Robinson, Edgar Lee Masters, Amy Lowell, Vachel Lindsay, Gertrude Atherton, Ida Tarbell, Hamlin Garland, and Alice Corbin Henderson.[111] The Division also exerted considerable coercive pressure on wartime writers, which pushed some into extreme actions. Carl Sandburg, for example, wrote pro-war pieces under his own name for the American Alliance for Labor and Democracy, a government-backed body with close connections to the CPI, while simultaneously publishing numerous articles lambasting government war policy in the *International Socialist Review* under the pseudonym Jack Philips.[112]

The long-term impacts of the CPI on American culture were manifold. Katherine Anne Porter thought it analogous to the influenza epidemic that ravaged America at roughly the same time: endemic, inescapable, and devastating. Her short story "Pale Horse, Pale Rider" has a protagonist who both contracts the flu and struggles to resist the coercive pressure to buy a war bond, peddled by two men with "a stale air of borrowed importance which apparently they had got from the same source," and who insist she "make a pledge of good faith that she was a loyal American doing her duty."[113] Shortly after listening to their "little set speech," she wonders "does anybody here believe the things we say to each other?"[114] As Matthew Stratton has observed, this new level of distrust over the sincerity of public language was central to the CPI's legacy, which had revealed "the notion of a rationally formed and informed public opinion not just as hopelessly naïve but as actively harmful: a disposition toward the world of ideas that would invariably favor the interests of those who control the means of information production."[115] Indeed, his fine reading of Dos Passos's treatment of the CPI in *1919* sees it as having obliterated the public sphere in its entirety, if such a sphere is understood as "a pluralist collectivity capable of making choices that might be at odds with the desires of industry and capital." For Dos Passos, such a public was "destroyed by the information campaigns rather than the trenches of World War I."[116] Yet

Dos Passos also saw that this transformation of the public sphere – with the government as a new controlling agent in the production and regulation of information – had inescapably altered and delegitimized the meaning of American political vocabulary in much of its habitual and classic forms; this incursion represented a hijacking by "strangers who have turned our language inside out who have taken the clean words our fathers spoke and made them slimy and foul."[117]

A similar view is on offer in some of E.E. Cummings' verse about World War One. Like Dos Passos, his wartime experiences were defined by state control of speech: while working as an ambulance driver for the famous Norton-Harjes Ambulance Corps in 1917 he was scooped up by Allied authorities investigating "seditious" utterances in the letters of his friend, William Slater Brown. Both he and Brown spent three months in a French concentration camp as a result, an experience that informed his autobiographical novel *The Enormous Room* (1922). Both this and his 1931 poem "I Sing of Olaf Glad and Big," which deals with the torture and jailing of a conscientious objector, are fierce indictments of the carceral institutions and practices used to police dissent during the war. Yet Cummings was also critical of both the languages of patriotic obedience and their new means of mediation, as was evident in the following sonnet from 1926:

> "next to of course god america i
> love you land of the pilgrims' and so forth oh
> say can you see by the dawn's early
> my country 'tis of
> centuries come and go
> and are no more
> what of it we should worry
> in every language even deafanddumb
> thy sons acclaim your glorious name by gorry
> by jingo by gee by gosh by gum
> why talk of beauty what could be more beaut-
> iful than these heroic happy dead
> who rushed like lions to the roaring slaughter
> they did not stop to think they died instead
> then shall the voice of liberty be mute?"
>
> He spoke. And drank rapidly a glass of water[118]

The poem works by stitching together numerous snippets of the sacred texts of American nationalist celebration ("My Country 'Tis of Thee," "The Star Spangled Banner") into a jumble of confused speechifying that hopes citational fervor will substitute for grammatical coherence and denotational content. And although this speech mashes those citations together in a sequence of hyperventilating non sequiturs, they nonetheless coalesce around powerful political ideas that dominated the public sphere in the war. Primarily, the speaker supports a nativist vison of Anglo-Saxon national leadership, one staked in the primacy of Puritan heritage to national identity and normative citizenship ("land of the pilgrims"). And it endorses a sacral vision of male martial heroism as the supreme act of national service and the defining story of national formation, one that idealizes the nobility of dying for one's country irrespective of cause or context. Yet the tipping of these sentiments from patriotic fervor into nonsensical comedy helps deconstruct the hugely powerful "semblance of a unified national culture – that dream so devoutly cherished by virtually all Progressives" that the CPI had so influentially put forward.[119] Cummings' humor works to establish a series of dramatic ironies at the expense of his hapless speaker – the "heroic happy dead" who nonetheless rush into the "slaughter," suggesting their acquiescence to state command had already rendered them lifeless even before their reckless battlefield charge. Or the singularity brought about by his horrible mix of the abstract and specific, as "the voice of Liberty" becomes one voice – suggesting, in fact, the illiberalism of wartime speech, where only one way to think and speak about the war had been socially sanctioned. Yet this poem also, I think, apes the four-minute men speaking programs that were one of the most effective means deployed by the CPI to encourage support for the war effort. So named because these speakers often talked during film screenings, in the four-minute intervals it customarily took to change a reel of film, New York alone had 1,600 "four-minute men," who spoke to an estimated half a million people each week; 75,000 were at work nationwide by the war's close.[120] One of the major ways the CPI exerted firm and centralized control of the nationwide program, as well as the national bulletin it sent out to ensure speakers were talking on the same topic at the same time, was the stipulation that speakers keep strictly to the four-minute time limit.[121] The speaker's headlong rush through his clichés here suggests the pressure of adhering to the ticking clock of an inflexible form. Moreover, Cummings' use of the sonnet's inherent restrictions presents a brilliantly impish parallel to such formal constraint. On the one hand, the use of the sonnet generates much of the poem's bathos, in generating an absurd contrast between the elevated and elegant associations embedded within the form and the speaker's incoherent and fatuous utterance. But it also gestures to the limitations of the four-minute speech – suggesting that the formal constraint on speech in wartime, that is, the tight control exerted over the length, locations, and media platform of public speech during the war – was as responsible for the evacuation of deliberative political thinking as were the content-focused proscriptions of the Espionage Act. That the *formal* characteristics of the CPI's major communicative techniques had their own insidious politics is a message as clear in this parody as it is in Cummings' irreverence for formal convention elsewhere.

The first page of *The Enormous Room* also parodied wartime public speech, as Cummings begins by borrowing "a characteristic cadence from Our Great President" – a "cadence" that turns out to be bombastic, longwinded, and vacuous.[122] Indeed, if the "voice of Liberty" did narrow to a singularity in the war, as Cummings suggested, then that voice was Woodrow Wilson's, whose speeches were at the core of both the CPI's propaganda efforts and the linguistic strategies of those postwar writers keen to reject his legacy of interventionist progressivism. Wilson's speeches, typified by soaring eloquence, rhetorical force, and appeals through the language of abstract, nationalist idealism for American commitment to the cause, were printed into pamphlets by the CPI and were among their most popular.[123] His speeches were often printed verbatim in the national press. He even exploited the nascent power of broadcast radio; his famous Armistice Day speech in 1923, decrying the isolationism of current US foreign policy, was the most widely heard radio broadcast up to that date.[124] As Sean McCann has observed, Wilson shaped the modern presidency by dramatically expanding presidential power, an expansion he often framed as "a vital response to political crisis," whether the domestic crisis of the rule of party machines and oligarchic trusts or, in his second term, the great global crisis of the war.[125] Wilson legitimated such expansion through a specifically rhetorical vision of the presidency; as he explained, in the last academic writing he did before entering politics, "when [the president] speaks in his true character, he speaks for no special interest. If he rightly interpret the national thought and boldly insist upon it, he is irresistible."[126] As McCann notes, this idea positioned "The chief executive … [as] the sole voice of a national constituency otherwise excluded from power. The president, in this respect, occupied an always potentially redemptive, if not sacral position," a leader who could give voice to the submerged common will and thus bring it to self-awareness.[127] This imagined the nation as an organic and unified community that one privileged executive could speak for and guide, a vision that both privileged a singular voice and carried a coercive force that fell heavily on anyone dissenting from that "unity" that the executive had imagined into being.

As McCann and others have observed, the failures of this exalted vision – which combined a faith in national organic unity, a model of the presidency as the voice of the submerged national will, and a view of state power as merely the instrument of voluntary national consensus – led Wilson's rhetorical style to be a highly influential negative example to the following generation of writers.[128] Indeed, they "defined themselves in good part against Wilson's vision of democratic nationalism and presidential leadership," often invoking the local, the concrete, and the authentic against the vacuities of Wilson's abstracted and transcendent rhetoric.[129] As H.L. Mencken, one of Wilson's fiercest critics, put it, Wilson's style reduced "all the difficulties of the hour into a few sonorous and unintelligible phrases, often with theological overtones" cannily designed to "arrest and enchant the boobery with words that were simply words, and nothing else."[130] "Making the world safe for democracy" was, in his words, "a masterpiece of boob-fetching."[131] At their most forceful, postwar authors contrasted this style to the brutal consequences of what that rhetoric had done to specific bodies. Dos Passos's *1919* concludes with the hypocrisy of Wilson bringing a bouquet of poppies to the Tomb of the Unknown Soldier, a soldier whose death he had indirectly caused. Midway through Laurence Stallings' only novel, *Plumes*, which deals in highly autobiographical ways with a young, married veteran struggling with the process of reintegrating to American society after suffering a debilitating combat injury, two veterans watch Wilson arrive at Warren Harding's inauguration. As they see Wilson walking awkwardly, due to the lingering effects of the catastrophic stroke he suffered in the fall of 1919, one remarks "He thinks he's the only man who really was deeply disappointed in this hellish mess ... He's never known anyone else. It was killing him just now to hobble before a crowd. He thinks no-one else hobbles as badly."[132] Wilson's claim to speak the national will, in such readings, was only the ruse of an autocrat largely uninterested in the people he purported to speak for. It was this that made his awe-inspiring wartime singularity more that of an arrogant and overly empowered idealist who abused the conventions of the executive branch, rather than the singularity of being the exceptional orator speaking and enacting the popular national will. This was best summed up by John Dos Passos: as his biographical section on "Meester Veelson" in *1919* says, rather than becoming the voice of the nation in the heady days of 1917, "Wilson became the state."[133]

Federal Citizenship: The War and the Aesthetics of the State

Writers such as Dos Passos, Stallings, Cummings, Mencken, and Sinclair were prominent figures in the widespread postwar reaction against the new powers and institutions forged by the state in 1917 and 1918 – and against the public discourse it devised for "the manufacture of consent," in Lippmann's famous phrase.[134] They would be joined by a swathe of veteran-novelists who depicted the United States' citizen army as a place of brutal dehumanization and institutional failure, a view apparent in Thomas Boyd's *Through the Wheat* (1923), James B. Wharton's *Squad* (1928), and William March's *Company K* (1933). The racial dimensions of the US war effort were also cause for much disenchantment with the federal state; the literature of the Harlem Renaissance, for example, frequently bridled at the way the new federal institutions of the war erected a new architecture of racial stratification onto American civic life, as the United States forced most black draftees into labor units, fought with a segregated military, and staffed the hugely expanded federal bureaucracies in Washington with a newly segregated workforce. Moreover, there was widespread disappointment among African Americans that their extensive wartime service failed to secure a better political postwar settlement. Yet many authors, including W.E.B. Du Bois, Nella Larsen, E.C. Williams, and James Weldon Johnson, believed the war had conferred an invigorated male martial citizenship on the 40,000 African American combatants, especially the officer corps, and embraced the political and cultural opportunities this held – a phenomenon I have written on extensively elsewhere.[135]

A narrative of postwar disillusion and recoil from statist ambition, therefore, is the most familiar one for charting the politics of mature modernism in the United States. But this book aims to tell a more complex story, of how authors considered the politics of the new forms the state had assumed in the war in manifold and usually equivocal ways. In 1928, on the tenth anniversary of the Armistice, Harriet Monroe reflected in *Poetry* on how "no one has yet been able to discover any good things [the war] accomplished in exchange for its ten million dead."[136] Yet she sounded a positive note, hopeful that the recent Kellogg–Briand Pact for the Renunciation of War as an Instrument of National Policy (signed or agreed to by forty-five nations) represented a move toward a "new and beautiful world-patriotism."[137] Moreover, this expansion of what she called the "boundaries of devotion" forged by a globalized economy was paramount "material for poets."[138] As Chapter 1 explains, these hopes were not wholly dissimilar to those she had voiced in 1917. And in balancing a disgust at the new kinds of state violence and coercion developed in the war with a continued hope that literature would play a central role in new kinds of state production – in her case, that poetry might produce "the world's new song" to help orchestrate innovative global forms of political community – she was far from unique.[139] Typically wary of the state's new coercive capacities, many postwar writers were nonetheless fascinated by the new social structures (and infrastructures) of the state, and explored the new possibilities – and even pleasures – these portended. Inevitably, this project looked different to the heady optimism for a reformed global democracy so current in the spring of 1917. But many saw the task of representing Bourne's shadowy state – mystical, depersonalized, and distant – as a political necessity that often blended skepticism with an investment in the function and potential of its new powers.

The book is organized roughly chronologically, with Chapters 1 and 2 considering how US authors – including modernists such as Wallace Stevens and the editors at *Poetry* magazine – saw the new size and scope of the wartime state as a representational challenge that modernist techniques were well-fitted to address. Chapter 1 considers debates over free verse during the war, focusing on three publications – the modernist little magazines *Poetry* and the *Little Review*, and the national mass-circulation *Saturday Evening Post*. Even before the war, the *Post* (and titles like it) had brought both ridicule and attention to the innovations of early modernist poetry, but during the war it ran a series of parodies that characterized free verse as not merely pretentious, elitist, and hermetic but as unpatriotic in selfishly withholding accessible artistic labor from the state. In contrast, magazines such as *Poetry* and the *Little Review* fostered a counterpublic sphere of debate on the war, one that frequently defended the relevance of modernism, and free verse, to a moment of collective emergency. *Poetry* identified free verse as the only poetic form capable of accommodating the vastness of the war, and even argued for draft exemptions for American poets. The *Little Review*'s ostensible policy of ignoring the war masked a complex set of practices that resisted many of the patriotic obligations expected of the American press in the wartime moment. Its free verse competition in 1917, which included its printing of a traditional and "patriotic" poem submitted by an unwitting reader, showcased many of the arguments then raging around the relationship between political and aesthetic freedom, or how rights might balance against obligations.

Chapter 2 considers the prevalence of the fictional letter home in the American fiction and poetry of World War One. Prior to the war, the *Post*

Office had been arguably the most dynamic, substantial, and transformative federal agency of the Progressive Era. The single most important agent in the development of America's transport and communication network, it also assumed an important representational role in American life, often serving as a synecdoche for the federal state in its entirety. The US Army devoted immense resources to its wartime mail system, even hosting huge publicity drives to encourage soldiers to send mail – most notably on Mother's Day 1918, as well as initiating the airmail system that would catalyze the development of the United States' civilian aviation infrastructure. While scholarship on wartime letters has usually focused either on state censorship and surveillance of mail on the one hand or on mail as an intimate exchange between sender and addressee on the other, I argue that these broader understandings of the mail system made it a dominant trope for writers to consider the new intimacies forged between state and individual in the war, and a useful vehicle for exploring the new forms of sociality the war had brought about. The chapter reads epistolary war fiction by Ring Lardner and centers on a reading of Wallace Stevens' wartime poetry sequence "Lettres d'un Soldat." Partly, this poetry sequence reflects Stevens' assessment of the various systems of government at conflict in the war – an assessment that closely tracks his reading of similar discussions in the *New Republic*, as his own letters attest. But the sequence also reflects on the mediating power of the state in handling the mail, and moves toward a language for framing intimacy between state and individual. The chapter finishes by reading Edith Wharton's satirical short story "Writing a War Story," which centers on the cliché of the letter home in war fiction as a way of considering the decline of traditions of voluntary, patrician philanthropy that the war's new centralized and state-run systems of charity had replaced.

The remaining chapters track developments in writing of the 1920s and early 1930s, as authors considered the legacies of the wartime state, both in terms of its transformation of the balance between centralized, federal power and local autonomy, and regarding the new infrastructures and institutions it put in place. Many of the authors discussed registered that these infrastructures and institutions were products of what Marc Allen Eisner has called the "compensatory state" that emerged from the war. As he explains, a poorly funded and weakly institutionalized federal state leaned heavily on US industry's superior production, information, and governance systems to mobilize for war. This embedded corporate structures (and often corporate self-interest) at the heart of America's new systems of governance – a state form that became an enduring feature of how the United States would organize federal responses to crises, whether the twentieth-century's military conflicts or the Great Depression that prompted the New Deal.[140] America's large corporations emerged as winners from the war; to go back to the opening example of the railroads, even amid their nationalization Congress passed a bill guaranteeing their postwar return to private control, and the United States Railroad Administration "was able to pay for its generous wage settlements and capital equipment purchases with record high freight-rate increases, gaining for the railroads revenue structures for which they had long, but unsuccessfully, lobbied."[141]

Chapter 3 examines how authors working in traditions of regionalist writing considered the shifting balance of power between local autonomy and federal-corporate centralization that attended the growth of that compensatory state during the war. The war prompted several literary critics to argue that local color writing had become redundant, due to its focus on smallness and personal immobility. Others, however, saw its reliance on concrete local detail as an essential ingredient for articulating visions of national community, a necessary supplement to the often abstract and metaphorical forms of civic nationalism and the ghostliness of the expanded federal state. Thinkers critical of the state's wartime coercions also began to articulate radical visions of regionalism as a viable counterweight to the forces of national political, cultural, and economic standardization. These debates are visible in Willa Cather's *One of Ours* (1922) and Ellen Glasgow's *The Builders* (1919), war novels that use regional fiction to frame what political theorists like Lippmann and Harold Laski were then calling "federal" modes of citizenship, a political form capable of dealing with (sometimes conflicting) obligations to ethnicity, region, religion, and nation. While *The Builders* strains to map Southern domestic morality onto imaginations of global progressivism, *One of Ours* celebrates the power of a nationalized, standardized industrial economy to successfully prosecute the war, while simultaneously gesturing toward the costs of that economic power. Hinting strongly at the corporate self-dealing underlying the exalted abstractions so typical of wartime discussions of the state, Cather also decries the effects of a standardized economy on localized cultures in both Nebraska and France. The chapter finishes with a reading of Zane Grey's *The Desert of Wheat* (1919), a novel that rejects the complex "federal" modes of affiliation proposed by Cather and Glasgow in favor of a glorified vision of unalloyed nationalist masculine martial citizenship. Yet Grey's location of ideal wartime citizenship in strenuous nationalism and what Anthony Rotundo has called the model of "passionate manhood" so

important to early twentieth-century US gender identity strikingly collides
with his simultaneous concern to preserve forms of regional exceptionalism
and the republican autonomy of the family farm in an era of federal and
agricultural consolidation.[142]

Chapter 4 considers John Dos Passos, a novelist obsessed with World
War One who increasingly identified its most important domestic legacy as
an enormous expansion of state power that would resurface in the New
Deal. The chapter reads his epic trilogy *U.S.A.* (1938), a work where the
atomization and loneliness of its twelve leading characters are often taken
as a leftist critique of a globalized world wherein capitalism had destroyed
earlier forms of connection and community. Yet my chapter argues for the
powerful connectivity provided by the symbiotic wartime growth of the
federal state and the global oil industry in *U.S.A. 1919*; the middle volume
carefully tracks the emergence of oil as a strategic resource for the world's
military superpowers during the war, but also explores how oil became a
commodity that increasingly enmeshed all aspects of daily life in the agency
of the state. This generates one of the defining features of liberal "petromodernity," as oil facilitates characters' social connections and often helps
them feel free in moments of motorized speed, while simultaneously
enfolding them into ever-denser networks of state infrastructure and control. In fact, as the editors of the *Little Review* also intuited in their wartime
numbers, this was one of the characteristics of the liberal state more
generally, namely that its characteristic experiences of freedom were generally not moments of escape from the state but were rather thoroughly
produced by it. A key part of the trilogy's political work is to show that
production as thoroughly infrastructural; *U.S.A.* renders visible the habitually occluded infrastructures of oil to reveal its organizing presence in the
sociality of everyday life, and to track the dense interconnections between
corporate, governmental, and individual investments in oil. Ultimately,
Dos Passos's innovative modernist form in the novel, and his suggestions
on how to carve out positions of relative autonomy from the liberal state,
are reliant on these networks. This suggests a deep ambivalence within Dos
Passos's ostensibly despairing account of the growth of the "compensatory
state."

The book's final chapter examines fictions of rehabilitation in World
War One, with a focus on Laurence Stallings' *Plumes* (1924). *Plumes*
focuses on a wounded veteran negotiating the bureaucratic nightmare of
federal health care in Washington, and reflects on changes to veterans' care
instituted after the war – changes that replaced the costly Civil War
pensions system with programs promoting rehabilitation into the

workplace. As part of that shift the federal government created the Veterans' Bureau, and undertook a massive hospital-building program to develop the nation's first federal health care system. It also embarked on an extensive program of cultural work to suggest that wounded veterans now held an obligation to undergo rehabilitative treatments and make a successful return to the workforce rather than relying on meager pension stipends in the family home. Even for those with combat wounds, being a "home slacker," in the parlance of the time, was incompatible with full male citizenship; and the more extreme voices in this new rehabilitative discourse suggested that no injury was too severe for the right kind of willpower to overcome. This cultural work was effected through publications such as *Carry On: A Magazine on the Reconstruction of Disabled Soldiers and Sailors*, a multigenre magazine designed to reconfigure dominant understandings of the relationship between male citizenship, wartime injury, and governmental support. As the chapter suggests, novelists working in sentimental genre traditions took issue with this rehabilitative discourse, because it located rehabilitative care solely within institutionalized and professionalized contexts, and away from family-based traditions of affective care. In contrast, veteran, disabled writers often rejected its refusal to countenance the stubbornness of lingering injuries and the material reality of pain. Yet both these traditions engaged with the institutional formation of veterans' care following the war years, and helped cement an acceptance of large-scale federal involvement in health care.

These fictions of rehabilitation attempted to both understand and shape a new state institution through the unique possibilities of literary representation. They exemplify how authors engaged the "creative statecraft" of an era too often presumed to have given up on such Progressive ambitions, even as they remained wary of the overinflated optimism about the overlap between statist and literary creativity that characterized the early days of US involvement in the war. As such, this chapter serves as a fitting conclusion to the broader ambitions of this book. In their now-seminal *PMLA* manifesto for the New Modernist studies, Douglas Mao and Rebecca Walkowitz noticed the curious absence of the subjectivity of the citizen from recent modernist scholarship, how it is often overshadowed by prioritizations of consumption as the prime motor of modernity's public practices. They suggested we remember that "modern subjects have been not only consumers but also citizens and voters and resident aliens – members of masses capable of being organized and harangued in countless ways yet in varying degrees conscious of themselves as embedded in political situations that they may in some way affect."[143] This book seeks to assert the centrality of those issues to the middle years of American modernism. At this defining moment of state formation in US history, writers often sought to understand the changes to political institutions, sovereignties, and civic subjectivities the war had produced; and they considered how literary representation might help interpret and shape these novel political situations they themselves inhabited. Often this exercise worked by exploring the porous boundaries so characteristic of the modern liberal state, bordered on the one hand by America's extensive culture of voluntarism and obligation, and on the other by the immense bureaucratic and infrastructural resources of its large private corporations.[144] It also looked for the politics of affiliation in the new infrastructures bequeathed by the war, such as America's road network and oil industry; and it saw old infrastructures such as the Post Office as ideal vehicles for considering the new socialities and even intimacies this moment of state innovation had generated. And authors considered and negotiated new models of citizenship that emerged from the war – configurations that delivered significant changes to how civic belonging related to disability, regionality, and gender. These changes newly insinuated the federal state into everyday lives in ways both mundane and irruptive, both negotiable and overbearing, and habituated Americans to the everyday experience of federal power in ways that informed their subsequent consent to the statist ambitions of the New Deal. The literary culture of that process is the subject of what follows.

CHAPTER I

Freeloading in Hobohemia
Antimodernism, Free Verse, and the State in American World War One Periodical Culture

In January 1916, just as President Wilson began a national speaking tour to explain to the American people his decision to expand America's military as part of a program of war preparedness, the *New York Times* hosted a discussion of an issue that would loom over American modernist poetry's relationship to World War One: What are the politics of free verse?[1] The poet Josephine Preston Peabody opened the question by critiquing free verse as undemocratic, claiming that *vers libre* was "in the worst sense of the word . . . aristocratic" and exclusionary because its irregular rhythm and lack of rhyme made it impossible to memorize and therefore to share.[2] In contrast, regularized poetic meter was "the most democratic thing" in mimicking "the rhythm of the heart-beat," producing a form that was inherently collective because it ran through all "the great moments of life." She predicted that the war would "make poetry democratic again," and would discourage "mere experimenter[s] with words, making intricate verbal patterns for the entertainment of [their] friends." A week later, the poet James Oppenheim gave the modernist reply, decrying Peabody's equation of democratic art with popular appeal, and arguing instead that "democratic" art should not be understood as a formal quality. For Oppenheim, the vitality of art in a democratic society was conditional not on formal choices but on free speech, on tolerating a constelated set of practices and modes of expression, wherein each man "should be pre-eminently himself, whether that means being a hodcarrier or a philosopher."[3]

Oppenheim and Peabody's argument may now struggle for footnote status, but it exemplifies a broader phenomenon: how questions about literary modernism's public and political instrumentality became especially acute during World War One, and frequently revolved around the issue of free verse. The debate over the civic responsibilities of American modernism – and the formal choices that responsibility entailed – was highly public; not confined to little magazines, it spread to the *New Republic*, the

New York Times, and even the *Saturday Evening Post*. Modernist "bohe-mians" were alternately dismissed as esoteric, insincere, pretentious, elitist, and hermetic; and by 1917, this shaded into charges of "slacking," unpa-triotically withholding labor (and money) from the state. In contrast, magazines such as *Poetry* and the *Little Review* fostered a counterpublic sphere of debate on the war, one that frequently defended the relevance of modernism, and free verse, to a moment of collective emergency.

This chapter seeks to recover the contours of that debate by focusing on three publications: the *Saturday Evening Post*, *Poetry*, and the *Little Review*. These periodicals took dramatically divergent positions on modernist instrumentality during wartime, and did so in dialogue with one another. Of particular importance to them all was how experimental poetics could engage the rapid expansion of the state, and the role of poetry in accom-modating the new forms of sociability this expansion entailed. As outlined in the Introduction, within months of the declaration of war, the US federal state had initiated several powerful new institutions and asserted control over the spheres of private enterprise, the press, and domestic economy in unprecedented ways, often to the delight of Progressives who had long agitated for more direct governmental agency over American life. Yet much of this expansion occurred through governmental partnerships with preexisting corporate infrastructures, often reconfirming an already powerful discourse that aligned civic participation and political agency with consumer choice. In this circumstance of dramatic state expansion and the alteration (or innovation) of how a variety of social services were provided and administered, citizens' relationship to govern-ment and one another underwent substantial changes that posed both challenges to representation and transformations in what modern citizen-ship entailed. As this chapter explains, in this rapidly transforming situa-tion, "freedom" became an elastic term that focused a host of competing political, economic, and aesthetic debates as citizens and authors struggled to understand and shape new practices of citizenship, debates that extended to free verse, free speech, and freeloading. And for these maga-zines, it was this nexus that became a site for considering not only the legitimacy of American participation in World War One, but the longer-term issue of the rapidly changing social experience of American citizenship, and the question of whether writers engaged in developing experimental aesthetic forms had obligations to mediate these new social relations. In doing so these magazines developed arguments and hosted debates about artistic autonomy, state sociality, and the obligations of the aesthetic to the collective well-being that would resurface in the 1930s. Just as Wilsonian progressivism provided an important template for the policies of the New Deal, so did this early aesthetic engagement with the Progressive wartime state help shape the debates of the later era.

The enormous transformations of the American state and the flourishing of modernism that took place in the 1910s should therefore bear increased scrutiny as interrelated phenomena, and this chapter seeks to develop that scrutiny by examining how two American modernist magazines – *Poetry* and the *Little Review* – imagined the relation between individual and state, and the function of literary modernism in mediating that relation, during wartime. Despite their widely acknowledged status as the two most influential modernist little magazines of the decade published in America, the fact that they were largely unmolested by the postmaster general's aggressive implementation of the Espionage and Sedition Acts has contributed to a surprising lack of scholarship on how they articulated a commitment to experimental aesthetics as inextricable from a politics of the war.[4] The chapter also examines how this commitment was achieved in dialogue with antimodernist critics who perceived modernist experimentation as contrary to the aesthetic necessities of the wartime state, critics who took enormous pleasure in poking fun at the modernist project in lead articles of the *Saturday Evening Post*, the nation's favorite weekly magazine. For both sides, free verse focused this discussion; ripe for parody, grandiose ambition, and political investment, it became a locus where questions about aesthetic experimentation, aesthetic value, and artistic obligation were forcefully asked.

Antimodernism and Materialist Nationalism in the *Saturday Evening Post*

As the cartoon (Figure 1.1) from the *New York Tribune* in January 1917 demonstrates, even before American entry into World War One, free verse had frequently been the focus of mainstream mockery of modernists' disconnection from civic seriousness and responsibility.[5] Yet as the instrumentality of all public and economic activity underwent increased scrutiny in the war years, so calls for writers to support the needs of the state became louder. The shrillest accusations of modernist "slacking" appeared in the *Saturday Evening Post*. In 1918, it ran Wallace Irwin's "Patrioteers: The Red War and the Pink," a poem satirizing the attitude of New York's bohemian poets toward the war. Irwin mocked Greenwich Village's writers as an "Amateur League of Self-starting Messiahs," vainly considering themselves the unacknowledged legislators of the world; in actuality, their verse

A Free Science Family Emancipated from the Law of Gravitation

Figure 1.1 "Shouting the Battle Cry of Freedom: Free Verse and Free Art Having Shown the Way, Free Science May Now Shake Off Its Shackles and Help to Swell the Ranks of Emancipated Knowledge. With Science Unfettered, Only Old Fogies Will Observe the Rules of Gravitation." *New York Tribune* (January 21, 1917), 8. Image courtesy of Chronicling America: Historic American Newspapers, Library of Congress

consisted of "patent unworkable war panaceas." Sheltered from the reality of public emergency in "a mauve mildewed hole/Full of sawdust and soul" in Greenwich Village, their "rare inspirations/Were limited mostly to rare publications/Of small circulations."[6] These writers later settle at the "Pink Magazine," whose editor is reluctant to print anything connected to the war; he welcomes them as "souls so refined that of war they can make/A toothsome confection, quite pleasant to take."[7] Pointedly, the modernists' understanding of freedom leads them to freeload; as they leave the bar with the well-intentioned cry "to our work–/let none be a slacker or conscience-less shirk!", they "left the poor waiter to ponder and think:/'It's all very well – but who pays for the drink?'"[8]

Irwin's mockery of modernism's interconnected mixture of elitism, pacifism, impracticality, squeamishness, abstraction, experimentalism, pretentiousness, and anticommercialism was typical of the *Saturday Evening Post*, which during the war proudly positioned itself as the opposite of all these things. By 1913 the *Post* had sales of over two million; estimates suggest it reached an astonishing 10 percent of Americans.[9] The *Post*'s phenomenal success relied on a loss-leading cover price of a nickel to encourage mass circulation, a cover price subsidized by advertising – which occupied around 50 percent of the 100-page plus weekly.[10] As Jan Cohn brilliantly demonstrates, this business model gradually developed into an identifiable "*Post* style," typified by a celebration of business, self-reliance, personal upward mobility for the hardworking (guaranteed by the progress of a classless America), and moderate consumption as the visible marker of progress.[11] As Thorstein Veblen noted in 1905, this pro-business policy was delivered consistently across fiction, nonfiction, editorials, and advertisements, dissolving differences between genre and register.[12] Moreover, the magazine flourished partly because of its aggressive campaign of nationalization, as the *Post* style aimed to interpellate the *Post*'s readers, employees, and even the newsies who delivered it into an ideology of America.[13] Cultivating national (rather than sectional or local) habits of taste was attractive to the *Post*'s advertisers, who were keen to foster national habits of consumption; as Cohn notes, "the *Post* was created to echo and re-inforce in its contents the emerging concept of America as a nation unified by the consumption of standardized commodities."[14]

Moreover, the interlocking reliance of advertising and a national readership in the *Post*'s success occurred as consumption was beginning to be formulated not just as patriotic but as civic participation in its own right. The *Post* represents an influential artifact and motor of what Charles McGovern has called material nationalism; as he explains, between 1890

and 1940, "Americans came to understand spending as a form of citizenship, an important ritual of national identity in daily life. Explicit political
and civic language, images, and practices that equated voting with buying
shaped common understandings of consumption."[15] The *Post*'s adverts,
fiction, and editorials configured consumption in this way; a discourse that
"conferred Americanness through and in things," material nationalism also
framed individual liberty as freedom of choice – a freedom best expressed
and reproduced in the marketplace.[16]

An example of this material nationalism is this Hyatt ball bearing advert,
where Hyatt ball bearings make possible the public *sphere* by providing the
architectural frame to public *space* (see Figure 1.2). Found in mines, race-
tracks, farms, factories, and advertised on billboards situated above theaters, dancing-halls, and vacant lots, Hyatt bearings form the material and
commercial infrastructure of this panoramic view of national space. Their
products allow the citizenry to travel to the town's public square, as they
are installed in the motor cars that transport them, and each corner of this
square bears their advertisements. The square's function of public assembly, debate, and celebration is thus enabled and structured by this fantasy
of monopolistic corporate dominance, so much so that citizens choose the
language of the Hyatt adverts to affirm their national loyalty. In this vision,
nationalist public assembly and speech, military and auxiliary service (there
are prominent signs for the YMCA and the Red Cross), quieting the
Kaiser, and choosing the quietest ball bearings become aligned as symme-
trical and inextricable acts of wartime civic participation and patriotism.
Hyatt ball bearings literally articulate, in both linguistic and mechanical
terms, the points of contact between social forms and identities: between
individual and state, citizen and consumer, corporation and community,
wage-laborer and volunteer.

The *Post*'s material nationalism meant that its hostility to modernist
experiment frequently focused on the economies of modernism, as Irwin's
poem suggests. In 1917 and 1918, the *Post* ran several articles ridiculing what
it called the "hobohemian" movement in Greenwich Village – reserving
particular scorn for ideas of modernist "freedom." Days after the United
States declared war on Germany in April 1917, Sinclair Lewis – who would
famously mock bohemian affectation in *Main Street* (1920) and *Babbitt*
(1922) – published the satirical short story "Hobohemia," the week's lead
feature. "Hobohemia" features a young businessman, Dennis Brown, who
follows his aspiring-bohemian sweetheart to Greenwich Village in an
attempt to persuade her to return to their home of Northernapolis.
Forced to ingratiate himself into "hobohemia" – "the place and state of

Figure 1.2 Hyatt Ball Bearings advertised in the *Saturday Evening Post*, July 6, 1918

being talented and free" – to win her back, he pursues modernist literary success by applying business methodology to writing literature; he hires an office, a press agent, an ideas man, and a Russian translator.[17] Together, the staff of the D.J. Brown Literary Productions Incorporated churns out

avant-garde poems and stories with astonishing success; Dennis reflects
that "the reason these guys [bohemian writers] get away with literature is
because no business man has taken the trouble to go in and buck them."[18]
He concocts a Russian novelist called Zuprushin; several of his stories are
accepted by the little magazine *Direct Action*. Soon, "The Zuprushin
brand ... became their chief line of manufacture," and after his first two
stories – "The Faun of Folly" and "Fog of the Samovar" – appear, the
company is deluged with "dozens of letters from small but fiercely icono-
clastic magazines asking for contributions."[19] When Zuprushin's novel,
Dementia, comes out, it is a sensation.

The story charts a complex relationship between modern American
business and experimental, bohemian modernism. Primarily, modernism
has unacknowledged concordances with consumer capitalism, which
Lewis's work seeks to impishly uncover. Brown finds modernism's hunger
for conceptual novelties, especially ones that can be easily formulated and
quickly circulated, to be akin to his experience with public relations.
In promoting Zuprushin, Brown understands his market, builds curiosity
in his product, and carefully controls information flow to increase antici-
pation for his novel and thus maximize its impact. Free verse imagist
poetry, with its supposed stress on unity, concision, and iconoclasm, recalls
his work on advertisements, although most free verse poems are "not so
well done."[20] Brown finds his experience writing reports on lumber-tract
conditions helpful in forging Russian naturalist fiction, due to their
mutually laborious accumulation of quotidian detail. The joke is modernism's unacknowledged reliance on a business system it claimed to repudi-
ate; Lewis suggests that modernism would, in fact, be helpless without the
methodologies of information management and brand recognition developed by advertising and public relations (PR). This neatly reverses one of
the truisms about modernism's relationship to mass consumer culture,
namely the ease with which its subversive potential was co-opted into
cultures of fashionability and commercial design, ultimately serving as
a "kind of research and development arm of the culture industry."[21]
Instead, for Lewis, business serves as the unacknowledged R&D arm of
modernism. Lewis's formulation therefore categorizes bohemia more as "a
transitory and acceptable form of urban slumming," to draw on Janet
Lyon's genealogical account of bohemianism, than as "a self-marginalizing
and generationally determined artistic community whose work heroically
transcends the economic pressures and prescriptive norms of bourgeois
aesthetics."[22] Bohemia's vaunted iconoclasm is actually plagiarism.

Lewis's smug formulation seems to dismiss bohemia as nothing but derivative, but for one caveat. Brown's press agent tells him that the latest poetic style is free verse, "so called because it doesn't pay ... A kind of poetry you wouldn't know it was poetry if it wasn't printed that way."[23] Later, Brown abandons writing *vers libre* for exactly this reason: it "didn't sell very well, and it attracted no attention."[24] Glossing "free" verse as valueless verse was such a good joke that it was repeated in Irvin Cobb's piece on Greenwich Village, "Improbable People of an Impossible Land," which appeared in July 1917. Drawing heavily on Lewis's portrait in "Hobohemia," Cobb opined that "real artists almost without exception are smart businessmen who dress and behave unostentatiously."[25] In contrast, Greenwich Village bohemianism is represented as indulgent posturing incapable of producing anything valuable, where "free lunch, free verse and free love, fattens the greasy he-alien who has hit upon the delectable knack of existing without working."[26] Cobb aims at some predictable targets: bohemian disdain for bourgeois standards, bohemian dress, costume balls, bohemian restaurants, and little theaters. Yet, in a twist on Lewis's piece, the "one true Bohemian" of Cobb's acquaintance has just been drafted, and is being forced to work. Bohemian nonproductivity, therefore, becomes particularly offensive during wartime, as Cobb, the *Post's* star reporter on the war in Belgium in 1914–1915, obviously felt qualified to judge.[27] Partly, Cobb was critiquing those who prioritized their individual liberties above their obligations to the state at a moment of national crisis, a commonplace view at the time. But there was a more specific aspect to this. Surrounded by advertisements aligning wartime patriotic service with forms of consumption newly attuned to civic purpose, Cobb's piece cast modernists' refusal to produce or to consume (except when things were free) as outside a sphere of national consensus in ways that were at best risible, and at worst seditious.

Cobb's synchronization of patriotism with consumption aligned with a series of hand-wringing editorials in the *Post* pondering whether prewar habits of consumption were patriotic or unhelpful during wartime. This anxiety was partly caused by the contradiction between the encouragement of consumption by the *Post's* extensive advertising and the advice of agencies such as the Food Administration to reduce consumption of key commodities to assist the war effort. That the Food Administration made these exhortations within the pages of the Curtis publications only sharpened that sense of contradiction.[28] Predominantly, however, material nationalism remained the keynote of the *Post* throughout the war, as advertisers strove to link consumption of their products with national service. Parker, for example, boasted that their pens were "used in the armies and navies of the world," and cajoled mothers that "your boy needs a Parker." Del Monte proudly announced it was "working to win the War"; Paige Automobiles advertised itself as a "national utility"; Victor Victrola boasted it was "thrilling the soul of the nation," including soldiers in camp; and Kodak launched a successful campaign to market cameras to soldiers.[29] Cobb's criticism was therefore consistent with the *Post*'s overall policy in its attack on modernist "freedom" in economic terms, and in two key respects. First, if consumption did, as material nationalism implied, amount to civic participation, then by not paying for the goods one consumed, one defaulted on one's civic obligations. A "free lunch" stymies the fiscal exchange that served as the symbolic and functional equivalent to democratic choice; without this exchange one could not validate oneself as part of the state. Secondly, "free" verse, for both Lewis and Cobb, was an economic failure from the perspective of the recent neoclassical "marginalist revolution" in economics – which argued that demand for a product, not the labor time or material costs involved in producing the product, was the condition that configured value. As James Livingston observes, this theory, which was gaining orthodoxy in the early century, asserted that "unless effective demand validated the prior expenditures of labor-power, commodities would have no value regardless of the labor-time contained in them."[30] Given that free verse is free because "it doesn't pay," it is effectively valueless as a commodity in the literary marketplace, despite the labor-time it might take to produce. It therefore became *wasted* labor, which could have assisted the wartime economy elsewhere. Dennis Brown abandons free verse because he cannot generate demand for it, unlike other modernist forms; for Cobb, it vacates normative systems of exchange (along with "free love") to exist as a solipsistic and unsocial indulgence.[31] Emerging at a time when the national instrumentality of all forms of labor and consumption was under scrutiny, these forms of being "free" therefore became un-American, marking bohemian free versifiers as "greasy he-alien[s]" in a nativist rhetoric that the *Post* would ramp into hysterical proportions in 1918.

Poetry, the State, and Modernist Freedom in Wartime

In the face of such hostility, modernist magazines contested the meaning of freedom in wartime. The struggle of magazines such as *The Masses* and *The Seven Arts* to protect their freedoms to criticize the war in print are well known, as is their ultimate failure to do so in the face of the Espionage Act of June 1917, in the case of *The Masses*, and declining support from patrons, in the case of *The Seven Arts*.[32] Yet other little magazines, those which focused less on direct political confrontations with government war policy, nonetheless articulated visions about the distinctive contribution of modernist verse to wartime public discourse. *Poetry* magazine, edited by Harriet Monroe, was especially ambitious in this regard. As John Timberman Newcomb has recently argued, Monroe repeatedly asserted the exceptional contribution that poetry could make in the representation of complex modern and social systems. This was central to the brilliance and the long-standing influence of *Poetry*'s project, which was to rescue poetry from a widely articulated crisis of value in the early century and reinvigorate the medium, delivering it from the stagnation and near obsolescence it had experienced under the decades-long stewardship of "genteel custodians bent upon protecting it from the sullying forces of modern life: urbanization, organized labor, commodity culture."[33] Moreover, Monroe emphasized the historical and social contingency of poetic form, pointing out that the complexity and scale of modern social organization necessitated formal novelty and experiment. As Newcomb notes, even in her initial editorial in *Poetry* in 1912, "The Motive of the Magazine," Monroe had identified an "immediate and desperate need" for a poetic medium that could accommodate the "confusion of modern immensities" that resulted from a global scale of sociality, as every individual "through something he buys or knows or loves, reaches out to the ends of the earth."[34] This situation was rendered even more "immediate and desperate" by the war, and Monroe's ambitions for poetry expanded accordingly.

Monroe's orientation of *Poetry* as a magazine devoted to showcasing the responsiveness – and even the unparalleled representational resources – of modern verse in the face of the new technological and social conditions of modernity meant she published war poetry in the magazine right from the outset of hostilities. Indeed, as early as September 1914 *Poetry* was advertising a $100 prize for the best poem to be featured in a forthcoming war number, an issue which appeared that November and included war verse by Amy Lowell, Wallace Stevens, Carl Sandburg, and Maxwell Bodenheim, among others.[35] During the conflict, it published some of the central texts in what would later form the canon of World War One verse, including Rupert Brooke's "The Soldier" (April 1915), Isaac Rosenberg's "Break of Day in the Trenches" (December 1916), and Wallace Stevens' "The Death of a Soldier" (May 1918); it featured extended reviews of the work of Wilfred Owen, Siegfried Sassoon, Rupert Brooke, and Alan Seeger during the war and its immediate aftermath. In common

with most of the American press, its attitude toward the war shifted over
the course of the conflict. At the war's outset Monroe asserted that the
pressing, contemporary job of poetry was to provide a counternarrative to
the glamorization of war – a narrative that poetry had been foundational in
establishing in the first place. As she wrote in September 1914, "the feeling
that war is beautiful still lingers in men's hearts, a feeling founded on
world-old savageries – love of power, of torture, of murder, love of big
stakes in a big game. This feeling must be destroyed, as it was created,
through the imagination. It is work for a poet."[36] When her co-editor,
Alice Corbin Henderson, provided the editorial comment that framed the
poems in the November 1914 issue, she took a similar line, asserting that
"the American feeling about the war is a genuine revolt against war, and we
have believed that POETRY might help to serve the cause of peace by
encouraging the expression of this spirit of protest" – a spirit that stressed
how the war's "collective naked waste" had caused war to lose "its illusion
and glamor."[37]

However, by early 1917 Monroe and *Poetry* saw the relationship of poets
to the state at a time of war as far more conciliatory, or even cooperative.
In a series of extraordinary editorials, Monroe outlined a utopian vision for
a new era of concordance between poetry and the state, wherein a formally
liberated verse would be the appropriate representational vehicle for
a universal state that would supersede local nation-states. As Allesandria
Polizzi has discussed, in several *Poetry* editorials Monroe outlined utopian
hopes that the war would usher in the end of nationalism, and see the birth
of this global, universal state.[38] In January, for example, Monroe expressed
the hope that "through the war the spirit of man is to be reborn. ... men
and nations are just about to begin their militant march toward the
common goal of a universal state organized for joy and beauty through
mutual service and universal brotherhood."[39] By the time the United States
was a combatant, Monroe was still decrying the bloodiness of war, but
nonetheless celebrating it as "a builder," a force capable of "sweeping away
old accumulations of falseness and ugliness, clearing the ground and the air
for great artists, great poets, great leaders, who shall see and reveal. We may
be fighting for greater issues than now appear: for the federation of the
world."[40]

For Monroe, this transformed political landscape posed profound representational challenges. Monroe perceived the war had delivered
a dislocating representational crisis of scale, stretching to incomprehensi-
bility the distance between the complex global connections that underpinned modern life, and atomized, immediate, individual experience.

In her postwar volume of poetry *The Difference and Other Poems*, Monroe remarked on the "terrible enforcement of that change through the immense and wasteful disaster of the World War," explaining that if "A century ago each man's world was small, each neighborhood supplied of its own needs . . . Today each man's world is enormously enlarged, each village makes demands to the ends of the earth, and governmental issues seem to outgrow the capacity of the individual human brain."[41] Here she anticipates Robert Wiebe's classic account of the decline of "island communities" at this moment in American life, when local systems and networks were being rapidly replaced by new and increasingly complex systems in the fields of economy, communication, and governance that were national in scope.[42] For Monroe, the war cemented this process; the dislocating cognitive shift it provoked was primarily caused by the size of contemporary government rather than the size or trauma of contemporary conflict, connected though they were. Rather than the affective particularity of modern, technological combat, it was the state's expansion beyond the capacities of individual cognition that challenged poetic language.

Monroe, therefore, identified the discrepancy between the individual and the size of the wartime state as the supreme feature of modern political experience, a discrepancy that modernist aesthetic innovation might adequately mediate. Monroe was not alone in such assessments; as discussed in the Introduction, some of the most influential political theorists of the era, such as Walter Lippmann and Randolph Bourne, were also turning their attention to the problem of representing the state, especially given its recent and rapid expansion. She shared the sense of these political commentators that the state was "a mystical conception," in Bourne's words, whose "glamour" and "significance linger behind the framework of Government and direct its activities" – an entity sublime in its depersonalized formlessness and scale.[43] In this circumstance, Monroe believed poetry could do crucial political work; she would have endorsed Michael Walzer's claim half a century later that the state must be "personified before it can be seen, symbolized before it can be loved, imagined before it can be conceived."[44]

During the war *Poetry* regularly argued that traditional verse forms could not mediate this colossal disparity between individual and state, but that modernist poetry could. In the June 1917 issue Alice Corbin Henderson argued this point while assessing *Life* magazine's wartime poetry contest. *Life*, which ran some of the crudest US propaganda cartoons during the war, had advertised a $500 prize for a poem of up to twenty-four lines that "should be a song of modern Democracy, typifying the spirit of Liberty,

Fraternity, Equality and the Allies." Criteria included the poem's "adaptability to music" and its "correct metrical rendering." This was quite in contrast to the war poetry competition *Poetry* had run in 1914, which had no such formal prescriptions (and which received an incredible 738 entries).[45] Henderson found risible the idea of treating such complex political systems within such a formal straightjacket; as she sniggered, "Any poet who can tackle modern Democracy, the spirit of Liberty, Fraternity, Equality, and the Allies, and get away with it in twenty-four lines, is entitled to all that is coming to him. Nevertheless, we hope for the miracle."[46]

Both Henderson and Monroe took to heart criticism that *Poetry* had not published enough patriotic poetry, and repeatedly asserted their "desire to print with the utmost promptitude any 'song for America' sent to its office which may seem worth printing."[47] As part of this effort to encourage submissions, even as they worried that "[v]ery little real poetry is written in the heat of battle," they ran publicity material for The Vigilantes, the writers' syndicate devoted to turning out pro-Allied fiction and poetry which by 1918 had become a byword for the worst kind of nativist, red-baiting propaganda material (Henderson even contributed a poem to them).[48] And both Monroe and Henderson published their own war verse in *Poetry*. Monroe remained optimistic about finding a truly modern war poem; in her July 1917 editorial "Will Art Happen?" she dismissed most American war verse produced thus far as "good journalism," but still held out the hope that "the new war song, when it comes, may well express a terror and beauty, and an over-arching infinite love, beyond the highest or deepest possible reach of the singers of lesser ages."[49] Monroe's identification of elasticity in a potential "New war song" as its most salient quality is telling; as the modern age grew in governmental complexity, and the distance increased between the individual experience of agency and the bureaucratic operations of state power, scope became the most important formal requisite for a modern poetry of statehood. *Poetry*, Monroe eagerly emphasized, was eager to support such efforts, and "to be the medium of . . . interpretation of the present crisis."[50]

In March 1918 Monroe produced her fullest consideration of the wartime role of art, which began with the contentious issue of the instrumentality of devoting wartime labor to poetry. Considering "what right has the thinker to his problem, the artist to his vision, the poet to his song, while fresh lives are giving up their hope of thought and art and song?" she admitted that "the arts seem at first glance to be a pottering with toys . . . out of the current of great events." Yet, she suggests, this view overlooked how art helped form a nation's "spiritual forces," the way traditions of aesthetic practice configured moral and political consensus. As she claimed, "every painter of his own wood-lot, every poet singing the beauty of working-girls instead of queens, or the bravery of common men instead of princes, has been doing his bit to democratize the world." The power of this cultural normalization of democracy was such that "the Kaiser is a man of straw against a force like this. Whitman and Millet beat him before he was born – our soldiers have but to finish the job."[51] Poets and artists' celebration of quotidian, working-class experience was a form of aesthetic enfranchisement, a form that asserted an irreducible claim to democratic, political enfranchisement for all; governments could thereby only gain assent within a range of political possibilities that a cultural milieu had established. Culture – and poetry – thus set the parameters of a state's political options.

Moreover, in the current crisis poetry had a second political role, one of heroic mediation and the ability to illuminate the sublimity of modern governmental forms:

> When the whole world is in the melting-pot, when civilization is to be reminted and no-one can tell what stamp its face and reverse will bear; when ideas, which flowed hitherto in separate channels, are gathering into vast tides that overwash the boundaries of nations ... then the stand of the individual against immensities, a stand always hazardous, becomes a gesture of incredible power and pride, an attitude of almost impossible heroism, the lonely uprising of a naked pigmy between overpowering hordes and the abyss. ... Puny unit of the unconquerable will, he must hold up his little torch between the old and new.[52]

That Monroe chose the reminting of coinage as her metaphor for geo-political change is also significant; it suggests both the *historicity* of systems of monetary value and the symbolic elasticity of money (a feature made especially palpable in wartime, as many belligerent European currencies abandoned the gold standard for fiat currencies). In this way, monetary value was hardly the fixed and indisputable system for pricing aesthetic products that magazines such as the *Saturday Evening Post* suggested. Paradoxically, free verse's value resided in its capacious ability to accommodate diverse and complex systems of fluctuating value, of which money was one.

Later issues of *Poetry* ran letters from YMCA workers, relating their encounters with devoted *Poetry* readers among the ranks of the American Expeditionary Force. It also included adverts from the Red Cross, the YMCA, and the Fourth Liberty Loan Drive asking for readers to send in "publicity rhymes" to aid the war effort.[53] It ran war verse by Carl Sandburg, Richard Aldington, Vachel Lindsay, John Reed, and Wallace Stevens. And in April 1918, Alice Corbin Henderson argued for American poets to be recognized as "official government agents" and given access to the front lines for the purposes of "see[ing] and record[ing] this war for future generations." In a pointed rebuke to magazines such as the *Saturday Evening Post*, she mused "what big magazine will be progressive enough to send an American poet to the front as an accredited correspondent?" – as poets, she suggested, were uniquely suited to giving American readers "more than journalism." Indeed, the government and the magazine industry would do well to accommodate modern verse in its sanctioned spaces of war culture, for "our poetry is now in closer touch with our lives than any other form of native art."[54]

In November 1918, *Poetry's* vision of the symbiotic partnership between state and modernist verse went a step further, as it exulted in Conrad Aiken's gaining a draft exemption for being a poet, which the War Department, in his (isolated) case, had granted through classifying poetry as an "essential industry."[55] Rather than apply for exemption on the typical grounds of being a husband and father, Aiken had filed on the basis of being a poet, and some "ultimate Solomon" in Washington had arbitrated in his favor. Monroe welcomed the fact that Aiken's impish claim had accorded poetry "what it has never before . . . received in this country – official recognition, a definite legal status." For Monroe, this was not merely a reciprocal acknowledgment by the state of poetry's instrumentality to its effective functioning – was not just a confirmation of the position she had outlined in "The War and the Artist." It was also a definitive statement indicating a structural position for the poet within the expansive apparatus of the state. Aiken's deferral positioned the writing of poetry as instrumentally equivalent to front-line military service, but in addition also suggested that the state had itself embraced the possibility of a poetics of the state, was aware of its own aesthetic nature. Monroe's argument was twofold: that the state was the representational object of supreme importance and challenge to modern poetry, and one that only formal experiment could approach; and that the expanding ambitions of scope held by both the modern state and modern poetry would inevitably be symbiotically developed. This saw modernism and the state as bedfellows, not antagonists, as the *Saturday Evening Post* had claimed; and in classifying Aiken as an essential worker Monroe could at least entertain the possibility that the War Department agreed with her.

The *Little Review* and the War

Poetry's ambition to align modernist experiment with state expansion – perhaps even beyond the confines of the nation – was not widely shared across the spectrum of American little magazines. Other publications dwelt on how wartime legislation had limited political speech, and how wartime material nationalism was circumscribing understandings of freedom. The quintessential modernist little magazine, the *Little Review*, was perhaps most innovative in this latter critique. Founded in Chicago in 1914 by Margaret Anderson, and co-edited by her partner Jane Heap, it was famous for the airily elitist masthead: "Making No Compromise with the Public Taste." During the war it relocated to New York, and began the serial publication of Joyce's *Ulysses*, which resulted in one of modernism's defining censorship battles. But the *Little Review* also ruffled feathers with Jane Heap's declaration in 1917 that "none of us considers this war a legitimate or an interesting subject for Art," and its consequent refusal to reproduce the jingoistic tenor of most of the American press.[56]

Heap's seemingly dismissive remark, as well as the *Little Review's* prewar attachment to Emma Goldman and anarchism – which brought it under Bureau of Investigation surveillance, and led to it being labeled as a (potentially nonmailable) "Publication of Anarchist Tendency" on the Post Office list of publications – has led many critics to ignore the complexity of the *Little Review's* politics of engagement with the wartime state.[57] For example, both Jayne Marek's and Mark Morrison's work on the *Little Review* explores how the "Reader Critic" section of the magazine – which presented readers' letters alongside replies from the editorial team – functioned as a vibrant discursive space that "ascribed an equal status to correspondents and primary authors alike," and established an important counterpublic sphere where modernism was defined and contested.[58] But they pay little attention to how, in 1917, the *Little Review* used this section's dialogic capacity to consider the war, and especially the question of what responsibilities artists held to the broader civic community during wartime. The *Little Review's* strategy acted to assuage the sharpening dilemmas of the war years for an avant-garde that could no longer blithely dismiss citizenship by linking it to bourgeois rationalism (Pound, in February 1914, had labeled the term "bourgeoisie" as "one of opprobrium, used by the bohemian, or the artist in contempt of the citizen").[59] As Janet Lyon notes, during the war years "the avant-garde program of integrating the realms of the political and the aesthetic was increasingly threatened by the Scylla of bourgeois instrumentalism and the Charybdis of solipsistic aestheticism."[60] The reader-critic section of the *Little Review* seemed to offer passage through that channel by presenting contributions from a variety of perspectives and in multiple formats, a strategy that fragmented the Manichaean options for a political aesthetic that Lyon identifies.

During 1917 the *Little Review*'s reader-critic section featured a letter from a front-line soldier criticizing the *Little Review*'s aesthetic, and requesting instead a more masculine, vital, practical, and passionate art to match the contours of his own transformed perspective. They published Margaret Anderson's defense of the *Little Review*'s editorial policy against this plea. They published Jane Heap's critique of vigilantes and police breaking up an antiwar demonstration, and letters from readers canceling their subscriptions in disgust at Heap's seemingly antiwar sentiments. They published letters from readers asking why there was not more material on the war, and letters protesting Heap's reply that the war was not an interesting subject for art. And they engaged with readers suggesting that the war was being fought to preserve just the kind of art and freedom that the *Little Review* prized so highly, a conversation that took place over the *Little Review*'s review of Henri Barbusse's searing war novel *Le feu*. (This featured Margaret Anderson's testy dismissal of the virtues of martial heroism: "I thought we needn't argue any longer about the vice of self-sacrifice."[61])

Outside the reader-critic section, the *Little Review* also courted war-related controversy for its publication of Wyndham Lewis's short story "Cantelman's Spring Mate." This related the tale of a Dionysian young officer in the British Army in the spring of 1917; he gets a young English girl pregnant while stationed in camp, abandons her, and then relishes killing Germans in the trenches (his "Spring mate" is both the "ruined" young woman and the German whose head he bashes in during the spring offensives, in ecstasies of sexual and violent energy respectively). The story's inclusion in the October 1917 number resulted in the issue being banned from the mails for its purportedly obscene depictions of sex, a decision the *Little Review* appealed. The *Little Review* then published the legal decision upholding the banning of the issue, written by Judge Augustus Hand, in the December number – along with a rebuttal from Anderson of the decision's main contentions. In the March 1918 issue, Pound printed the entire section of the Criminal Code the story had purportedly violated in his article "The Classics Escape."

Despite tepidly upholding the postmaster's ban, Hand was clearly uncomfortable with the prevailing guidelines for categorizing publications as obscene, the so-called "Hicklin test." This allowed censors to evaluate excerpts out of the context of the work as a whole, and to consider its effects on all readers (especially young children) rather than a work's probable readership. (Hand would be a part of the judicial team that put the nail in the coffin of the Hicklin test; he wrote the majority opinion for the three-judge New York appellate court decision upholding Judge Woolsey's overturning of the ban on James Joyce's *Ulysses* in 1934 in *United States v. One Book Called Ulysses*, which effectively did away with this prevailing approach to obscenity.[62]) In his 1917 decision on "Cantelman's Spring Mate," Hand demurred that

> few would . . . doubt that some prevention of the mailing of lewd publica-
> tions is desirable, and yet no field of administration requires better judge-
> ment or more circumspection to avoid interference with a justifiable
> freedom of expression and literary judgement. I have little doubt that
> numerous really great writings would come under the ban if tests that are
> frequently current were applied. . . . It is very easy by a narrow and prudish
> construction of the Statute to suppress literature of permanent merit.[63]

In a section that delighted Pound, he noted that many such "really great writings" "escape [censorship] only because they come within the term 'classics,' which means, for the purpose of the application of the statute, that they are ordinarily free from interference, because they have the sanction of age and fame and usually appeal to a comparatively limited number of readers."[64] As it happened, the *Little Review* found its appeal handled by one of the most speech-protective judges then at work in the United States, and one who, along with his cousin Learned Hand, was at the forefront of First Amendment jurisprudence in the first half of the twentieth century. (Learned Hand had been one of the first judges to interpret the recently passed Espionage Act, overturning the New York postmaster's decision to ban the August issue of the left-wing magazine *The Masses* from the New York mails for its opposition to conscription under the terms of the act.[65]) "Cantelman's Spring Mate," therefore, brought the *Little Review* into contact with a relatively liberal, and ulti-mately influential, member of the twentieth-century US judiciary on the topic of free speech at a moment when First Amendment jurisprudence was at a formative stage. As Christopher Capozzola notes, this was a crucial time in the evolution of an American political culture of the right to speak free from the interference of the state, as "out of this wartime crucible emerged the American Civil Liberties Union, modern First Amendment jurisprudence (articulated, at the beginning, only in dissent), and understandings of individual rights in popular political culture that would transform American politics in the twentieth century."[66] As has long been understood, that jurisprudence had a long and significant interrelation with the fate of modernist publishing in the United States; and although Anderson read Hand's opinion as the overreach of a federal state devoid of any respect for individual rights to speech or to the broad civic value of aesthetic experimentation, in fact it represented an early part of a broad reframing of the right to free speech that was one of World War One's enduring legal legacies in the United States.[67]

Pound, in contrast to Anderson, intuited more of Hand's nuance on this issue from the outset. He had privately commended elements of Hand's decision to Anderson, and had urged her to print it in the magazine "EVERY MONTH" as "a labour of patriotism wherefrom we must not shrink."[68] Although Anderson declined Pound's suggestion, Pound re-printed sections from Hand's decision in his March 1918 editorial "The Classics Escape," along with sections of the US Criminal Code dealing with the definition of "obscene" material, the mailing or circulation of which was cause for criminal prosecution. (He also thundered that he would "continue to publish the text of this law until the law is amended."[69]) In his editorial, Pound averred that "no more damning indictment of American civilization has been written than that contained in Judge Hand's 'opinion'"; although Hand had upheld the postmaster's ban, Pound clearly reveled in – and seconded – his blunt observation that the classics only "escaped" censorship due to their comparatively small readership, a judgment that indirectly echoed Pound's often-expressed disdain for American provincialism and the aesthetic mediocrity of its mass culture.[70] Hand's opinion also informed his short satirical poem "Cantico del Sole," also in the March issue, with its refrain "The thought of what America would be like/If the Classics had a wide circulation/Troubles my sleep."[71] The upshot of the affair, therefore, was a complex discussion in the pages of the magazine of the prevailing standards of obscenity in the jurisprudence of free speech, what "classic" status meant in relation to those standards, and whether in effect sedition had become a form of obscenity and therefore a reason for suppressing material. It also showed that, despite decrying the state's limitations on free speech, Pound at least recognized the state as the best potential guarantor of free speech, the agency most likely to protect speech under a discourse of rights from the tyranny of a provincial majority.

While ostensibly claiming that the war was "not interesting," then, the *Little Review* in fact produced one of the most insightful considerations of the war's effect on American cultural life, and of the question of whether or not artists had particular obligations at a moment when the relation between state and individual had been so radically transformed. At the center of those considerations was Anderson's most provocative image of the war, her one-page editorial in April 1917 (see Figure 1.3). At one level this page supports Heap's statement that the *Little Review* had nothing to say about the war. But to read it solely as having nothing to say overlooks its status as a response to the growing call for magazine pages to be effectively nationalized as a wartime resource. Even in the first month of American participation there were calls for magazine and newspaper space to be donated to publicizing the Liberty Bond campaign.[72] In April 1917, shortly after Wilson had created the CPI, the so-called Chicago Plan was supporting the First Liberty Loan Drive.[73] The plan solicited donations from clubs, businesses, and individuals to be used to promote Liberty Loans by purchasing advertising space in the nation's newspapers and magazines. Newspapers and magazines alone donated space worth $160,000 per month to the government, and advertising agencies also donated space.[74] As well as Liberty Loan publicity, this space was used to convey information about the facts of selective service, registering for the draft, and following the guidelines of the Food Administration. The Advertising Division of the CPI was praised by the Provost-Marshal-General, E.H. Crowder, for perfecting a system "genuinely American in its method – [a] voluntary union of individual citizens to accomplish those results which in some continental countries are left to the vast army of government officials."[75] As Creel thrilled in his autobiography, *How We Advertised America*, advertising had shaped the methodological, ideological, and discursive nature of the CPI; the Committee's work had been, in his words, "the world's greatest adventure in advertising."[76] The state had been explained and legitimated through this medium, which simultaneously solicited political and financial support from its citizens. And yet this process was not wholly controlled by the state, by Crowder's vast army of bureaucrats; instead, the state had been marketed through the "American ... method" of utilizing the infrastructure of commercial information production, management, and placement. As advertising provided the institutions and the rhetoric with which the state conducted much of its wartime communication with its citizenry, it therefore set up deep structural homologies between the activity of the consumer in the marketplace and how citizens could exercise agency within the institutions of the state.

Anderson's blank-page editorial anticipated these contexts by rightly suggesting its own seditiousness. On the one hand, it defied the wartime

4   *The Little Review*

The War

Margaret C. Anderson

[*We will probably be suppressed for this.*]

Figure 1.3 Margaret Anderson's War Editorial in the April 1917 *Little Review*

culture of coercive voluntarism. As Christopher Capozzola has suggested, the language of obligation – usually rendered in terms of duty and sacrifice – was dominant in Americans' conception of their relationship to the state at the outset of World War One. Men who did not register for the draft, women who did not knit socks, and citizens who refused to buy Liberty Loans faced fierce pressure from their communities and less frequently from the government. Failure to volunteer – or, in this case, to speak – Anderson rightly saw as contrary to popular traditions of citizenship in the United States, where simple inaction or having nothing to say threatened the principles of voluntarism the state relied upon for its successful operation.[77] By definition, a blank page volunteers nothing, and she rightly predicted that having nothing to volunteer would be subject to intensive coercion in the months to come.

However, her editorial also addressed the culture of material nationalism exemplified by the *Post* and underpinning what would become the modus operandi of the CPI's Division of Advertising. In this context Anderson's editorial becomes even more challenging; it is wasted space and wasted money, space conspicuously not donated to the government, used for her own editorial, or filled with advertising. As critics such as Mark Morrison and Lawrence Rainey have shown, the *Little Review* was not perpetually hostile to advertising, and indeed relied on it for some of its revenue. Anderson was also acutely aware of the value of magazine space in wartime; in April 1916 she had apologized to readers that "because of the war – paper is going up. We can't help looking ugly this month."[78] Moreover, Anderson had already tried the editorial trick of identifying blank pages in the *Little Review* as unsold space; in the June–July issue of 1915, when advertising had dropped off, Anderson printed seven mostly blank pages with only a small box of type indicating the ads that might have appeared (and the price they would have cost).[79] In wartime, this strategy looked very different; the commodity of magazine pages had become a nationalized resource, and consuming them became an act of wartime civic participation. Anderson's blank editorial demonstrated her concern with both the nationalization of consumption and the analogism of consumption to citizenship, the reduction of the notion of liberty to freedom of choice. The page sardonically chooses not to choose, and thereby presents a defamiliarizing break from a national-material ideology that only really worked when one's freedoms were framed solely through operations that had marketplace parallels. Moreover, in being free of content, it flirts with the semantic (and economic) plurality of "free." Readers were free to insert their own editorials here; and by flaunting its status as valuable space deliberately unsold, the page itself represented a moment of qualified economic and political freedom from the quasi-compulsory and interconnected systems of national and consumer currency. And the page is free in the sense that the *Saturday Evening Post* frequently invoked in its satire of modernist freedom; it is a commodity evacuated of libidinal content, a product that nobody would want to buy. In 1917, to be free in those terms, the *Post* declared and the *Little Review* cheekily accepted, was to be outside the obligations of the wartime state.

There was one further articulation of "free" contested in this April issue. This came in the *Little Review*'s free verse competition, jointly won by H.D. and Maxwell Bodenheim. Anderson lambasted the quality of the majority of contributions, though, and as an example printed what she described as an "involuntarily humorous" poem entitled "A Mother's Sacrifice." Noting that this poem was "a sample of the rest of the contest, and speaks for itself," Anderson also paraphrased the accompanying note to the submission, which expressed the hope that "it may win one of the prizes in the contest, being original free verse and very patriotic." While the authors of the other poems in the issue are identified, the name of the contributor of this poem was strikingly withheld. This is the first stanza:

> The day has come, beloved son –
>   When duty's call resound,
> Your father fought, and laurels won
>   He firmly held the ground.
> Now honor calls you to be true,
>   To the dear flag, red-white-and blue,
> Long may it wave o'er land and sea –
>   Thou sweet land of liberty.[80]

Anita Helle contends that in being printed as a laughable example of what could never win a free verse competition in the *Little Review*, the poem "appears, in effect, under erasure, and not only for its poetics of form, but its rhetoric of feeling"; Anderson was asserting that "only certain forms of consolation would be acceptable within the bounds of the new art."[81] It was laughable because its author had labeled this belabored use of the four-teener meter as free verse, terms that were formally antithetical. But arguably its appearance under erasure is rather due to the poem's inter-twined *politics* of form and feeling – for this author's definition of "free verse" might have been very different from Margaret Anderson's. The poet calls this "free verse" because it articulates a passionate, maternal defense of political rather than formal freedoms, because it is a poem about fighting for political liberties. Indeed, it exemplifies a widespread discourse of citizenship, what Kathleen Kennedy has called "patriotic motherhood," which suggested that women's citizenship was guaranteed not by fighting but by willingly sending their sons to battle. (Indeed, Kennedy goes on to observe that mothers who protested the war were liable to prosecution as "disloyal mothers and scurrilous citizens."[82]) It also participates in what Mark Van Wienen calls a culture of partisan poetry in this era, wherein occasional poetry served as a legitimate language of public, political debate capable of shaping public opinion through its unique resources of feeling and cultural authority. As he notes, poetry then had a much more prominent place in newspapers and magazines than it does now; the *New York Times* printed a poem on its editorial page in almost every issue during World War One, the majority of these on war topics, many of which were similar to "A Mother's Sacrifice."[83]

Anderson registered her contempt for the poem by refusing to print its author's name. Within the homogenizing discourse of maternal nationalism, she implied, any one poem is indistinguishable from another, making individual authorship impossible. Where the writer of the poem sees the vital body politic, Anderson sees what Mina Loy called corpse poesy, a set of poetic structures of both lyrical and gendered conventionality that are both dead and deadening.[84] Yet the unnamed author literally gets the last word in this competition; the poem appears under erasure but it does appear, "speak[ing] for itself" in defining free verse as free not from regular meter, but as free in the terms of Wilsonian purpose. In speaking thus it has several effects. It reconfirms the *Little Review*'s commitment to printing a contentious breadth of opinion to generate its counterpublic sphere. The friction caused by the presence of "A Mother's Sacrifice" alongside imagist lyrics of war such as John Cournos's "Assault" and Horace Holley's "The Soldiers" identifies "freedom" as the semantic and political location of conflict between modernist and traditional poetic responses to war. And more than this, it confirms the idea put forward, in different ways, by both Monroe and Josephine Preston Peabody: that poetic formal strategies were not merely analogies for different forms of civic subjectivity, but were their very articulation.

*

What these various examples demonstrate was the intense discussion about modernist freedom that occurred in the United States in 1917 and 1918 across the entire scope of America's press. Modernists were criticized for not saying enough, doing enough, consuming enough, or producing enough to assist the war effort, and these critiques frequently centered on

the political-economic implications of free verse. Modernist little magazines indirectly made various responses to this charge. *Poetry* suggested that
only free verse modernist poetry had the capacious formal resources for
dealing with the sublimity of the state, its hugely expanded and often
inscrutable dimensions and structures. Perceiving that the expanded federal state had bequeathed a crisis of representation, one embedded in the
problem of effectively mediating the gulf between atomized individual and
gargantuan institution, *Poetry* advanced the utopian hope that this challenge would be the privileged representational task for modernist poetry.
The *Little Review*'s anarchistic, radical individualism was less interested in
this project; but it did intuit that this aesthetic vacuum had already been
effectively corporatized. In contrast to Monroe, who hoped the war would
serve as a "renewer, a vitalizing force, a reorganizer" that could "wash away
much of that accumulated materialism which clogs our souls," Anderson's
blank-page editorial suspected that expansions of state sociability would
only facilitate the extension of market systems and corporate activity into
federal structures.[85] The prospect of such extensions helped her frame
a concern that material nationalism was narrowing definitions of liberty
to freedom of choice. The ghostly outline of the state was implicit in far
more of the *Little Review*'s discourse than has regularly been admitted, and
is figured in its citations, silences, and explicit erasures. Most pointed was
its insistence on the importance of rights before the state, whether the right
to speak freely – or the right to say nothing. This presented a counterpoint
to the prevailing climate of coercive voluntarism, which located obligation
rather than rights as the defining term of citizenship. At the same time,
antimodernist satire in the *Saturday Evening Post*, along with the maternal
nationalism of the anonymous contributor to the *Little Review*, began to
outline the default position on the politics of modernism for a generation,
namely that by stressing aesthetic understandings of freedom, modernists
had placed themselves at best at the periphery, and at worst in opposition,
to the cultural and political economy of the modern state, a criticism that
would be replayed with yet greater force in the Depression. In thereby
neglecting the obligations of the citizen-artist, this argument ran, modernists had drastically misunderstood the social role of art.

CHAPTER 2

Letters from a Soldier
Letters and States of Intimacy in World War One American Literature

Mother's Day in America in May 1918 was a special one. The *Stars and Stripes*, the official newspaper of the AEF, had launched the so-called Mother's Letter Plan, designed to maximize the volume and speed of correspondence from American soldiers in France to their mothers at home. On the day, extra stationery was delivered to billets and trenches across France; and by writing "Mother's letter" on the envelope, priority for this mail was assured. As the *Stars and Stripes* boasted, "those two words will have precisely the same effect as though the highest postal official in America had, with his own hand, written 'Rush' across the envelope."[1] No one escaped their tone of bullying sentiment: military censors and mail orderlies were exhorted by the newspaper to work night and day to deal with this surge of mail, and soldiers were encouraged to "plan the best letter you ever wrote in your life . . . write it from the bottom of your heart, and the boat that carries the Mother's Letters to America will be a boat laden with as rich a freight as ever craft bore from shore to shore."[2] As the *New York Times* reported the next day, "Americans in every quarter of the globe yesterday united in one tender thought – the memory of their mothers."[3] (One of those Americans was G.P. Cather, Willa Cather's cousin, who sent a letter to his mother on May 18, just ten days before his death; he became the model for Claude Wheeler in *One of Ours*.) In the final weeks of May, 1.6 million Mother's Day letters crossed the Atlantic.

The Post Office was essential to the American prosecution of the war. Its surveillance of the second-class mail – the rate at which most publications were circulated – was where the Espionage and Sedition Acts' restrictions of permissible speech took greatest effect. The draft was largely administered by mail, and the Post Office delivered a staggering 50 million items to American troops stationed in Europe between June 1917 and July 1918 – all via a transatlantic shipping system already straining to transport the AEF and its necessary supplies.[4] It inaugurated America's airmail system – designed initially to fly mail between New York and Washington – a program that, in the decade that followed, largely subsidized the growth of America's civilian air infrastructure.[5] Yet the Post Office also assumed a cultural prominence in the war for reasons exceeding these vital contributions. In part, this was because before the war the US mail system was the most familiar and quotidian experience of federal power to ordinary Americans, and thus became an important template for Americans to understand the new wartime activities of state power. It served this role particularly well because of the simultaneous experience of systemic vastness and intimacy it provided: it was an infrastructure that combined intimate communication with sublime scale. This duality was exacerbated during the war as the mails registered both newly coercive forces of top-down control in the action of censorship and, conversely, the demotic exchanges of emotional and informational sustenance between ordinary citizens experiencing the anxieties of wartime separation and danger. It was precisely the wartime mail's unique mix of familiarity and intimidating novelty, local dynamics and international scale, institutional coercion and individual self-expression, and depersonalized bureaucracy and intense intimacy that led it to being so often used as a representational vehicle for thinking about the totality of the new relationships between state and individual that the war had unleashed. This chapter explores the literary culture of this phenomenon. In particular, it examines how a range of authors looked to the mail to consider the state's new imbrications in what are commonly considered the experiences and institutions walled off from state intrusion – the private, and intimate, spheres of the family and sexual relationships; and private organizations of charitable benevolence.

Unsurprisingly, some of this writing argued that surveillance of the mails – whether the domestic postal surveillance of publications under the new censorship powers of Congress, or the military censoring of soldiers' mail – infringed liberal freedoms. Yet there was another tradition fascinated by the thoroughgoing transformations in American patterns of sociality and even intimacy that accompanied the changing relationship between state and individual in the war years, and that looked to the mail as both symbol of and conduit for those transformations. If, as postal historians have suggested, the post had essentially produced certain social forms of intimacy and even ideas of the private individual, especially since the advent of cheap postage in the 1840s in the United States had embedded affordable private correspondence as a staple of ordinary life for middle-income Americans, its wartime innovations brought that productive capacity into sharp relief.[6] The 1918 Mother's Day campaign is one of the most compelling examples of this, one that sought to draw what Fredric Jameson has called the "uniquely relational system" of the mail into the service of the wartime state.[7] The campaign sought to shape personal cultures of correspondence in ways that were coercive – Mark Meigs calls it a moment when "the army turned individual soldiers into propaganda agents" – but could never be entirely so.[8] It sought to parlay a widely shared feeling of trust in the Post Office (a trust essential to its systemic success) into a trust in the American wartime state more generally. It served as a structure of affection that augmented affinities between soldiers and their familiar addressees, but also between citizens and the state apparatus that made this exchange possible. Such dynamics help explain why fictional or poetic letters became such an omnipresent motif in American war literature, a motif found across the spectrum of politics and aesthetic style. For modernists such as Wallace Stevens – whose underregarded poetry sequence "Lettres d'un Soldat" is one of the most sophisticated experimental poetic responses to the political transformations of the war – the letter home was the perfect vehicle to ruminate on new affective and aesthetic dimensions of the state, especially its role in the production of new kinds of intimacy. For Ring Lardner, wartime innovations in postal sociality were ripe occasions for epistolary comedy. For Edith Wharton, the fictional letter home's status as a shopworn cliché became a mode for considering wartime challenges to types of privatized moral experience she held as central to both her political and her aesthetic life – challenges occurring in both the wartime transfer of private charities to state control and the aesthetics of modernism. Yet many of these writers understood that intimate relationships would not merely be mediated by these letters, but would be indelibly shaped by them and the systemic practices that made them possible. That this wide array of writers chose the wartime letter as a central structural device suggests its nature as the perfect relay between individual and state, the personally intimate and the structurally impersonal – and as the object that demonstrated how deeply interconnected and mutually contingent those categories had become.

The Post Office, Progressivism, and War

That this literary device was so popular in wartime was in part because before the war the US Post Office was the most visible institution of the federal state, and the one most deeply embedded in daily American life. For the historian Christopher Capozzola, pre-1917 America existed as a political culture that "saw little role for the federal government other than delivering the mail."[9] In Upton Sinclair's novel *100%*, as the political ingénueprotagonist is being educated about socialism from socialists, they tell him "What they wanted was to have the State take over the industries, or to have the labor unions do it, or to have the working people in general do it. They pointed to the post office and the army and the navy, as examples of how the State could run things. Wasn't that all right?"[10] In 1917, the Post Office was the United States' largest civilian employer, as it had been since the 1790s.[11] Moreover, it had been arguably the central federal institution within Progressive Era reform, principally in how it shaped truly nationalized markets and access to information. From the 1870s onward, the Post Office heavily subsidized second-class postage for publications, a system that represented "what amounted to an informal nationwide educational system based on second-class mail," in the words of postal historian Winifred Gallagher, and that also facilitated the boom in the magazine industry that helped shape nationalized tastes and habits of consumption.[12] Rural Free Delivery in 1902 and the inception of the parcel post in 1913 were also significant Progressive innovations. The former brought free delivery to rural homes, obviating the need to collect mail from local post offices; the latter saw the US mail accept parcel post of items heavier than four pounds, a business previously only managed by private corporations. The parcel post was an immediate success, with over 300 million parcels mailed in the first six months of operation, and facilitated exponential growth in the catalog mail-order business; Sears handled five times as many orders in 1913 as it did in 1912. Few innovations of the Progressive Era state altered the triangulated material relations between individuals, state, and corporations, or between America's manufacturing and warehousing centers and their rural customers, as these changes.[13] Even then, the Post Office was often used as an example by those on the right of everything that was wrong with a large, federally run bureaucracy. For example, in 1915, Henry A. Castle, the former Post Office Auditor, published an article in the *North American Review* assaulting what he called the Post Office's "state socialism" and resistance to reform. Part of the problem was the Post Office's sublime unintelligibility, and therefore unmanageability; as he bewailed, it "has already grown beyond the power of the human mind to grasp it as a whole, and reform and control it. And still it grows!" Unrepresentable and therefore unaccountable, for Castle, the Post Office bore all the failures of what he called the "policy of public ownership."[14]

Castle would doubtless have been aghast at what happened to the Post Office after America entered World War One in 1917. Wars in American history effected some of the most significant changes in Post Office services and practices; City Free Delivery and Money Orders were introduced during the Civil War, and V-Mail (microfilming mail to make it easier to transport in bulk) was launched in World War Two. World War One was no different; during the war, the Post Office underwent significant expansion to handle the increased volumes of mail and to transport large quantities of mail across the Atlantic. Even before the huge troop buildup of spring and summer 1918, 450,000 letters per week were going out to troops in France, and by the war's end, 169 Army Post Offices had been established in Europe.[15] In addition, the Post Office was charged with registering enemy aliens, assisting with recruitment, aiding the Red Cross, and helping enforce the Espionage and Trading with the Enemy Acts. Mass letter-writing campaigns were orchestrated around occasions such as Christmas and Mother's Day, and stories documenting delays in the mail between home and front lines featured regularly in the national newspapers – and even sparked a congressional investigation.[16] As well as campaigns to elicit letters from soldiers, the CPI placed numerous pieces in major slick magazines such as the *Woman's Home Companion* and the *Ladies' Home Journal* exhorting wives, mothers, sisters, and sweethearts to write to their men in camp or in France; one such piece by "An American Soldier at the Front" went so far as to claim "I believe this war may be won largely by successful letter writing on the part of the women at home."[17] Mass-drives were also organized to have women write or send gifts to soldiers from their local communities, and even to servicemen they had never met before.

That the Post Office was simultaneously the most visible arm of the federal state, was the preeminent example of Progressive Era ambitions for what a service state should provide, but was also a lightning rod for conservative attacks on the inefficiencies of state institutions, meant that it both produced and became a central imaginative mechanism for comprehending the new structures and socialities of the American wartime polity. This accounts, at least in part, for why the letter became such a central genre in American war literature. Many collections of letters from American servicemen were published during the war and its immediate aftermath; the fullest bibliography of personal accounts of the war produced by Americans lists forty-eight collections of war letters published from 1919 to the late 1930s, and many more were published during the conflict.[18] Particularly popular (and poignant) were those collections of letters written by young men who had been killed in battle; as well as the letters of Eugène Lemercier (so important to Wallace Stevens and discussed extensively in the section "Wallace Stevens' Epistolary Politics in 'Lettres d'un Soldat'" below), such posthumous collections by Quentin Roosevelt and Alan

Seeger also attracted a wide readership. Seeger's appeared in May 1917, less than a year after his death at the Battle of the Somme, and was widely reviewed (and even given a two-page spread in the *New York Times Magazine*, two days after Wilson signed the Selective Service Act into law).[19] This public appetite for letters was also reflected in the prevalence of fictional letters, which appeared embedded in stories or novels, formed the basis for poems, and frequently appeared as standalone pieces. The latter were particularly apparent in American mass-circulation magazines in World War One, and imagined missives from wives to servicemen husbands, soldiers to mothers, and parents to sons on the battlefield. Such letters became staple features of publications like the *Ladies' Home Journal* and the *Saturday Evening Post*: they served simultaneously as conduct literature, propaganda, popular narrative, and a cultural form that mediated anxieties over separation, combat, death, and life outside of the intimate confines of the family home. American humorists such as Ring Lardner, George Pattullo, and Edward Streeter wrote popular serials for these magazines composed of rookie doughboys' unwittingly hilarious letters home, serials often collated into what were essentially epistolary novels. Within more canonical work, Wallace Stevens, Ellen Glasgow, Edith Wharton, Willa Cather, Edna Ferber, and F. Scott Fitzgerald all used the letter home in their war poetry and novels.[20]

This prominence of the fictional letter in exploring new wartime socialities worked in several ways. It marked that the military assembled after the Selective Service Act of 1917 was a conscripted citizens' army, quite different from the small, professional prewar cadre that often contained men who had served for many years, if not decades. Accordingly, these new men had complex and deep ties to localities, professions, and communities that the original army often did not – ties that relied on the mail for their upkeep. In William March's 1933 war novel *Company K*, for example, the old army company sergeant ruminates that "one thing that puzzles me about these new men is why they are always writing letters home, or getting packages from their mothers or sweethearts. You didn't see much of that in the old days, when I came into the service. Most of the boys then didn't have any people to write to."[21] Secondly, letters both registered and promised to assuage anxieties about distance, anxieties particularly acute for American combatants fighting thousands of miles from home. They became the material bridge between Europe and America, parents and children, home front and war front. The emotional power of this is registered in the very title of John Allen Wyeth's fine war sonnet "Home Mail," which begins with soldiers jostling to access the "seven sacks of mail" that have just arrived.[22] "Home Mail" presents a neologistic conjunction that, in dispensing with a preposition (i.e., "Home Mail" rather than "mail from home"), represents mail as offering the comfort of an embodiment of home, a literal piece of it, rather than merely emanating from home. Moreover, that such gaps were formed not only by geographical distance but by how the war front had scrambled prewar norms of geographical rationalization and liberal legibility was registered in how often wartime fictional letters dwelt on the state's paratexts – the codes, stamps, and information included on the letter to ensure its accurate delivery. Few soldiers' letters appeared in print without the ubiquitous return address of "somewhere in France" for members of the AEF. And in Edna Ferber's "Long Distance," a letter arrives to a rehabilitation facility in England "bearing an American postmark and addressed to Sergeant Chester Ball, with a lot of cryptic figures and letters strung out after it, such as A.E.F. and Co. II."[23] As postal historians have argued, "addressability" was a significant way in which modern postal technology had bequeathed modern identities – fully rationalized house numbering and street naming followed on from cheap postage, not the other way around.[24] The prevalence of new kinds of address in the war's fictional letters therefore both suggests an anxiety about how the war would disrupt prewar identities and also often bespoke a faith that the state would find ways to maintain prewar social ties within novel – albeit bewildering – systems of communication, and even that it could impose order on terrain whose geographical intelligibility had been so challenged by the war.

However, all these tropes did not deliver a consistent politics. As well as being a staple feature of patriotic wartime writing, and often precisely because of that centrality, fictional letters were prevalent in antiwar writing too. This was especially so in British wartime poetry, where, as Susan Schweik has contended, the device of the imaginary letter accentuated "the temporal and spatial distances between soldier/author and civilian/reader," and was often used in order to place "bitter emphasis on the ignorance of the woman who served synecdochically as a figure for the poet's audience, and insisted on a disjunction, not a gratifying identification, between poet and reader."[25] In the US tradition, perhaps the foremost example of such an antiwar poem based in the epistolary conventions of the wartime mail is E.E. Cummings' "my sweet old etcetera" from 1926. Beginning with the line "my sweet old etcetera/aunt lucy," which playfully mocks the conventions of epistolary salutation, the poem repeats a series of clichéd statements from the speaker's family during his time at the front – "my/mother hoped that/i would die etcetera/bravely of course."[26] These flights of

formulaic, patriotic rhetoric become obscene when placed alongside the
actual conditions of the speaker's time in the war, as

> meanwhile my
> self etcetera lay quietly
> in the deep mud et
> cetera (dreaming,
> et
>   cetera, of
> Your smile
> eyes knees and of your Etcetera)[27]

Here, the temporal, spatial, rhetorical, and experiential distance between
home front and battle front so characteristic of the antiwar poetry that used
the letter as a motif is fully on display. Moreover, the use of "etcetera"
changes throughout the poem, and those moves account for much of its
fun and satirical sharpness. It begins by marking the sheer *expectedness* of
the rhetoric about war used at home, which has become so familiar and
limited that once a phrase is initiated, "etcetera" is all that is needed to
complete it ("my/mother hoped that/i would die etcetera"). Yet when the
speaker refers to "my/self etcetera," with both a line and a stanza break
fracturing "myself," he suggests how this rhetoric authorizes the blasting
apart of subjectivities at the front. This occurs in both political and
potentially physical terms: firstly, the force of this rhetoric's coercive and
institutional logic tramples on any possibility of individuated feeling,
opinion, or language about the war, thus loosening the possessive and
sovereign connection between "my" and "self" – now that self is largely
controlled by, and beholden to, others. Moreover, that rhetoric has helped
place these young men in positions of extreme danger where their bodies
might literally be blasted apart. And the "etcetera," here, has diminished
the importance of his life to the extent that its value and complexity can
effectively go without saying. Subsequently, the use of the word then shifts
to what strictly cannot be said in a military letter; now, the word serves as a
place-marker for the unsayable. That unsayable becomes both geographic
and sexual: the "etcetera" of his precise return address in the deep mud in
France, and the innuendo substitution of a capitalized "Etcetera" for a part
of his girl's anatomy at the poem's close.

The poem, therefore, pithily makes two central points about the war's
effects on language that would be repeated so often by modernist writers in
the 1920s. First, as I discussed in the Introduction, its heavy irony insists
that the slew of state-sponsored pro-war rhetoric, originating with
Wilson's rhetorical style and disseminated through all levels of the

enormous apparatus of the CPI, was so abstracted, formulaic, and grotesquely detached from the immediacies of war that its vocabulary had been ethically rendered beyond further use. Secondly, the poem suggests that the wartime state's circumscription of what could be written or said had overstepped the realm of protecting military secrecy to police moral and political opinion in ways that represented a gross intrusion into the contents of personal mail – which Cummings understands here as a private sphere of liberal freedom. The Post Office was indeed the crucial institution in the federal policing of speech during the war; as Christopher Capozzola notes, "to state that the wartime Espionage Act authorized the federal government to regulate speech is to say that it handed over those powers to employees of the Post Office department," and Postmaster General Albert Burleson even boasted that the Federal Mail was the only institution with an adequate infrastructure and personnel to police American speech.[28] Cummings had bitter first-hand experience of such policing during his service as a volunteer ambulance driver in the war, having been imprisoned at La Ferté-Macé concentration camp for three months after French censors read letters home from his friend William Slater Brown expressing misgivings about the Allied war effort. When Cummings was questioned about this by French authorities, he refused to incriminate Brown, leading to their detention – which only a frantic calling in of favors by Cummings' father brought to an end, experiences memorably described in his *The Enormous Room* (1922). In both his novel-memoir and this poem, therefore, the liberal state has abrogated what was widely understood as its responsibility to ensure the mails as a sphere of privacy (and therefore individuality), not only by surveilling the mails and punishing elastically understood iterations of "disloyal" speech but by insidiously pushing letter-writers into the self-censorship of empty, patriotic cliché.[29]

Yet, despite the importance of the antiwar tradition in American writing about the letter home, there was also a quite different, and particularly American, dimension to much of this literature, which took a different approach to the place of the state within private life. This was to see state-structured forms of sociality in war as productive of new forms of private and intimate experience rather than intruding on them, a move that challenged the exteriorization of the state from a letter's "private contents" in the manner of Cummings' poem. Such literary work registered that wartime letters were at once personal and intimate – freighted with the tactile individuality of handwriting, fragrance, or keepsakes – and controlled both physically and linguistically by the state. It acknowledged that they were handled by the intimate addressees of lovers and family members, and by state employees of postal officials and mail orderlies; that they were read by military censors as well as spouses, siblings, and parents. Many authors contemplating the letter in wartime considered the reciprocal action of these two spheres, the way that both intimate and subjective experience and state institutions were being shaped by this interaction.

Scholarship on war letters, however, tends to stress one or other of these scenes of epistolary production and readership. Paul Fussell, for example, in his classic section on letters home in *The Great War and Modern Memory*, pays particular attention to the British Field Service Postcard, which he finds is the prototype of the modern bureaucratic "form." This is the paradigmatic "letter home" for Fussell; with its highly limited (and mostly reassuring) range of communicative options (soldiers were asked to strike through any of the preprinted statements not applicable to their situation, and then sign it) and its absolute proscription of individual embellishment – any personal message written on the postcard resulted in its immediate destruction – it is a medium hobbled by the state's intrusiveness. For Fussell, censorship is the governing feature of war letters. This works both externally, with the handling of soldiers' mail by military and civil postal authorities, and through servicemen's self-censorship in the face of a supposed unwillingness or inability of those on the home front to comprehend the horrors of combat. Accordingly, he finds letters a poor medium for communicating what is most real and important about war.[30] In contrast, more recent critics – particularly Santanu Das – stress war letters' potential for meaningful, especially intimate, communication, often as evident in their role as sensory and tactile objects as in their linguistic content. The introduction to Das's *Touch and Intimacy in First World War Literature* features reproductions of the file of Private George Bennett, including Das's experience of opening a letter and experiencing the crumbling feeling of dried flowers under his fingertips, flowers picked on the western front and included in Private Bennett's letter to his wife. For Das, the sensation is "intimate and unsettling," an intrusion on a realm so private, intimate, and fragile that it literally crumbles under the fingers of an intruder.[31] Such analysis exalts the personal communication – and tactile exchange – between two people, with the necessary evil of the state – which collected, read, transported, delivered, and archived this intimate missive – placed in the background. Finally, Cary Nelson has recently written about the wartime poem postcard, drawing from his archive of 10,000 items that mingle personal communication with cheaply printed popular poetry. He finds that such poetically engaged correspondence served state ends by cementing citizens' consent to war through the discourse of sentimental nationalism, but also that it cannot be reduced to that discourse; he observes that "As an ideology crafted to romanticize one's transformation into cannon fodder, [the romanticization of absence in the poem postcard] is largely repellent. As a complicating model of interpersonal politics it cannot be so readily dismissed."[32] His essay demonstrates the manifold ways that writers and readers of such correspondence were more than interpellated dupes, and yet the state is an insidious presence for the most part, with his readers and writers gaining their fullest humanity when they resist the state's imperatives most energetically.

Postal Intimacies in World War One Popular Writing

This either/or approach fails to accurately replicate the culture of wartime letters in America during World War One. To consider how the mediation of intimacy by the state became a form of intimacy with the state it is worth turning to the AEF newspaper, the *Stars and Stripes*. Launched in February 1918, at its peak it had a circulation of 526,000 readers. High-spirited and often jocular, the *Stars and Stripes* was an immediate success with rank-and-file soldiers; and, as Mark Meigs observes, it was frequently masterful in finding "a way to move between the impersonal generality of the war and its destructive power and the individual soldiers." Led by prominent journalists (including Harold Ross and Alexander Woollcott, who went on to found the *New Yorker*), this negotiation was frequently achieved by "the special quality of its style: that of the soldier made skeptical by experience but who allows himself to be persuaded by reason, and can surprise himself with heartfelt enthusiasm."[33] Part of the way that style balanced skeptical individualism with enthusiasm for the collective mission was to take soldiers' own writing and language seriously; launched as a magazine for soldiers by soldiers, it took great interest in soldiers' poetry, soldiers' slang, and soldiers' mail. Articles on the latter often addressed censorship, and the dilemma of how a citizens' army could honor the personal and private dimensions of soldiers' sense of individuality – particularly the erotic and sentimental so usually confined to domestic spheres – within a military organization that treated the control of information flow between war front and home front as an imperative. Framed as the war was as a struggle for liberal freedoms – fought by free individuals who had "volunteered in mass," in Wilson's words, to fight autocracy – and also as a war fought to defend the sanctity of intimate domestic spaces, the US Army's surveillance of soldiers' mail put considerable pressure on the rhetorical strategies of papers such as the *Stars and Stripes* to legitimize the state as a reader of intimate correspondence.[34]

The paper's agony aunt column, "Free Advice for Lovelorn Lads," showcased those difficulties. In the March 29 issue, for example, all four of the letters to "Miss Info" deal with anxieties from doughboys about letters to their lovers; two dwell on how the state is controlling their correspondence. One worries that he is not receiving letters from his girl at home every day, only to be told that "Nobody gets letters every day in France except the Quartermaster and the Post Office Department." Another dealt with a doughboy's worry about beginning a romantic correspondence with a girl in America because of his concern that his commanding officer would read it in the act of censoring his unit's mail and "kid the pants offa me."[35] The reply to that letter was typical in reassuring "Bashful" about the impartiality of the censor. This was also stressed in one of the longest articles on army mail, one that explained the work of the base censor, whose morning mail "was 8,000 letters," 600 of them in languages other than English. It detailed the case of a doughboy carrying on a clandestine affair with a local French woman; the soldier had feared his letters being read by his company officers, and so had used the French mail system, which was prohibited to AEF servicemen. Yet he was caught out, and his mail opened and read. The article reassured doughboys that "he needn't have worried a bit. For the bogey-man isn't a likely rival of anyone. In fact, he isn't a man at all, but a System – just as impersonal as if he wrote his name, 'Base Censor, Inc.'"[36] In basing its reassurance on the systemic nature of censorship, the article relied on a commonplace understanding of systems at the time as both automatic and predictable, and as essential to "new visions of order, control and regulation."[37] Moreover, its choice of the corporate metaphor to best achieve this reassurance – base censor as "Base Censor, Inc." – was telling; it nods toward what Susan Edmunds has recently labeled the formation in the period of a space she calls the "domestic exterior," a "modern sentimental space developed to coordinate and moralize a triangle of relations emerging among market, home, and state."[38] The presence of corporate or state systems in intimate life was no cause for concern, the metaphor of "Base Censor, Inc." suggested; it was both benign and impersonal, and already a fact of life within the "modern sentimental space" of contemporary domestic experience. This reassurance was therefore not so much a guarantee of privacy as its total reformulation, in suggesting that modern, mediated communication was and would never be strictly interpersonal but would feature multiple, benign, and depersonalized readerships within systems. These

"MOTHER'S LETTER"

Figure 2.1 "Mother's Letter," Abien A. Wallgren, *Stars and Stripes*, 1.13 (May 3, 1918), 1. Image courtesy of Library of Congress, Serial and Government Publications Division

readerships would not attend to the intimate content of those communications but smooth the alignment of state and corporate structures with private interests.

This idea was replicated elsewhere in the *Stars and Stripes'* representation of the mail. For example, their exhortations to send letters on Mother's Day in their May 3 issue were accompanied by an image on the front cover by their resident cartoonist, Abien A. Wallgren (see Figure 2.1).

The postman is both inside and outside the domestic space here, inside the gate but not on the porch, a perfect representation of Edmunds' "new sentimental space" in figuring a state that through "domestic infrastructure" had "penetrated and reconfigured the home and the domestic sphere."[39] This liminal placing of the letter carrier at the margin of the home also reinforces the particularly conflicted nature of the wartime letter carrier's duties, a duty toward both a nonintrusive political neutrality that preserved the "sanctity" of the private mail and a simultaneous duty toward vigilant surveillance. From the outset of the war, they were advised by their superiors to be "extremely cautious in voicing opinions on the war situation," especially with "citizens of foreign birth or with those having extreme views," but were also ordered to report any "suspicious characters [or] disloyal and treasonable acts and utterances," reports then forwarded to the Justice Department.[40] Moreover, the letter carrier's gesture is strange and awkward: he is holding the letter out, yet not to the eager mother rushing down the path; nor does he make eye contact with her. In holding his head to the side he half-faces the mother and half-faces the reader of the piece, which would have been the soldier; his very embodiment, therefore, is poised between these two addressees. The embodied impossibility of being at the front and at home simultaneously is caught in this awkward pose, which shows the representational strains of personifying an institution structured around such systemic simultaneity. Respectfully outside the home but shaping (and surveilling) much that happened within it, and handling this personal exchange with a depersonalized aloofness that hints at the impossibility of personifying the vast mail system at all, Wallgren's carrier's strangeness suggests how new and unsettling was the US wartime state's alteration of domestic sentimentality.

Indeed, it was the radical nature of how wartime censorship and the kind of organized sentimentality of the Mother's Day letter campaign had opened familial intimacy out into wider commercial and governmental networks that accounts somewhat for the *Stars and Stripes'* unease in these pieces. There is an uneasy jocularity to the "Base Censor" article, and an uneasy embodiment in the postman, an unease doubtless originating from both pieces' assault on what Lauren Berlant has called the "mirage" of an intimate and often hermetic domestic sphere – a powerful notion that represents the "endlessly cited elsewhere of political public discourse" in its status as a fantasized oasis and "home base of prepolitical humanity."[41] Yet the *Stars and Stripes* would hardly have reached for the corporate metaphor in defining the activity of censorship without the confidence that the "domestic exterior," the nexus between corporation, home, and state, was a widespread, positive, and quintessentially modern understanding of domestic space and its associated affects of privacy. That space was grounded in the domesticized systematics of both corporations and the postal state, and ultimately it was the sense of depersonalized predictability, constant availability, and trust that were so central to the operations of all those systems that this article sought to engage.

The *Stars and Stripes'* guarded enthusiasm for the new socialities rendered by the wartime letter was amplified in their treatment of the erotic possibilities they generated, which became the subject of humor rather than awkward reassurance. Perhaps the most interesting example was provided by Wallgren (see Figure 2.2).

The cartoon pokes fun at the dilemmas of a doughboy writing back to a woman who had sent him a "comfort kit," as women's voluntary organizations were urged to do. The doughboy is stumped by the fitting register of familiarity to use in responding to a gesture that is both generous and coerced, to a woman simultaneously identified and anonymous, and to say thank you for a gift exchanged between individuals that is organized and mediated by the state. He ranges through forms of address, dismissing them as overfamiliar, patronizing, or too brief. In his search for the appropriate linguistic term he is looking for a register to accommodate new forms of sociality and connection that have elicited both his gratitude and his irritation; and his irritation is more at this situation's perplexing novelty than anything else.

Michael Herzfeld's theories are pertinent here, particularly his work on what he terms "cultural intimacy." For Herzfeld, moments when citizens criticize the nation-state, or work seemingly at odds with its rationalizations and interpellative apparatus, can in fact be moments when the state is most robustly constituted. States are made not just by faceless technocrats but by the rueful familiarity of ordinary people, who in their complaints about state bureaucracy are recognizing the fallibilities of the all-too-human state, complaints that paradoxically cement their allegiance to it. For Herzfeld, "In the intimacy of a nation's secret spaces lie at least some of the original models of official practice"; for if social actors find advantage "in using, reformulating and recasting official idioms in the pursuit of often highly unofficial personal goals," then frequently "these actions – so often in direct contravention of state authority – actually constitute the state."[42] We can see something of this constitutive dialectic between conformity and frustration, familiarity and the official, in Wallgren's cartoon, which is an artifact that both rues the unintelligibility of the new socialities of the state and helps render them manageable. Intimacy,

Figure 2.2 "From: To: Subject:" by Abien A. Wallgren, *Stars and Stripes*, 1.13 (May 3, 1918), 4. Image courtesy of Library of Congress, Serial and Government Publications Division

therefore, becomes a crucial mode for the functioning of the liberal state, even as its own nature is reciprocally transformed by putting strangers in unfamiliar situations of intimacy.

This dynamic could also be observed in arguably the most popular writing about the soldier's letter home in the United States at this time: Ring Lardner's so-called "busher" stories. These were one of America's favorite serials: fictional letters from the laughably naïve narrator and Chicago White Sox baseball star Jack Keefe to his friend Al Blanchard in Indiana. Keefe's semiliterate and hilarious stories about life in baseball had been a star feature of the *Saturday Evening Post* since 1914, with Lardner's stories commanding $1,500 each from George Horace Lorimer, the formidable editor of the *Saturday Evening Post*.[43] Widely regarded as an influential innovator in American vernacular writing, and praised by Virginia Woolf as the most promising American prose stylist of the modern era, as the United States prepared for its first summer with a large number of troops in Europe, Lardner began a series of stories for the *Post* that embroiled Jack Keefe in the war effort.[44]

The Curtis magazines had invested heavily in the wartime letter. Both the *Saturday Evening Post* and the *Ladies' Home Journal* printed numerous fictional letters from war front to home front. The *Ladies' Home Journal* specialized in what were essentially template letters for epistolary conduct – from sons to parents at home, from fathers to sons at the front, from sweethearts at home to their boyfriends overseas.[45] These guided its readers in the sentimental codes of wartime; they stressed uncomplaining self-sacrifice, cheeriness, and sexual continence, and typified the war as what Stanley Cooperman called a "great crusade" of Christian and civilizational righteousness. In line with the prevalent culture of citizenship that Christopher Capozzola has called "coercive voluntarism," they often exhorted their readers to adopt the proper tone and content to inspire their men at the front; one fictional letter from a "drafted man" to his sister reprimanded her to "cut out the sob stuff in your letters," and ended with the caution that "I'll look forward to that next letter, because I know it'll be the kind I want."[46] A different register was struck with Lardner's eleven wartime "busher" letter-stories, written between March 1918 and April 1919. Minus two stories, these were later collected as two slim volumes entitled *Treat 'Em Rough: Letters from Jack the Kaiser Killer* and *The Real Dope*.[47] These dealt with Jack's being drafted, his training and promotion at Camp Grant, his rocky relationship with his beautiful wife, and his service overseas. They explored his failure to qualify for a marital draft exemption due to his wife's profitable beauty-parlor business, and his eventual patriotic response to his number being called. But perhaps the biggest joke in *Treat 'Em Rough* – and the one spun out the longest – is a situation similar to Wallgren's cartoon, the erotic charge of a correspondence with a strange woman who sends him a gift.

The storyline begins as Jack receives a sock from the Red Cross, which has a note tucked into it from "Miss Lucy Chase" in Texas. This immediately connects Jack to the huge (and overwhelmingly female) volunteer network of American knitters in the war; knitters for the Red Cross alone produced a staggering 22 million items for hospitals, 1.5 million refugee garments, 15 million military garments, and 253 surgical dressings.[48] As Christopher Capozzola notes, this effort was wracked with tensions; the volunteer network of knitters was an exemplary case of the voluntarism so central to American political sensibility in 1917 in that it simultaneously "denoted an expression of consent . . . referred to organized activity outside state auspices . . . [and] was also an act of unpaid labor."[49] Exactly what the place of the volunteer was in the massive war effort was both unclear and contested, and shifted during the course of the war; for example, by 1918 contracts for soldiers' sweaters had been parceled out to factories, as many volunteers did not possess the necessary skills to make garments to military specifications. (By fall 1918, the *Red Cross Magazine* was urging its readers "Don't Make Sweaters!"[50]) Yet the letters between Jack and Lucy transform this uncertainty over the relation between the volunteer and the state into an uncertainty over the interpersonal and potentially erotic relationship between volunteer and soldier, especially as it was mediated by the mail. The awkwardness and misunderstanding that characterize their relationship are both the grounds of Lardner's humor and suggest the perplexing novelty of the new relationships between previously unconnected and unconnectable individuals that the wartime state had conjured into being.

In her initial letter, Lucy flirtatiously asks "Dear Solider Boy, you may never see me but if you can spare time to write me just a few lines it will make me happier than any one in the world for I am oh so lonesome. You won't disappoint me will you Soldier Boy?"[51] Yet Jack is perplexed by this anonymous amorousness: he speculates on "where she seen me" (with the caustic aside that "it must have been a picture without my feet in it or she would of made the sox bigger"). Troubled by the simultaneous desires to remain faithful to his wife, Florrie, to express the requisite gratitude to a generous volunteer, and to explore what is clearly presented as an intriguing erotic opportunity, Jack's letters break into a characteristic pattern of anxious dithering and self-justification as he pursues a correspondence with her. All the while he is flummoxed by the question of "where we met," never comprehending the exchange's anonymity; both the nature of the gift-giving and the coquettish tone of Lucy's letters can only accord with his prewar sense of normative heterosexual relations, which stipulate that they must have had a visual encounter.

Unsurprisingly, Jack's perplexity embroils him ever deeper into this farcical situation, until he arranges a face-to-face meeting with Lucy in a hotel lobby. This results in him discovering that Lucy is in fact "old about 35," and that his wife and young son have made a surprise visit to the hotel to see him. Red-faced, he writes to Al that "I couldn't help from feeling sorry for her the way she looked but a woman her age should ought to know more than start writeing [*sic*] letters to a guy she never seen."[52] That their encounter does not "fit" the expectations of their correspondence echoes the fact that the socks Lucy knitted do not fit; and this ill-fitting mismatch between garment and body, gift-giver and gift-recipient, encodes a whole host of gendered anxieties about the place of volunteerism and its relation to the state in operation at this time that are also embedded in Wallgren's cartoon about the flummoxed soldier. What was the appropriate place of the volunteer, and indeed of women's participation in the war effort: For did not gift-giving place obligations on the receiver disquietingly similar to those in operation in romantic relationships? Was social contact with soldiers initiated by women always shadowed by the overtones of an erotic advance, even when mediated by an "anonymous" letter? Did this assertiveness of the female volunteer, as Jennifer Haytock suggests, give women on the home front an agency in the stakes of the war that actually troubled narratives of separate spheres – an agency that some men found troubling?[53] And how could prewar social and linguistic customs structuring heterosexual relationships accommodate these vastly expanded and newly mediated forms of exchange? That none of these questions are resolved only highlights their baffling novelty. What Lardner's fiction and the artifacts from the *Stars and Stripes* demonstrate is that the culture of the wartime letter in the United States cannot be explained simply by seeing the mediating state either as an Orwellian censor that coerced content through its intrusive surveillance or as a necessary evil that left a pristine and intimate interpersonal content largely untouched. Instead, wartime correspondence had greatly expanded the potential readers and writers of intimate content, sometimes in ways that felt like uncomfortable intrusion, and sometimes in ways that felt like exciting and/or erotic expansions of the social.

Wallace Stevens' Epistolary Politics in "Lettres d'un Soldat"

While fictional letters were prominent in wartime popular literature, the unique role of letters in mediating new wartime forms of sociality – and therefore in producing new modes of political subjectivity – also informed arguably the most important American modernist poetry sequence of the war. Indeed, letters provided Wallace Stevens with one answer to a question that preoccupied and transformed modernist poetics – how to write a war poem. As James Longenbach argues, it was the war-as-subject that shifted modernist poetics from the limits of imagist diminishment into the epic achievements of the long poems of the 1920s.[54] Yet that move to epic involved its own challenges; for Wallace Stevens, it involved formulating how to replace older rhetorical models while avoiding "the easy aestheti-cization or internalization" of "the sheer brutality of experience."[55] He felt that mission as a historical necessity; Stevens later claimed that the "pres-sure of the contemporaneous" had begun with World War One, and that "if politics is nearer to us because of [that] pressure . . . poetry, in its way, is no less so and for the same reason."[56] Faced with the fact that the war was not merely a military conflict but a conflict of political systems and their allied forms of rhetoric, and, as his noncombatant status placed his perso-nal experience behind manifold and unavoidable filters of mediation, it was unsurprising that Stevens turned to the letter as the medium for crafting his major poetry sequence of World War One. In doing so, he engaged the role that letters home played as a privileged structure of affection facilitating the newly expanding state that I have been discussing so far, as well as their obvious potential for sentimental propaganda.

Stevens' poetry sequence "Lettres d'un Soldat" first appeared in *Poetry* magazine in May 1918. As Susan Schweik notes, the sequence "has a complex textual history with one general teleology: poems and other apparatus fall away at each stage, each new editing moving the remaining poems further from the politics and topoi of the war and further toward an insulated modernist lyric privacy."[57] Yet, in its early incarnations, it pre-sented a remarkable political meditation on the various forms of govern-ance in conflict during the war. Stevens had sent thirteen lyrics to Harriet Monroe at *Poetry* in September 1917, but in March 1918 – on a visit to Chicago – he and Monroe "weeded out the bad ones" in preparation for the eventual publication of nine for the May 1918 issue.[58] Interestingly, it was the most antiwar poems – such as poems I and XIII – that ended up being "weeded out," a testament to Monroe's stated desire to have *Poetry* support the US war effort, and to "print with the utmost promptitude any 'song for America' sent to [our] office which may seem worth printing," as she put it in June 1917.[59] Formally, the sequence is characterized by having every poem in the sequence prefaced by excerpts from letters from a French soldier to his mother; and, as virtually all commentators on the sequence have observed, the fluctuating ironic distance between a letter and its subsequent poem is the key tonal determinant of the collection. Stevens chose not to include any of these poems in the 1923 version of *Harmonium*, and only included four in the second edition (1931), and all without the prefatory letters. In 1972, the full sequence, including four sections omitted from the 1918 *Poetry* version, was established by A. Walton Litz; this was republished in Milton Bates' 1989 edited *Opus Posthumous*.[60] (The numbering I use here refers to this full sequence of thirteen poems.) The letters that prefaced each of Stevens' poems were drawn from a collection published in France in 1916 as *Lettres d'un Soldat: Aout 1914–Avril 1915*. Stevens had read both the original and the American translation, a translation he recommended to Monroe, should she wish to include an English version in the *Poetry* printing (she chose not to).[61] The letters had initially appeared anonymously, because of concerns that the author – who was reported as missing in action in April 1915 – might be a prisoner of war who would be endangered if his name was revealed. But he was never found, and after the war, it was revealed that the soldier in question was a young artist, Eugène Lemercier.

Stevens' critics have claimed that these prefatory letters function as opportunities for Stevens to explore his noncombatant anxiety, and to register his concern that in writing about war without combat experience he ran substantial risks of ethical and representational failure.[62] In April 1918, Stevens addressed these concerns to Monroe, observing that the war "absorbs me, but that is no excuse: there are too many people in the world, vitally involved, to whom it is infinitely more than a thing to think of."[63] Much has also been made of how Stevens uses Lemercier's letters and this sequence to consider the limits and the appropriate function of the aesthetic when facing a violent reality. For James Longenbach, the poetry sequence maps out the parameters of Stevens' major collection *Harmonium* of 1923, in presenting a continuum between poems of hubristic idealism at one end and poems stressing the implacability of the real at the other. It has also been seen as a watershed poem in Stevens' career, as well as in the modern aesthetics of death and consolation; for Sandra Gilbert, the poem "The Death of a Soldier" – its most famous individual poem – is a central exhibit in "a crucial turning point in the history of both death and elegy."[64]

Yet few critics have seen this sequence as Stevens' meditation on forms of political authority, and on the various ways in which consent to forms of sovereignty are generated. However, these issues were important to Stevens' consideration of the war. Stevens was a keen reader of the *New Republic* at the time; when he was finished with an issue he would mail it to his wife, often along with the London *Times'* regular monthly summary of the war, and sometimes directing her attention to what he felt were the most interesting articles.[65] One letter of his from July 1915 records an excursion to Long Beach to spend his day off reading the *New Republic* on the shore.[66] At this moment, the magazine was full of concrete examples of exactly the kind of "creative statecraft" Lippmann had called for in 1913, and from a variety of distinguished contributors. In July 1915 alone, H.G. Wells wrote on "Ideals of Organization," predicting that the future of Western governance would be a middle ground between German "authoritative state socialism" and Allied democratic voluntarism. It reviewed Thorstein Veblen's new work on the German dynastic state in the Industrial Revolution, which argued that German successes in the war had arisen because of its belated (and thus perfected) adoption of the techniques of British industrial economy, on which it had overlaid feudal traditions of paternal authoritarianism. And it featured a manifesto by Norman Angell proposing that economic sanctions levied against aggressor countries, and administered by a global committee of nations, would be a highly effective way for states to resolve disputes without resorting to military conflict.[67] In sum, the *New Republic* was engrossed with the relative merits of different political and governmental models, and was certain that the war was their great testing ground. Their articles carried a simultaneous excitement and trepidation about German industrial and political innovation, and an obvious desire to co-opt elements of this system into elements of postwar governance in the United States and Western Europe.

This experimental approach is very like Stevens' sequence, which maps out a contesting variety of political models – one per poem – as a mode of testing their efficacy through the action of contrast. By putting a variety of political philosophies in the voices of multiple speakers, Stevens replicates the format of the *New Republic*'s pragmatic experimentalism, their evaluation of different political philosophies through the juxtaposition of different voices and arguments. Yet Stevens highlights mediation as a crucial element in political subjectivities; by using a series of dramatic monologues, the political evaluation of Stevens' sequence often rests on the relationship between his speakers' situation and the language they have available to negotiate it. In the first and last poems in the sequence, for example, Stevens employs a strategy familiar to scholars of World War One literature, namely an ironic deflation of the nationalist-patriotic language and ideology that were so crucial in ensuring widespread social consent – and even enthusiasm – toward the war. This was the strategy Paul Fussell famously identified as the major tonal legacy of World War One, a war "more ironic than any before or since" because of the unprecedented challenge it presented to a prewar order wherein "values appeared stable and the meanings of abstractions seemed permanent and reliable."[68] An ironic challenge to such "abstractions" endorsing the link between national virtue and martial glory is evident in some of World War One's best-known literature, from Wilfred Owen's "Dulce et Decorum Est" to Erich Maria Remarque's takedown of the bullying schoolmaster Kantorek in *All Quiet on the Western Front*. The first section of "Lettres d'un Soldat," "Common Solider," takes this approach, as the solider announces he will dutifully "accept" the messages of his officers, clergymen, and politicians, in place of what he calls "introspective chaos":

> I have been pupil under bishops' rods
> And got my learning from the orthodox.
> I mark the virtue of the common-place.
>
> I take all things as stated – so and so
> Of men and earth: I quote the line and page,
> I quote the very phrase my masters used.
>
> If I should fall, as soldier, I know well
> The final pulse of blood from this good heart
> Would taste, precisely, as they said it would.   (*CPP* 538–539)

Each stanza of this poem suggests the violence and coerciveness inherent in habitual language. The "virtue of the common-place" is simultaneously the quotidian life of the yeoman and the "common-place" of the aphoristic phrase; the fact that the speaker does little to disentangle these two meanings demonstrates the interpellative force that makes the linguistic figurations of ideology seem common and natural. This force is just part of the continual menace surrounding these rote phrases, a menace amplified by the violence through which children are forced to learn these commonplaces (under the bishop's rod), and by the violent death that obeisance to these phrases entails – and that the speaker accepts with a sense of stoic inevitability. Any sense of the solider finding his own language is dismissed as "introspective chaos," but this leaves him with blood rather than his own words in his mouth. Ultimately, the grotesque implication that a moment as anguished, intense, and personal as one's own death can be neatly summarized in an aphorism speaks more to the power of the phrases of jingoist militarism than it does to the heroism of the uncomplaining soldier.

The final poem of the full sequence closes with a return to these "phrases" of the common soldier's political and spiritual masters. Yet unlike poem I, it contains an explicit dual imperative toward "men of the line," a phrase that gestures simultaneously to poets and soldiers. This requirement is that they renovate and replace the forms of language that have served to make death seem either purposeful or heroic, what the poem calls "symbols of sentiment." Instead, they should literally unearth a "new phrase/Of the truth of Death":

> 26 Mars
> *Rien de nouveau sur notre hauteur que l'on*
>   *continue d'organiser. . . . De temps à autre*
>   *la pioche rencontre un pauvre mort que la*
>   *guerre tourmente jusque dans la terre.*
> Death was a reaper with sickle and stone,
> Or swipling flail, sun-black in the sun,
> A laborer.
>
> Or Death was a rider beating his horse,
> Gesturing grandiose things in the air,
> Seen by a muse. . . .
>
> Symbols of sentiment . . . Take this phrase,
> Men of the line, take this new phrase
> Of the truth of Death –
>
> Death, that will never be satisfied,
> Digs up the earth when want returns . . .
> You know the phrase.   (*CPP* 545)

These bookend poems seem to mark a fairly familiar critique of how the nationalist public rhetoric of war, "the phrases," scandalously legitimated its excessive personal costs. They also signal how "a deep mainstream of established attitudes – call it public reason, call it civic rationality – was convulsing under the effort to legitimize this war," a convulsion that left an extensive mark on modernist poetry, as Vincent Sherry has ably discussed.[69] Yet the poems within the sequence map out a more multivalent politics, and present multiple voices and political traditions for readers to respond to. Partly, this is because – as is rarely noted in analyses of the sequence – Stevens deploys a series of dramatic monologues, each ventriloquizing a different political tradition. For example, in poem III, "Anecdotal Revery," a murderer boastfully strides through a town square full of blind men with the head of the mayor in a sack over his shoulder, perhaps signifying the revolutionary decapitations of the czarist state then taking place in Russia, or at least the anarchist and revolutionist energies of the decade (*CPP* 539–540). Poem IV, "Surprises of the Superhuman," is a brief, six-line meditation that assumes the voice of a German soldier fantasizing about storming the hilltop French *palais de justice* of chambermaids (a *palais* filled with tempting political and fleshy objectives). He voices the hope that swamping the *palais* in "Übermenschlichkeit" would make "our wretched state . . . come right." And yet, the "brave dicta" of the "kings" who had built the *palais* are making "more awry our faulty human things"; the lyric voice seems perturbed by the disconnect – enforced by the exacting dualism of the poem's couplet form – between the stern and abstract imperatives of Ubermenschlichkeit (roughly translated as the condition of the overman) and his experience of wretchedness, human frailty, and sexual desire (*CPP* 541). And Stevens looks forward to his *Harmonium* poem "Anecdote of Canna," often presumed to be referring to Woodrow Wilson, with "Negation," a poem warning about the excesses of political idealism when applied to war policy. In what may well be a dig at Wilson's lofty rhetoric of international progressivism, the lyric voice ruefully observes that "the creator too is blind/Struggling towards his harmonious whole." This blindness of a "too vague idealist" ensures "we endure brief lives" through struggling to be shaped into "The evanescent symmetries/From that meticulous potter's thumb" (*CPP* 543). In short order, then, Stevens mobilizes critiques of the political systems of socialist revolution, German racial imperialism, and the ambitions of Wilsonian internationalist progressivism.

Yet this recurrent skepticism about the exercise of various forms of state power is far from the Wallace Stevens who thrilled in a letter to his wife at the sight of a trainload of African American draftees departing for the training camps in the spring of 1918: "I feel thrilling emotion at these draft movements. I want to cry and yell and jump ten feet in the air; and so far as I have been able to observe, it makes no difference whether the men are black or white. The noise when the train pulled out was intoxicating."[70] To find this version of Stevens we must look to the heart of the sequence, poem VIII, and to the only moment at which we hear Lemercier's addressee, Bien chère Mère aimée, most dearly beloved mother. We have heard the voices of the uncomplaining soldier made docile by the disciplines of nationalized religion; the existential braggadocio of the decapitating socialist; the critique of the Progressive technocrat; and the Prussian soldier doubtful of the order bequeathed by Ubermenschlichkeit. But this poem deploys a symbol that has not been degraded or rendered obsolete by the events and experience of war, as the lyric speaker mobilizes a series of mothers, each bound to him by bonds of affection and intimacy:

> There is another mother whom I love,
> O chère maman, another, who, in turn,
> Is mother to the two of us, and more,
> In whose hard service both of us endure
> Our petty portion in the sacrifice.

Not France! France, also, serves the invincible eye,
That, from her helmet, terrible and bright,
Commands the armies; the relentless arm,
Devising proud, majestic issuance.
Wait now; have no rememberings of hope,
Poor penury. There will be voluble hymns
Come swelling, when, regardless of my end,
The mightier mother raises up her cry;
And little will or wish, that day, for tears.   (*CPP* 542)

For Jahan Ramazani, the mother is a frequent and consolatory figure in Stevens' war elegies, a "supreme fiction" of "ultimate consolation, an imaginary being who shields one against pain, suffering, and death by making them a part of her eternal life."[71] Yet here that consolatory figure undertakes a multiple, or a modulated, presence for the lyric speaker: the mother is both his own mother, the motherland of France, and an unnamed mother who nonetheless wields supreme sovereignty over the battling nations. Owing to this instantiation of the mother as a female, helmeted, warrior figure, it is not too outlandish to suggest this is Athena, the goddess of civilization, wisdom, war, and justice – and presiding deity over the prototypical democratic city-state of Athens. His affections move through these different registers, familial, national, and finally the cosmopolitan sphere of universal justice and European civilization embedded in the liberal-democratic state.

The fact that the superior mother is not named aligns her with the sublimity of the liberal state: too vast and numinous to be named, this figure is characterized by the abstracted principles of freedom, and transcendent justice, but also by the focused and local actuality of "relentless" violence. It recalls Woodrow Wilson's deft definition of the global ideal of liberal citizenship to a group of newly nationalized citizens in 1915; Wilson told them they "had vowed loyalty to no one, only to a great ideal, to a great body of principles, to a great hope of the human race."[72] The mother here is characterized by the capability to subject and annihilate citizens in the name of the welfare of those selfsame citizens, yet still compels the filial loyalty of the speaker, faithful as he is that the political content of her "proud, majestic issuance" is worth his sacrifice. Devoid of the cultural trappings and sentimental machinery of nationality – there is no "will or wish" for tears when this figure speaks – this mother is absolute, "terrible," impersonal, and all-powerful. Yet this figure remains maternal and familial. How to have an intimate relation with an entity that cannot be named; how to register linguistically the simultaneous personal indifference of a social macrostructure and its penetration into the most intimate aspects of quotidian life; whether it is possible to bring new forms of social relation within the communicative and affective structures and terms of the old, are questions asked by this poem. And these were the same questions implicit in the epistolary cultures going on with the doughboys in the trenches. This is where strangers gave gifts to each other by letter but struggled with how to address one another; and where the state reified the mother–son relationship on Mother's Day – but in the process facilitated a mass mailing that doubtless went well beyond this idealized and sentimentalized vision. The letter to mother sustained not just intimate communications between two people but an intimacy with an entire bureaucratic-state structure that elicited affection as one of its sustaining features, and this dynamic runs through the epistolary culture of doughboys in the trenches just as it does Stevens' poem. While Stevens is far from blind to this new state's coercive and often deadly features, he thrills at the new aesthetic and social forms it seems to promise, just as he thrilled to the trainload of draftees in Tennessee.

Of course, such a reading engages critiques of what Lauren Berlant has called "public intimacy," the use of familial ties and affections to articulate nonfamilial political relationships, and thereby to generate a situation wherein "the intimacy of citizenship is something scarce and sacred, private and proper, and only for members of families."[73] Marxist and feminist critics in particular have sought to uncover the conservative and patriarchal ideologies that often underpin such representational strategies, which in the twentieth century were especially prevalent in wartime, and which surfaced in the United States in World War One as what Jennifer Haytock calls a "cult of patriotic motherhood."[74] It is also true, as Patricia Chu has recently noted, that "women's relationships to the state [whether actual or symbolic], particularly because their status as citizens is not ideologically naturalized in the way male citizenship is, can become flashpoints for thinking about state subjection generally."[75] Susan Schweik reads this sequence this way; she finds poem VIII quoted above to be the most conservative of the sequence, in its replacement of the suffering and bereavements of real women by this symbolic woman who demands sacrifice in the name of some higher purpose.[76]

Yet I think such propositions run the risk of ignoring the multiple, and even self-contradictory, statements made by the sequence when considered in its entirety about the way an individual death gains significance beyond itself. In contrast to poem VIII, Stevens' most famous lyric from the sequence (entitled "The Death of a Soldier" in *Harmonium*) has been lauded for refusing the elegiac tradition of pathetic fallacy, as it rejects any suggestion that death gains metaphysical or political significance by some kind of sympathetic concordance with the spiritual or natural world.[77] Similarly, the mother figure is both a presence inspiring feats of martial heroism in lyric VIII and a moon enfeebled and elderly, barely illuminating a scene of rotting leaves, in "Lunar Paraphrase." This poem, seventh in the sequence, intones that "the moon is the mother of pathos and pity," which seems little more than mawkish sententiousness. (This is quite in contrast to the Lemercier letter prefacing it, which rhapsodizes over a scene during a moonlit march the day before, when the moonlight had cast "shadows of houses which we know to be only heaps of ruins but which the obscurity of the night presents as if peace had built them up again" [CPP 541].[78]) To recognize these kinds of internal contradictions within the sequence is to confirm Patricia Rae's insight that Stevens' poetry is often marked by "the method of 'presenting' materials side-by-side, without commenting definitively on their relation to one another."[79] Perhaps most famously employed in Stevens' better-known sequence "Thirteen Ways of Looking at a Blackbird," this technique, as Rae goes on to observe, is central to a pragmatic reading of Stevens, for "pragmatic hypotheses may have the effect of transforming the very world against which they are tested: they 'emerge from facts,' but also 'dip forward into facts ... and add to them.'"[80] In the "Lettres d'un Soldat" sequence, Stevens presses on the political potentialities of such pragmatic method by juxtaposing the rhetoric and subjectivities produced by sentimental nationalism, revolutionary fervor, racial entitlement, technocratic idealism, and democratic cosmopolitanism. He does so not to validate one proposition over another but to see what happens when these propositions collide, and to leave his readers to choose which rhetorical/political attitude to imagination, service, and death they prefer.

In doing so, this poem seems to reflect on the very nature of political subjectivity: the multiple ways in which polities are organized across geographical, imaginative, symbolic, violent, and intimate territories, and how individuals struggle to make sense of the geopolitical forces and available discourses that control their destiny. Given this investigative impetus, it is no surprise that he prefaced the individual poems with Lemercier's letters, which were of course originally a private exchange but then were published as what Schweik calls "that most populist type of wartime and postwar epistolary publications, the collection of a dead soldier's letters home."[81] From a "private" exchange read by his mother and military censors, to published and widely read populist wartime fare in France, England, and the United States, to epigraphs to a wartime modernist poem in *Poetry* magazine, Lemercier's *A Soldier of France to His*

Mother demonstrated the manifold ways in which letters both reflected and conditioned the relationship between individual and state during wartime. This connected Stevens' poem to a broader cultural awareness of how wartime letters engaged often disconcerting new circumstances of intimacy, and forged new social relations that frequently defied conventional sentimental or symbolic representation. Stevens was surely aware of this phenomenon, and how letters represented a particularly rich location for thinking about the ongoing and dramatic transformations in the American state. His skill in the "Lettres d'un Soldat" sequence was not just to assemble a series of monologues that test different rhetorical and political models against one another in a form of poetic-pragmatic warfare that mirrored what he saw as the militarized clash of ideologies taking place in Europe but to enfold them all under the umbrella of the letter form whose mediating and habituating force was inseparable from those ideologies. The medium of the letter was the privileged location where "creative statecraft," linguistic coercion, and a simultaneous reification of nationalist gender conventions and their explosion through networks of expanded sociality came together.

Edith Wharton's "Writing a War Letter," Modernism, and Charity

This overdetermination of the letter, seen by Stevens as such a rich source of creative potential, was not universally so regarded. Edith Wharton was much cooler in her enthusiasm for the aesthetics of the wartime letter and the politics it encoded, and continued to see the kinds of intimate dynamics discussed so far as the proper dimension of private and voluntary spheres rather than the province of the state. She was totally committed to France's cause in the war; she lived in Paris for most of the duration and worked intensively for a number of private wartime charities, many of which she had personally organized and funded. Just three weeks after the mobilization of France, Wharton had established a workroom for seamstresses put out of work by the war; later she organized charities for Belgian refugees and sanitaria for tubercular soldiers.[82] In 1916, she published *The Book of the Homeless*, whose proceeds went to Belgian refugees; it contained a preface bemoaning America's persistent neutrality by her friend Theodore Roosevelt (a view that echoed Wharton's own) and contained writing by John Galsworthy, Henry James, George Santayana, William Dean Howells, Joseph Conrad, and W.B. Yeats. She delivered medical supplies to Verdun, Ypres, and the Vosges, and wrote about these experiences for *Scribner's* magazine, articles later collected in *Fighting France*

(1915); these pieces were essentially designed to mobilize wealthy American philanthropic support for the wide array of war-related medical and refugee charity agencies at work in France.[83] For Wharton, who had moved permanently to France in 1913, her adoptive country was a "luminous instance," a country typified by "intellectual light and ... moral force" that had been "for centuries the great creative force of civilization," and was now menaced by a militarism that was "stupid, inartistic, unimaginative and enslaving."[84] For her service, Wharton was made a Chevalier of the French Legion of Honor in 1916.

The war demonstrated and deepened Wharton's commitment to two political ideas. The first was her idealization of a moral-aesthetic unity in France that informed all aspects of its national life, and had produced a civilization and society far superior to both what she called German "state paternalism" and American materialism.[85] She praised France as the "most homogeneous and uninterrupted culture the world has known," a "continuity" that deeply informed France's status as an intellectual and artistic beacon to the world; in her fiction, she called it "a second country" "to thinkers, artists, to all creators," "a luminous point about which striving visions and purposes could rally."[86] And what the French shared with America was a love of liberal democracy rather than a faith in technocracy; for as she explained:

> The Frenchman and the American want to have a voice in governing their country, and the German prefers to be governed by professionals, as long as they make him comfortable and give him what he wants.
>
> From the purely practical point of view this is not a bad plan, but it breaks down as soon as a moral issue is involved. They say corporations have no souls; neither have governments that are not answerable to a free people for their actions.[87]

The second idea was the value of charity work as a necessary supplement, and even corrective agency, to the actions of the state. This was especially important during the period of American neutrality; Wharton was infuriated by Wilson's reluctance to aid France by joining the war, and often referred to it as a cause of national shame. (After Wilson's reelection in 1916, under the slogan "he kept us out of the war," she remarked that "it was the saddest moment of my life when I realized that my country wanted him to be what he is."[88]) Accordingly, she felt it a personal duty to support the French effort however she could. She threw herself into this; within two weeks of the mobilizations, she had joined the committee of the American Ambulance, and soon after returning to Paris in September 1914, she founded a new charity, the American Hostel for Refugees, which, as Shari Benstock notes, raised funds "on a scale that in our time only corporations could undertake." This was made possible by Wharton tapping her extensive connections in America's social and financial elite for donations.[89] This followed a well-established model wherein charitable work was one of the few avenues for American women of Wharton's class to participate in public life, a participation steeped in ideologies of *noblesse oblige* and sentimental benevolence. Yet Wharton was careful to separate selfless wartime voluntarism from the kinds of social function charity work customarily played for women in her own elite transatlantic class in peacetime. Indeed, she excoriated American women who took on wartime charity activities as part of a status-building extension of the public social rituals and network-making that her fiction anatomized so well. In wartime Paris, this seemed little more than "dancing and flirting and money-making on the great red mounds of dead" (*ASATF* 176).

Charity work was also where Wharton had her most direct – and bruising – contact with the American state in wartime. As Alan Price has ably discussed, after American intervention in April 1917, the American government designated the American Red Cross as the official US wartime charity and the specified relief agency for the AEF. Over the summer of 1917, it absorbed charities run by private American citizens in France as well as embarking on a $100 million fundraising drive, the largest of any charity in history. Simultaneously, it dispensed with the prewar leader of the Red Cross, Mabel T. Boardman, a woman in many ways similar to Wharton – born to a prominent Cleveland family and with extensive connections among the American social and financial elite. The reorganized Red Cross was led by an all-male "war committee" made up of dollar-a-year men, headed by Henry P. Davison, a vice president at J.P. Morgan. As Price observes, this shift represented "a dramatic transformation in the nature of American philanthropy. Before April 1917, control of civilian war charities rested primarily with the socially and economically privileged classes. . . . After America's entry into the war, however, philanthropy and civilian war relief increasingly took on the look of a corporate organization dominated by large-scale efficiencies."[90] Wharton was at the center of this change from "a noblesse oblige model to a corporate model" of charity, and her letters from the time reveal her anger at its effects.[91] She resented the often high-handed and blundering management of "her" charities by the Red Cross, finding that "it did not care about national or personal sensitivities, only about imposing American control and ensuring efficiency."[92] And she bridled at being shunted out of work she found civically meaningful and rewarding. As recent critics such as Annette Benert have noted, Wharton's war work with refugees was "the only occasion in which she entered full time into a public cause." Wharton took great pride in it and relished this experience of institutional leadership and management. But the amalgamating actions of the Red Cross effectively made her one of the many women "forced further from the industrial workplace and public responsibility after the war," as she was "thrown back into private life."[93]

This preamble serves as an important introduction to one of Wharton's most interesting but least-discussed war fictions, "Writing a War Story," which appeared in 1919. Wharton still has a reputation for sinking to the depths of crude propaganda in her war fiction; this charge was leveled most forcefully by Stanley Cooperman, who saw Wharton as spearheading a band of much less talented American "lady authors" who "seriously portrayed God-fearing boys blondly carrying the banners of Christian faith against a simian foe."[94] Moreover, as Robin Peel has suggested, the war is often seen as contaminating her postwar fiction through its sharpening effect on Wharton's illiberal, reactionary, and nativist political views.[95] Yet this story – written in the war's aftermath – is a much more humorous take on the war than the often stern moralizing found in *A Son at the Front* or *The Marne*; and the humor stems from a situation that paralleled Wharton's own – how to write war fiction as a noncombatant woman. Yet that the story-within-the-story is entitled "His Letter Home" also connects this piece to Wharton's thinking on how art might engage the new incarnations, and even the new intimacies, of the state.

"Writing a War Story" concerns the pretty and privileged Ivy Spang, a Croton-on-Hudson heiress and poet who had "published a little volume of verse before the war" entitled *Vibrations*. It was praised by her local newspaper but also the "editor of *Zigzag*, the new 'Weekly Journal of Defiance,'" which opined that her poems' "esoteric significance showed that she was a *vers-librist* in thought as well as in technique."[96] "But then the war came," and we next find Ivy "pouring tea once a week for a whole winter in a big Anglo-American hospital" in Paris. There, she is identified as an author, and tapped by the editor of the new soldiers' magazine *The Man-At-Arms* to contribute a "rattling war story" for their initial number. The editor tells her he wants "the first number to be an 'actuality,' as the French say; all the articles written by people who've done the thing themselves, or seen it done." Nonetheless, he seems unconcerned that she has never visited the front, and urges her to write a trench story, "a tragedy with a happy ending."[97] He also secures her permission to print a photograph of her in nurse's uniform alongside the story, and this is where Ivy's troubles begin.

Well aware of the modernist dicta received from the editor of *Zigzag* that one should "not [allow] one's self to be 'influenced,'" and that "people don't bother with plots nowadays," she struggles to make progress with her story. A recent copy of *Fact and Fiction* is promising but turns out to be of little help.[98] However, inspiration arrives from her governess – formerly a student of the famous philosopher Henri Bergson at the Sorbonne – who has a notebook full of stories related to her by convalescing *poilus* during her year-long stint at a local military hospital. Ivy eagerly works to adapt one of these stories; she adds "a touch of sentiment," and her governess "revised and polished the rustic speech in which she had originally transcribed the tale."[99] Eventually, her story – "His Letter Home" – is published. Yet all that the young soldiers at the hospital seem interested in is the photo that accompanies her story. She then encounters the renowned soldier-novelist Harold Harbard, who is convalescing in her hospital. The only serviceman to have actually read her work, he tells her that she has "mauled" an "awfully good subject," and schools her that the subject of a story is all-important; "it's only the people without invention who tell you it isn't."[100] The final indignity comes when he asks her for a copy of her photograph.

For such a short piece this story does a considerable amount of work. As Julie Olin-Ammentorp has noted, it ventriloquizes Wharton's own insecurities about her war fiction, particularly her reluctance to describe military combat for fear of misrepresenting a subject her gender prohibited her from experiencing. The fact that Harbard draws his status as an authority figure in the story from his confidence in both war and writing, and that both are staked in a specifically masculinized privilege, is significant; as Jean Gallagher observes, the story is a "satirical cautionary tale of the discursive constraints placed on women writers during wartime."[101] But it also voices in nascent form what would become Wharton's extensive postwar critique of modernism. In her 1925 collection of essays *The Writing of Fiction* – which, as Sharon Kim notes, she had been working on for many years and revised extensively following her reading of Joyce's *Ulysses* – Wharton outlined a series of criticisms of modernism that she held to for the rest of her career.[102] Her central contention was that modernism had abandoned core principles of fiction that had been carefully worked out by preceding generations, perhaps most importantly the necessity of embedding subject matter within a broader context of moral experience. This was particularly problematic in stream-of-consciousness narratives, for in attempting to mimetically capture the patterns of consciousness and psychological experience modernists had dispensed with what she called the "creative imagination," which in contrast to the "merely sympathetic imagination" was "two-sided, and combines with the power of penetrating into other minds that of standing far enough aloof from them to see beyond, and relate them to the whole stuff of life out of which they but partially emerge."[103] Modernists' passionate attachment to the idea of originality had led them to abandon the formal lessons that provided that perceptive distance; accordingly, "the distrust of technique and the fear of being unoriginal – both symptoms of a certain lack of creative abundance – are in truth leading to pure anarchy in fiction, and one is almost tempted to say that in certain schools formlessness is now regarded as the first condition of form."[104] She also defended the importance of subject matter in fiction, for "A good subject ... must contain in itself something that sheds a light on our moral experience. If it is incapable of this expansion, this vital radiation, it remains ... a more irrelevant happening, a meaningless scrap of fact torn out of its context."[105] In later critical writing, she traced what she believed to be modernism's wrong-headed commitment to iconoclasm back to the war, which had been a cataclysm of "moral and intellectual destruction" that was "shattering to traditional culture," and had caused an entire generation to avoid "the fecundating soil stored for it by its predecessors."[106]

The continuity between these precepts and the satire of modernism evident in "Writing a War Story" is very clear, particularly in Wharton's scathing opinion of modernism's supposed readiness to dispense with a "subject," and its purported overobsession with originality, both of which lead Ivy astray. Combined with Ivy's dilettantish attitude to volunteering, Wharton also seems to echo the views of many mainstream cultural critics that I explored in Chapter 1, which linked modernist experimentalism with a failure to properly dispatch one's wartime patriotic responsibilities. Yet there is an element of sympathy here, too, one staked in Wharton's own anxieties over how noncombatant artists, especially women, could function at all during the war when they were operating under such constrictive parameters for what wartime experiences they could imaginatively engage. Detached from the "actuality" of front-line experience owing to the gendered restrictions of her time – a definition of war experience that has, as many critics have noted, been central to the canonization of male combat veterans as the war's most important literary voices – Ivy has little to fall back on but the hollow forms of technique in fulfilling an assignment she does not really want. (As Claire Tylee notes, this was a situation

Wharton had personally experienced in the war, when she was pressured by her publisher Scribner's into writing a war story on a topic she had only encountered second-hand.[107]) Ivy is relentlessly sexually objectified by men, but also has her writing belittled by them, a belittling in no small part enabled by the very limits they have set on how she should write. The editor of *The Man-At-Arms* sets suffocating limits to the story – asking for an "actuality" and "stirring trench story" with "a dash of sentiment [but] nothing to depress or discourage," constraints that more or less doom the story to failure from the outset. And, as Tylee observes, at the conversation with Harbard at the story's close, and despite her attempts "to overcome the ladylike limits that convention sets for her," Ivy is met by "a super-cilious determination to keep her in her place."[108]

What appears as a fairly slight story, therefore, has some complex things to say about the relation of gender to war writing, and how modernist aesthetics might preclude the kind of moral engagement necessary to adequately represent the war. Yet what no critics have addressed is the detail of Ivy's failed story, its basis in the fictional letter between war front and home front. What readers are expected to recognize in this choice of title and subject is first and foremost its status as a cliché, the most obvious and well-worn vehicle for combining sentiment, "actuality," and a connection between the different geographical and gendered spheres of the war.[109] And I use "sentiment" here in the sense neatly formulated by June Howard: that "'sentiment' and its derivatives indicate a moment when emotion is recognized as socially constructed," where "we mark a moment when the discursive processes that construct emotion become visible."[110] By this point, as I hope to have demonstrated in this chapter, the fictional letter home had become a staple of comic writing, propaganda fiction in the nation's bestselling magazines, and war novels of every stripe. Yet it was also perhaps the preeminent form for writers to consider the new forms of sociality of the expanded wartime state, the new ways in which social connection and "cultural intimacy" were being forged and experienced in the new structures (and infrastructures) of Progressive civic life. "Writing a War Story" is withering about the implications of this kind of intimacy, a critique it enacts precisely by mobilizing two of the corner-stones of sentimental, gendered conventionality in the war – the letter from a man at the front to a woman at home, as well as the pretty volunteer nurse – in order to think not just about how women might write about war but about how they might work in it, especially within new state structures of both benevolence and literary production. Which is to say that the story is steeped as much in Wharton's experiences as a woman writing about the

war as it is in her experiences of charity organization in the war, and the
way that her gender privileged certain kinds of labor and sidelined her from
others.

To engage this issue fully, it is worth registering more fully Wharton's
thoughts about the Progressive state, and especially its role in establishing
social safety nets of medical care and the amelioration of poverty. At one
point in her 1922 war novel *A Son at the Front*, her artist-protagonist John
Campton muses over these things:

> Nothing hitherto had been less in the line of his interests than the large
> schemes of general amelioration which were coming to be classed under the
> transatlantic term of "Social Welfare." If questioned on the subject a few
> months earlier he would probably have concealed his fundamental indiffer-
> ence under the profession of an extreme individualism, and the assertion of
> every man's right to suffer and starve in his own way.[111] (*ASATF* 93)

Despite his musings on "large schemes of general amelioration," which
were the forerunners of the mature welfare state then being enacted in
Europe and to a lesser degree in the United States – schemes for unemployment insurance, social health care, and universal pensions –
Campton's views on charity never really shift from "eas[ing] his own
pain by putting his hand in his pocket" in cases of particular "poignancy"
(*ASATF* 93). This was the kind of affective and social structure Wharton
was most comfortable with for organized beneficence and its attendant
social relations, where private charities monetized sympathetic connection
outside of the parameters of the state. Indeed, William M. Morgan has
characterized Wharton's wartime writing as frequently offering nostalgic
evocations of a "classically republican masculinity with its sentimental ideal
of public benevolence," a form of masculinity that had been largely super-
seded by 1917.[112] In *A Son at the Front*, Campton is an erratic and impulsive
volunteer to war charities, generally only contributing his name or his labor
when moved to do so by the appeals (or the tragic deaths) of young men
who remind him of his younger self or of his own son. Indeed, this
emotional bond becomes one of the few left to him during the war, as
"pity was his only remaining link with his kind, the one barrier between
himself and the dreadful solitude which awaited him when he returned to
his studio" (*ASATF* 94). Of course, poignancy – so characteristic an affect
of the sentimental – is an emotional mode eminently capable of privatizing
issues of public policy; as Elizabeth Barnes observes, "the conversion of the
political into the personal, or the public into the private, is a distinctive
trait of sentimentalism . . . [wherein] family stands as the model for social

and political affiliations."[113] Such is true of *A Son at the Front*, where John Campton's relationship to his only son, George, forms the central emotional and artistic relationship in the book; George is both Campton's central artistic subject (in both life and death) and the only person he loves. His political commitments radiate out from this relationship and inform his understanding of most of the war's broader social and political implications. In these scenarios, charity becomes a way for Campton to organize his politics in a way that both provides the emotional sustenance of "pity" with his "own kind" and remains on the intimate scale of familial fidelity. "Amelioration" in *A Son at the Front*, then, operates not in the "general" terms of state systematics but on the largely privatized and personalized terms of charitable benevolence organized by social elites.

As Hazel Hutchison notes, it is seriously misleading to read the focalizing figure of Campton – marked by petulance, self-centeredness, emotional volatility, and inconsistency in his beliefs and affections – as any kind of reliable guide to Wharton's own feelings. Yet they seem to share the belief that charitable "sentimental benevolence" might be how social amelioration could best be institutionalized, and also that the difference between good and ineffective art is the difference between work that "sheds a light on our moral experience" and work that merely offered to record "scraps of fact." (The book is littered with Campton's scathing reflections on bohemian modernism; he prefers the "sounder goods" of "classic art," *ASATF* 89.) Both Campton and Wharton, therefore, share a set of moral and aesthetic precepts wary of new innovations in both state practice and artistic representation – precepts that are deeply intertwined. Accordingly, if letters function as the paradigmatic state form of facilitating – and even organizing – intimate life, it is telling that *A Son at the Front* pays as much attention to their mediating processes and their unreliability as to their content; an important letter from George to Campton "bore the military frank," and another is not in George's hand but in that of an "unlettered French soldier," George's orderly, who is writing after George has been injured (*ASATF* 160). Letters are prized for their ability to provide substitutes for bodily presence – George's handwriting and turns of phrase give comfort to Campton, and he marks time between letters from his son – but they are also deeply misleading. The second section of the novel, with the relation between George and Campton entirely mediated by letter as George is away from Paris in service, has Campton believing George is safely placed in a staff job, whereas in actuality George has secretly left that posting to fight – a deception he upholds through reassuring (and duplicitous) letters home. At the end of the novel, after George's death ends this epistolary relationship, Campton wonders whether he knew him at all; for "between himself and George lay the unbridgeable abyss of his son's experiences," an abyss that letters only served to widen (*ASATF* 212).

Yet the fullest consideration of the state's role in intimate life – and its related aesthetics – comes in the depiction of the fictional letter in "Writing a War Story," for this allowed Wharton to consider on different yet parallel grounds the competing merits of "general schemes" versus personalized "poignancy" in the new institutional paradigms of war. Although the Red Cross is never named directly, and Wharton changes dates and locations to avoid any overt allegorization of its wartime activities, it is easy to see Wharton's anger at this institution in the story too.[114] The work Ivy does marginalizes women's authority while drawing on their volunteer labor, and the story Ivy is coerced to write is stripped of the kinds of intimacy and first-hand knowledge Wharton felt was so important to effective charity work. Wharton denigrates the fictional letter in "Writing a War Story" partly by evacuating it of content: we hear nothing of Emile Durand's life, the *poilu* whose letters form the basis of the story. All we are left with is the title, "His Letter Home," the hollow shell of the form itself, which becomes a technical device that – devoid of any kind of "moral experience" – becomes not only bad art, but bad politics as well. If the modern state functions through depersonalized infrastructural systems such as the postal service, which, in Bruce Robbins' words, are "the object of no-one's desire," then Wharton sees this less as an exciting expansion of sociality and more as the draining of what makes social connection meaningful.[115] In the hands of Ivy's governess, sensitively transcribing Emile's first-hand experiences, there is a "good subject"; as soon as these become reworked into Ivy's fictional letter home, which hopes to expand that intimacy into the mediating structures of the state, that affective and therefore moral power evaporates. What the cliché is to literature – a form incapable of moral expansion or personal idiosyncrasy, stripped of the possibility of sympathetic connection, where our affective reaction is to the form rather than any kind of individuated experience – in fact comes to resemble the same affective flatness as the modern state's organization of labor and social connection, a form of bureaucratic depersonalization Wharton saw at work in the newly reorganized and state-sanctioned Red Cross. So, rather than being anathema to the modern state, modernism was in this case seen as its perfect counterpart – an unfeeling and technocratic prioritization of form over moral connection.

Wharton cannot quite let it go at that, however. Most volunteers in *A Son at the Front* seem to achieve benefits – monetary, social, or emotional –

from their work that seem more rewarding than the assistance they purportedly offer to the needy beneficiaries of their labors. And, later in the book, Wharton includes a withering description of how charities can be beset by the same kind of organizational infighting and corruption so often charged to larger governmental structures. This is of a piece with Hutchison's characterization of *A Son at the Front* as an unstable, self-contradicting book, unsure of its politics or its aesthetics. Ultimately, it is interesting to look at the two artworks that conclude the two pieces I have been discussing: "His Letter Home," and the memorial sculpture to his son that Campton begins in the novel's final pages. Neither the morally evacuated forms of modernism and the new Progressive state represented by "His Letter Home" nor the retreat to private grief and a "fix[ation] on the lost childhood of the son from whom he walked away," which represents Campton's final work, seem to offer good alternatives for the place of the artwork in the war's new political, aesthetic, and emotional structures.[116] The former is incapable of the moral experience Wharton thought essential for any kind of meaningful intimacy; the latter is a retreat into the solipsistic bath of pity that inevitably becomes self-pity, and so becomes a renunciation of the social altogether.

The first of these views would seem to endorse the views of later critics such as Lionel Trilling, that once the inherently progressive and enfranchising impulses of the "liberal imagination" become programmatic, which is to say institutionalized and rationalized in political institutions, they drift "toward a denial of the emotions and the imagination" that were their very fueling impulse.[117] It also limns a quite different Wharton from the flag-waving propagandist cheering on the wartime state that emerges in much of the critical appraisal of her war work. Moreover, Campton's breezy dismissal of "social welfare" on the grounds of needing poignancy to orient his benevolence chimes with one of the most persistent criticisms of the welfare state, both at its inception and in recent neoliberal times: that voluntary benevolence and private charities – often because of the affective richness of personalized and voluntary contribution – were materially and ethically better for the common good than state-organized assistance.[118] Yet the representation of voluntarism in *A Son at the Front* is simultaneously unsparing about the problems that social theorists have identified with charitable giving as a foundation for the common weal – its tendencies toward philanthropic particularism and philanthropic paternalism, wherein elites channel money to groups that either remind them of themselves or that serve their own interests.[119] Campton's attitude to charity brings into focus his major failure in the novel, which is a failure to be fully sociable and even social. Tellingly, he refuses to have a telephone installed in his rooms; he is both unable to master the technique of answering and placing calls, and resents it as a "live thing, a kind of Laocoon-serpent that caught one in its coils and dragged one struggling to the receiver" (*ASATF* 35). Like his views on "social welfare," he is uncomfortable with both the technological form of this new network and the social implications it invokes. He cannot ever broaden his concerns far beyond his son and form meaningful and fulfilling relationships or connections with others, whether in his peer group or within a commons of democratic community. Taken together – and with the letter home as an important mediating device for thinking some of these issues through – "Writing a War Story" and *A Son at the Front* suggest Wharton's awareness that the very nature of the social was being transformed by the agencies of the modern state; and while she disapproved of some of those transformations, the older models would not suffice either.

*

Wharton's sense that letters could flatten and sentimentalize the intricacies of moral experience was not new to the war – earlier fiction, particularly her 1910 story "The Letters," had made much of this. Yet what was new was her recognition of the expansion of letters' purposes, readerships, and audiences in the war – as company commanders, military censors, nurses, volunteer workers, and propaganda magazines read, altered, wrote, imitated, and prompted soldiers' correspondence. The suspicion of these extensions of intimacy evident in her war fiction in many ways reflected her politics, anchored as they were in principles of naturalized privilege and private affiliation rather than the leveling and impersonal "grand schemes of social amelioration" of state bureaucracy. But other authors saw those extensions of sociality in different terms. Those most directly aligned with the aims of official US war policy saw fictional letters as a key genre in the mass organization of national morale, a vehicle for codifying national sentiment in ways that exalted the private and familial sphere while tacitly reminding the nation that this sphere was deeply enabled by a system of reliable, private, and universal communication that represented a crown jewel of Progressive Era statecraft and institution-building. Others, like Stevens, used the uniquely mediating status of the letter to consider the filters of representation lying between noncombatants and combatants, but also how such mediation was central to a wide variety of modern political experience – including affiliation to the liberal democratic state. For some writers, illuminating the oxymoron of the "private" letter – read by censors or swapped between strangers, and handled by a state that somehow professed to protect the sanctity of the domestic private sphere by drafting millions of men away from their homes – carried rich potential for comedy and antiwar satire. And a few writers sited the wartime mail as a bracing transformation of national social experience, the full realization of the promise of a federal institution that had already done so much to effect national integration and social modernization, and might even play a key role in Wilson's dream of an international Progressive order. As N.W. Peterson, President of the Illinois State Association of the National Association of Letter Carriers, and writing in the *Postal Record* in 1917, put it, "there is no institution in the world which so tends to draw the nations together as the postal system ... when the clouds that today darken our storm-tossed world disappear, the Postal System, more than any other single agency, will help to establish the Universal Brotherhood among men."[120] The culture of the wartime letter, therefore, did not just exist within a polarized terrain of propaganda and censorship on one hand, and familial intimacy on the other; it registered that the war was reconfiguring intimacy and the state's role in producing it. In consequence, fictional and poetic letters, so important to the American understanding of the war's geographical, emotional, and political dimensions, both considered and were conditioned by the state's presence in intimate life, and the simultaneously productive and intrusive place it held there.

CHAPTER 3

The Regional Novel and the Wartime State

In 1916, at the height of the preparedness movement, John Dewey weighed in on the debate over the benefits of universal military service. He was responding to Major-General Leonard Wood's suggestion that such service not only was an obligation of American citizenship but would serve an especially useful role in integrating what Wood called "all kinds of human-ity seen on the docks at Ellis Island." Wood's nativist scaremongering suggested that many recent immigrants came "in racial groups, drift through our schools in racial groups and are controlled by a dialect press," possessing unassimilated identities that presented a threat to national civic cohesion – and potentially military cohesion, should America require a citizen army to fight in the world war. While Dewey sharply critiqued Wood's nativism and elitism, and was generally appre-ciative of America's distinctive cultural pluralism, he did little to challenge Wood's assessment of ethnic and cultural plurality as a problem for inculcating a desirable sense of patriotism and national affiliation. Yet instead of compulsory military service, he proposed instead "a vision of a national government which takes an interest at once paternal and scientific in our alien visitors." Dewey envisaged the building of national civic cohesion – and consequentially military cohesion, in the likely necessity of drafting a citizen army – through a compulsory educational program for every "foreign illiterate," including the mandatory learning of English. This, along with having "conditions of labor safeguarded in the interest of his health and his integrity as an economic agent," and being taught "to associate these things in whatever part of the country he found himself with the United States and not with the district, township or state," would mean such compulsory educational service would soon "be dis-cussed as a military proposition and not as an educational one."[1] Mandatory "educational service" following a federally coordinated sylla-bus, then, could trump both ethnic and regional loyalties, a nationalizing force that would have considerable military advantages in America's increasingly likely participation in the war then raging in Europe.

Following the war, however, Dewey sounded a very different note about the value of integrative national institutions. In "Americanism and Localism," which appeared in the *Dial* in 1920, he characterized American life as bonded by surprisingly weak national cultural and affective ties. Instead, Dewey argued that the "loose collection of houses, of streets, of neighborhoods, villages, farms, towns" that make up the national whole were typified by an "intense consciousness of what is going on within itself . . . and a languid drooping interest in the rest of the spacious land."[2] Nor was this a problem; nebulous concepts of Americanism and Americanization were too often deployed coercively in service of nativist arguments about assimilating the foreign-born, Dewey noted, confessing he often could not "tell very well . . . what Americanization is" and impishly suggesting that it might consist of "learning a language strangely known as English. But perhaps [the foreign-born] are too busy making the American language to devote much time to studying English."[3] As well as reversing his earlier position about mandatory English lessons for immigrants, Dewey also took care to differentiate the various kinds of affiliation that characterized country, nation, and state, seeing the nation as fundamentally an administrative rather than an affective unit; whereas "the country is a spread of localities," the nation was solely "something that exists in Washington and other seats of government."[4] Ultimately, Dewey declared that "the locality is the only universal," the only political unit possessing what he would later call "vitality and depth of close and direct intercourse and attachment" – qualities missing from "The Great Community" of the nation.[5]

"Americanism and Localism" would go on to be an influential blueprint for the cultural politics of US regionalism in the 1920s, a politics that sought increasingly radical alternatives to the political and economic centralizations that characterized the drift of recent American history. A large part of that influence resulted from Dewey's insight that regionalist politics was indelibly aesthetic; as he insisted, "Americanism and Localism" was not a "political treatise," but rather a reflection on "the literary career of our country," before going on to discuss local newspapers, Mary Wilkins Freeman, Bret Harte, and Mark Twain.[6] Of course, Dewey's dissociation from the political in this piece was a thin smokescreen; his disdain for the rhetoric of "100% Americanism" that had characterized the recent Red Scare is very clear. Yet that sleight of hand helped the essay signal two related things: that regionalist politics and regionalist aesthetics were often the same thing, and that both the aesthetics and the politics of federalism would, in the immediate future, be deeply colored by the American experience of the nation-state in World War One. This chapter explores that dynamic, examining how many of the major writers of regional fiction in the era – Willa Cather, Ellen Glasgow, Sinclair Lewis, Booth Tarkington, Zane Grey, and Ruth Suckow – wrote novels that often strained to consider the question of how local affinities articulated in specifically aesthetic terms might relate to the nationalizing imperatives of war and its concomitant centralization of political power. Such questions resonate with the recent preoccupations of literary scholarship on regionalist literature, which have often centered on regionalism's relationship with US nationalism, especially how nationalist cultural forms functioned to underwrite American imperial expansion and its frequent corollary of an increasingly globalized economic world. This scholarship has frequently diverged on the issue of whether regionalist literary aesthetics were constitutive of a nationalizing cultural and political project, becoming little more than a "henchman of the nation state," in Scott Herring's words, or acted instead as a critical counterweight to its operations.[7] The parameters of that debate are identifiable in the regionalist fiction of World War One. On the one hand, regionalist writers felt particular obligations in the pressurized search for nationalized cultural forms that overtook the nation in 1916 and 1917. On the other, the wartime surge in nativism, and the enormous cultural influence of the CPI and the extensive, pro-war national mass culture emerging from Tin Pan Alley and Hollywood, exacerbated regionalists' sense of needing to resist what Robert Dorman calls "the nationalizing, homogenizing urban-industrial complex."[8] This dynamic and this dilemma shaped regional fiction in the war era and its immediate aftermath. While, as Mark Storey has argued, the technological, economic, and demographic changes of modernity all subtly register on the superficially Arcadian fictions of American regionalism in the nineteenth century, World War One multiplies the traces of a greatly expanded state in regional fictions.[9] As they tracked those traces, regional writers also began imagining the forces of economic standardization and incorporation as threatening localized cultures beyond American shores, within an international framework that the war had made newly visible. They also frequently returned to the issue of the multiplicity of citizenship, and how affinities to domestic, regional, national, and even global spheres might be constellated. And struggling with the burden of how to establish representational homologies and lines of continuity between these differently scaled political and cultural units, their novels often showed strains that led reviewers to class them as failures, both in their own time and in ours.

World War One and the Politics of Regionalism: The End(s) of Local Color

The notion that American regional distinctiveness was in decline, as economic and political systems characterized by national reach and centralized power became increasingly dominant, was not new to the wartime moment. But it was more loudly articulated at a time when regional, ethnic, racial, and linguistic differences were often being downplayed or actively suppressed in the name of ensuring national, martial cohesion. In literary terms, this situation was frequently used to ring the final death knell of local color. In the immediate prewar period, the presence of local color stories in the nation's preeminent literary magazines had declined sharply from its late nineteenth-century heyday, but during the war and its immediate aftermath several literary critics identified the war as effecting the genre's complete obsolescence. For example, an unsigned editorial in *The Nation* in September 1919 proposed that "The classical episode of 'local color' in American fiction may now be said to have ended."[10] In an argument anticipating the more recent claims of critics such as Amy Kaplan, the editorial credited local color fiction with having helped effect nationwide homogeneity and unity; for as "different sections read eagerly about one another," a nationwide readership "became imaginatively aware of the enormous territory now being welded into a federal unity of spirit as well as administration."[11] The genre was partly a victim of its own success, therefore, in bringing constellated localities into a coherent, and nationalized, perspective. The piece also anticipated a recurrent feature of criticism on local color – its connection with smallness, "little plots, little scenes, little characters," a littleness rooted in the minuscule nature of regional differentiation – as any "local singularities which could be observed at all were more or less surface singularities, minor differences in accent or gesture, and little more."[12] The genre's obsolescence was due to these (increasingly) slight differences in local cultures, the piece proposed, and also because America had been so thoroughly centralized by the "administration" of a dramatically expanded federal state. One of the main ways this empowered wartime state had wielded homogenizing cultural power was through the mass mobility it had precipitated, a mobility that capped off the demographic sea change of the large-scale urban migrations of the recent past. Such widespread mobilization had made those people who stayed in the rural communities they had been born into seem "dull" and "timid" rather than quaint, the piece proposed – also intimating that the nostalgic tone that had been one of the genre's guiding characteristics and primary attractions was incompatible with the wartime exigency to mobilize populations and resources.[13] The scornful hint at rural slackerism embedded in this judgment on rural immobility partially explains why such obituaries for the local color tradition were not necessarily elegiac; as the *Literary Digest*'s piece "Is Local-Color Fiction Passing?" remarked, with Americans "being stamped by rapid communication and general education into more general likeness," "while in the old days it was proper for fiction to stress the disparate character of our communities, now it should stress their unity."[14]

Most famous of all such arguments, albeit one with a quite different political spin, was made by Carl Van Doren, who in *The Nation* in 1921 proposed a new "revolt from the village" school of novelists and poets including Sherwood Anderson, Floyd Dell, Edgar Lee Masters, and Sinclair Lewis. This tradition had blasted apart the "cult of the village," replacing the purportedly saccharine sentimentality of the local color tradition with portrayals of rural communities riven by isolation, boredom, transgression, and frustrated desire. And in Sinclair Lewis's *Main Street*, the runaway bestseller of this new tradition, Van Doren identified the village rather than America's urban centers as the center of a "monotonous uniformity," a vision that presented America's regions as a vast and undifferentiated hinterland "conquered and converted by the legions of mediocrity."[15] As with many of the pieces emerging on localism at this moment, Van Doren envisaged a landscape of "Americanized" regions whose original variety had been incrementally homogenized by the economic forces of an incorporating America. Yet this slow grind was also punctuated by moments of intense and violent coercion and conflict. His language of "conquering" and "conversion" strongly hints at America's recent history of the harassment and legal persecution of America's ethnic and linguistic minorities in the Red Scare of 1918–1920. Moreover, his deployment of the term "legions" nods to the American Legion, who played so prominent a role in those persecutions, and were synonymous with the extralegal, violent coercions that backed up the rhetoric of "100% America" in this period. All these pieces, therefore, saw regional homogeneity as the new norm; suggested that those who were not involved in the mass movements of the nationwide mobilization were retrograde and undynamic rather than organically rooted; and averred that the most promising sites of cultural innovation lay elsewhere than in America's regions. And all drew their evidence for this from the purported death throes of the local color tradition, death throes the war had hastened.

This debate had another side, however, which proposed that the war had revealed the primacy of regional identity, a primacy often shadowed by the concern that truly national cultural traditions did not exist. Such propositions suggested that America's aggregation of different ethnic, racial, and regional communities was tied by abstract political traditions and institutions alone, rather than the palpable materiality of cultural or linguistic practices. And these arguments intimated that a civic rather than culturalist nationalism lacked the bondedness that only a truly collective culture could provide.[16] This view was not unique to the wartime moment; as Leigh Ann Duck has noted, this was a "dichotomy . . . repeatedly proposed in U.S. history: where affiliation with the nation is represented as abstract and pragmatic, [whereas] affiliation with the region suggests commonality and rootedness."[17] But it was a dichotomy felt with particular force as America entered the war and sought affective strategies to assist the project of national cohesion. For some, the problem lay in a government that did so little for its citizens; Walter Lippmann ventured the hope that expanded national systems of welfare could inculcate the type of "thick" loyalty found in local cultural traditions, suggesting in 1916 that "our government is weak in the affection of the people because it is a weak government, because it rarely touches their lives . . . The great reality for most Americans is still the locality where they dwell . . . National loyalty is so generally a phrase without obligation because the national power is so much of an abstraction."[18] For others, a reluctance to embrace nationalized abstraction was a shameful failure of moral imagination rather than a failure of the state. Such arguments were made, in particular, about the Midwest, a region that historian Jeanette Keith avers produced "the best-documented incidents of protest" against the war (including the "Green Corn Rebellion" against the draft in Oklahoma, and Wisconsin US Senator Robert M. La Follette's opposition to US entry into the war).[19] Indeed, Willa Cather remembered how "again and again I heard New York business men and journalists say that the West wouldn't know there was a war until it was in the next county: the West was too busy making money and spending it."[20] Writing in *The Nation* about the citizens of the Midwest in 1917, literature professor Philo M. Buck opined that "The abstract idea of an injured and insulted state naturally had little meaning for them. They have no conception of the state." Excoriating its citizenry for their cloddish materialism and parochialism, Buck's remedy was a stern, and condescending, policy of compulsion from the centers of national political and economic power, which was "simply needed to have [the Midwest's] eyes raised from the problems of crops and markets, and to be told clearly one or two of the responsibilities of citizenship."[21]

As noted in earlier chapters, then, the quintessentially *abstract* nature of civic nationalism was considered a key problematic for "patriotic" aesthetics during the war. An editorial in *Collier's* on patriotic poetry in October 1917 mused that "Poetry must intrigue the imagination through the senses. Perhaps the trouble comes, then, from the fact that we never hear, see, taste, or smell 'patriotism,' 'democracy,' 'liberty,' or any of the staples of the too-ambitious poet-patriot."[22] And such abstractions were often posed against the kind of material solidity found in a localized aesthetics, a solidity that, as Buck testily complained, could put up a stubborn recalcitrance in the face of the kind of dematerialized rhetoric that framed American participation in the war as a shining episode of international progressivism. Even the army itself considered how to best craft representational and cultural forms that could square this circle. In 1918, the soldiers' magazine of the American armed forces, the *Stars and Stripes*, ran a piece entitled "A.E.F. Must Grow Lingo of Its Own," which mournfully observed that there was, as yet, no widespread or rich colloquial vocabulary across all the AEF branches of service to rival that found in the British and Australian forces. Noting dolefully that "the men of the A.E.F. continue to use the 'plain United States' as it grows in their particular home town portions of that beatific region," the lengthy article went on to detail examples of colloquial expressions it had found in different branches of service, presumably in the hope of seeing these become picked up and deployed more widely as building blocks for the kind of nationwide "lingo" it bewailed the lack of.[23] The *Stars and Stripes* also solicited poetry from its readership, receiving up to 500 submissions a week and printing 381 poems in its first year of publication; a selection was anthologized in the 1918 collection *Yanks: A Book of A.E.F. Verse*.[24] The volume's editors leaned noticeably toward dialect poetry in this collection, in a poetic continuation of the *Stars and Stripes'* desire to encourage and enshrine a vernacular that might sound like national ideals spoken in the accents of the local. Taking a cue from the collection's editorial principles, the poet Vachel Lindsay reviewed it with great approbation, enthusing that "it is written in the American language. It is colloquial, without too much slang, the easy American dialect of college boys and farm-hands alike."[25] Such enthusiasm for the value of "real" speech was taken straight from the regionalist tradition, which, as Carrie Tirado

Bramen observes, traded heavily on "the rhetoric of authenticity," whereby "to be from the geographic margins of the country was not a disadvantage but a privilege: it authorized one to speak for a distinct place and thus provided a way of gaining access to national letters."[26] Regionalism's "rhetoric of authenticity" prized vernacular speech for its supposedly artless artistry, its grounded distance from the rhetorical poses of the abstracted or aesthetic. As Lindsay averred, the verse in *Yanks* had the benefit of having "an embarrassed refusal to be aesthetic, heroic, or stoical." This nationalist linguistic form, Lindsay prophesied, would be "the future idiom for our informal verse."[27] If national cultural traditions did not exist, then figures like Lindsay and the editors of the *Stars and Stripes* suggested the war might present the ideal opportunity for their invention; moreover, they believed that this invention might well draw on the regional resources that had been so important to prewar American literary culture. Indeed, in one of the war's more bizarre cultural suggestions, the Progressive workers' rights campaigner (and co-founder of the NAACP) Florence Kelley, in an article entitled "The Menace of Localism" published in the *Yale Review* in 1920, suggested that local color writers might be recruited for a national publicity bureau devoted to increasing interregional understanding and furthering national cultural and political integration. Modeled on the wartime CPI, she mused, such a government-organized bureau would pursue "the work of making cities, States, and sections friends and admirers of one another and conscious co-workers for the general good." Movies, lectures, and exhibits about life in America's regions would assist that work, as would readings by "well-known authors of novels, poems, or sketches rich in . . . local color."[28]

The reverse of this position, and one that became increasingly vocal in the postwar period, was that regionalist writing should not serve as combinatory cultural raw material for projects of national integration but should, instead, serve as a medium for resisting such projects. Dewey's "Americanism and Localism" was an early and influential example of this new generation of regionalist thinking.[29] Subsequent iterations were unprecedentedly radical, in the view of historians like Robert Dorman, who contends that postwar regionalist thinkers such as Lewis Mumford, Howard Odum, Mary Austin, and Donald Davidson sought to press regionalism's "creed beyond its historic role as artistic seedbed and adversary culture." Instead, they attempted to "formulate regionalism as a full-fledged national *ideology*" capable of reintegrating the modern urban-industrial economy "with the folk-cultural myths and ideals it had so deeply violated."[30] In so doing, "regionalists were to plot an alternative route for modernization."[31] The deeply aesthetic nature of these radical programs for alternative modernization informs their thoroughgoing connections to the regionalist modernisms that sprang up after the war, connections that developed into an influential cultural politics among groups like the Nashville Agrarians, or the writers and intellectuals associated with what Dorman calls the "regionalist capital" of Taos, New Mexico.[32] As Lewis Mumford described, in a series of articles he published in the *Dial* of 1919 that explored his vision of a "nonstatist politics," Civil Society was in desperate need of revitalization following a period of obligatory deference to the nation-state during the war that had suppressed any competing allegiance to other groups, localities, or forms of community.[33] For Mumford, such affiliation to the state alone meant little more than acquiescence to perpetual war, to the "almost rhythmic alterations of passive and active warfare."[34] Instead, he urged a reinvigoration of the civil "institutions of peacedom" that "function freely only on a basis of divided loyalties and dispersed interests," institutions of religion, culture, and professional organizations; for a man's "civic needs are not met by the lean satisfactions of his life as the member of a political state."[35] Arguing that "the future of nations . . . lies in the success which greets the efforts of communities and associations to establish corporate autonomy and to carry on their functions without subservience to that large and jealous corporation called the state," he increasingly came to see regional "autonomy" as central to that mission.[36] And this resistance to state subservience was indelibly literary, for Mumford's regionalism was "a political possibility . . . located . . . not in a political idea or a movement but in the literary and artistic imagination," grounded in "the imaginative recovery of place."[37]

US Regionalist Fiction in World War One

These debates were everywhere apparent in the regional fiction of the war years, and while it is widely recognized that the war represented a watershed moment in the history of both literary and political traditions of US regionalism, relatively little attention has been given to reading how that transition is at work in the regionalist literature of war. For example, it was no accident that Dewey's prime example of a deracinated and disposable – because national – literature in "Americanism and Localism" was the fiction carried by the *Saturday Evening Post*. The *Post* had published arguably the most extreme nativist material advocating for 100 percent Americanism of any of America's large circulation national magazines in

1918 and 1919, and was at the forefront in identifying localism with anti-patriotic or obstructionist tendencies in the war era. In November 1917, it ran a piece by Samuel Blythe, which argued that before the war the United States existed as "A nation of villagers, some foreigner said, and that was so true it hurt – a nation of segregated groups" that "thought locally, acted locally, and existed locally in the main affairs of life."[38] Yet as Americans began to conceptualize the effects a German victory would have on their own localities, "our localization of the matter became a nationalization of it . . . we translated it into our own manner of thinking and conceiving, and then transmuted it into terms of America."[39] The *Post*'s sister magazine in the Curtis publishing empire, the *Ladies' Home Journal*, translated such ideas directly into one of its most popular and long-running wartime serials, *Mrs. Redding Sees It Through* by Grace S. Richmond, which ran in eleven installments from September 1917 to August 1918. A story of a mother and father whose son goes off to fight, and of their relationship to their small-town community as it adjusts to the demands of an international war, the action is set in a paradigmatic small town whose regional location is never specified. In this way, the aesthetics of place in Richmond's serial function as an example of what Ryan Poll calls the "dominant small town," a recurrent trope in US culture (think Smallville, Bedford Falls, Disney's Main Street, USA), and an important element of the "national imaginary" that helps cement an enduring "form of U.S. exceptionalism that imagines the nation as an autonomous, contained, and innocent island community."[40] Significantly, the "dominant small town's" combination of delocalization, boundedness, and innocence as a way of imagining *national* community is important in legitimating an expansionist foreign policy, and "proves central to the U.S. empire and to the development of global capitalism."[41] Rather than being a distinct element in a constellation of national unity, then, the small town in this story – and in the Curtis papers more widely – was often a synecdoche for national community, and a modality for erasing or suppressing regional difference and dissent from a homogeneous picture of national politics and cultural identity.

The small town's place in a "national imaginary" that could be easily turned to the purposes of militaristic nationalism perhaps explains why so many of America's "regionalist" writers rallied enthusiastically to support the war. Well-known regionalists including Vachel Lindsay, Edward Arlington Robinson, George Washington Cable, Edgar Lee Masters, Booth Tarkington, and Hamlin Garland all joined The Vigilantes, which, in Mark Van Wienen's words, functioned as "a union exhorting

its members to produce patriotic propaganda and a press syndicate distributing this propaganda."[42] A recruiting campaign brought 328 writers
into their ranks in 1917, even though its extreme opinions caused many
writers to discontinue their membership as the war progressed.
The Vigilantes exerted fierce editorial control over the publications produced in their name, publications that tended to endorse a "conservative
(and repressive) politics" regarding home-front mobilization.[43] Hamlin
Garland, for example, who remained a member of The Vigilantes throughout the war, wrote to Theodore Roosevelt in 1918 about his support for the
suppression of the German-language press in his home state, averring that
"Wisconsin would be a better state today if her German papers had been
forbidden twenty years ago."[44]

The most jingoistic and anti-German of the wartime writers who had
made their name as regionalists, however, was the Indiana writer Booth
Tarkington, who would win two Pulitzer Prizes for fiction and was
described in 1921 as "The most significant contemporary author" by
Publisher's Weekly. He published the article "The Separating Hyphen: A
Ringing Message for Americans and German-Americans" in *Collier's*
in October 1917, an article that informed German-Americans that
"Germany conducted the war with an unspeakable barbarity[,] and the
horror of the anguish inflicted by Germans on Belgians has sunk so deep in
the American's typically pacifist mind that he shivers (without the ability to
control his symptoms) when he hears the very word 'German.'"[45]
Tarkington's sentiments only intensified as the war progressed; in 1918,
Collier's turned down his short story "Captain Schlotterwerz" because it
was too rabidly anti-German and propagandistic; it was picked up instead
by the *Saturday Evening Post*.[46] In 1919, he turned this approach to his
novel *Ramsey Milholland*, a bildungsroman of an unremarkable young man
who ends the novel by becoming the first man to enlist in his year at
college; the action takes place in an unspecified Midwestern state.
Although Tarkington's renderings of Indiana were a core component of
his literary reputation, the only character who speaks in heavy dialect or has
a nominated place of origin in *Ramsey Milholland* is "Linski," a German-
American socialist from Chicago who is passionately opposed to the war.
Linski stands out dramatically against a backdrop of patriotic, bland,
deterritorialized WASP characters, one of whom offers the veiled threat
that "we can attend to him when we get back from over yonder."[47] Linski's
demonization in the novel, its casual endorsement of vigilante violence to
enforce ideological homogeneity (Milholland punches Linski after Linski
interrupts a college debate to interject his pro-socialist principles), and its

linkage of ethnic and geographical specificity with radical politics suggests the way that regionalism's rhetorical claim to speak for the nation could easily be turned to the purposes of exclusionist nativism. Within this ideological framework, *Ramsey Milholland*'s nonspecific territoriality works to dissolve a generic Midwest into merely a metonymy for a nation imagined as politically unified, and whose unification gains definition from the stark contrast to political, linguistic, and ethnic intruders whose rootedness is precisely a sign of their nonpatriotism. Linski intrudes on the debate, but he is also, effectively, an intruder onto the campus and into the national community; and his spatial specificity as a German-American from Chicago is a key indicator that he is incapable of being incorporated into a deterritorialized national community of abstracted ideals.

Tarkington's nativist politics in *Ramsey Milholland* can be productively read alongside the debate in the scholarship on America's regionalist tradition over whether the genre proposes an essentially ethnocentric and "ascriptive" model of nationalism and citizenship, in the words of the historian Rogers Smith, or rather represents a genre oriented toward more inclusive models of ethnic, racial, and cultural difference.[48] On the one hand, the nativism of much regionalist writing on the war seemingly supports the view of regionalism as "ultimately a reactionary genre that configures the region as a pure space pitted against the fear of a hybrid society," as Roberto Maria Dainotto argues.[49] However, other regionalist novelists producing work in the wartime moment and immediately afterwards sought instead to develop the genre's capacity for representations of plurality and diversity, not so much to oppose the imperatives of militaristic nationalism that swept the country in 1917–1919 but more to consider what multiple forms of affiliation, identity, and loyalty in a moment of dramatic political transformation might mean. Ruth Suckow's first novel, *Country People* (1924), for example, presented a sensitive account of German-American life in rural Iowa through the war years, and the alienation from American citizenship felt by the Kaetterhenry family as a result of the wartime harassment they faced from their neighbors. And Willa Cather's *My Ántonia* (1918) has often been taken as a rebuttal of the fantasy – so prevalent in wartime – of region as ethnically "pure space" in its portrayal of how migration from Bohemia, Norway, and Denmark rejuvenates a dully normative Black Hawk, Nebraska in ways economic, sexual, and cultural.[50]

Still other novels considered how specifically local affiliation and national martial solidarity could coexist, in both aesthetic and political terms. This issue was particularly acute in Southern writing; the South had long been perceived as the "nation's region," separated culturally, politically, and economically from the rest of the nation, still struggling with the legacy of being the defeated party in America's most devastating war, and with a long and distinctive tradition of regional fiction. A discussion of the place of Southern writing in World War One is a complex issue that deserves more extensive treatment than I can provide here.[51] But many of the preoccupations of that literature – its reassessments of the legacy of the Civil War now that the United States was collectively committed to another cataclysmic conflict; what part Southern traditions would play in a nationalizing cultural terrain the war seemed to have accelerated; and how Southern iterations of white supremacy would fare in national institutions – were evident in Ellen Glasgow's *The Builders* (1919). This was first serialized in the *Woman's Home Companion*, a popular magazine known for its interests in both middle-class domestic life and Progressive reform. In a contemporary interview, Glasgow voiced her hope that the book might help the South become "more and more a part of national life, and from that ... part of the universal life," and indeed *The Builders* placed its politics front and center with a sustained assault on the entrenched isolationism of the "solid South" dominated by a singular allegiance to the Democratic Party.[52] The novel's plot centers on the forbidden love of a wealthy Richmond manufacturer and aspiring politician, David Blackburn, and his daughter's nurse, Caroline Meade. Yet much of their dialogue is turned over to lengthy speeches by Blackburn, who is frustrated by the two-party system and the progressive stagnation it had delivered. Holding that the South's political traditions will be vital to both a national and a global postwar political order, he argues that a Southern heritage of Jeffersonian small-government republicanism must "act as a check upon the ... principle of centralization in government, the abnormal growth in Federal power" that had characterized the wartime state.[53] Moreover, Blackburn believes that the state can only be reformed through a revitalization of morally continent citizenship. Opining that "every American carries in his person the essential elements of the State, and is entrusted with its duties," Blackburn intones: "cultivate the personal will to righteousness, teach the citizen that he is the State, and the general good may take care of itself."[54] This awkward parallelism between private morality and institutional governance was replicated in the novel's narrative structure, which, as most of its critics have noted, infuses its animating love triangle with lengthy passages of political dialogue, thus mapping domestic incident onto the current dynamics of national and international politics. Many of the novel's reviewers took issue with this attempt to blend a plantation romance with an assessment of current international statecraft; the *Knickerbocker Press*, for example, judged that Blackburn was "somewhat overweighted by his political perplexities," distorted by "Miss Glasgow [being] carried away by her realization of the problems with which America is at present confronted, and by her anxiety to suggest some practical solution of the political deadlock. She has sacrificed her story in a good cause."[55] Other reviews, rather than faulting Glasgow for bad art, critiqued her for bad politics; a young Malcom Cowley, writing in the *New Republic*, felt "she seems to understand only the external features" of the political discussions the novel attempted, while James Sibley Watson in the *Dial* labeled her "third order" for skating "brilliantly on thin ice over deep waters."[56] More recent critics, as Mark Graves has assessed, often share these evaluations.[57] Then, as now, *The Builders* seemed like an awkward kind of novel: generically muddled, sacrificing characterization to political buttonholing, and marred by the contrivances of mapping domestic onto regional, and regional onto global, phenomena that in reality were quite incongruous.

Federal Citizenship in Willa Cather's *One of Ours*

Many of the problems these reviewers identified in *The Builders* – which often amounted to a recognition of the difficulty of adapting regional aesthetics to the demands of the war novel – were replicated in the responses to a much better-known regional novel of the war, Willa Cather's *One of Ours*. This novel, with its complex and multiple vision of citizenship, refused to turn the region into a mere metonymy for a national identity of "100% Americanism" along the lines of *Ramsey Milholland*. It also avoided suggesting that regionalist identities and cultures might provide the grounded specifics that would flesh out the ghostly abstractions of national community. Instead, Cather saw the play between regionality, ethnicity, and national identity as productive of an aggregated and often conflicted political identity that political theorists at the time had dubbed "federal citizenship," an identity her novel used as much to critique martial nationalism as it did to express a passionate affinity with it. *One of Ours* is Cather's fullest fictional consideration of the federal state, and in the negotiation it tracks between local and national affiliation (and between the characteristic political imaginaries of both scales of community), and in the critical debates it prompted in 1922 around these issues, it is an indispensable novel for any consideration of how regional aesthetics would both accommodate and challenge the increasing centralization of American political power in the war years and after.

Her thinking about these issues was in evidence in her wartime writing and in speeches she delivered in Nebraska the year before the publication of *One of Ours*. In 1921, she had panned the so-called Siman Act, enacted in Nebraska in 1919, which prohibited teaching in any foreign language, or the teaching of any foreign language, to children younger than the ninth grade in any of Nebraska's schools. While its effects were scattershot, its real target was Nebraska's German speakers.[58] This law would be struck down by the Supreme Court in *Meyer v. Nebraska* in 1923, a decision that also invalidated similar laws in twenty other states; Meyer's lawyer, Arthur Mullen, characterized the legislation as an example of the "hatred, national bigotry and racial prejudice engendered by the World War." Christopher Capozzola finds the Supreme Court decision became a "bedrock for civil liberties movements throughout the twentieth century" on the question of "whether the obligation of loyalty was singular or multiple," a decision that turned on the right of states to "create a singular national loyalty by legislative means."[59]

Cather excoriated the language laws, wondering whether it would "make a boy or girl any less American to know one or two other languages? ... According to that sort of argument, your one hundred percent American would be a deaf mute."[60] Yet she also broadened her critique, seeing the legislation as part of a coercive discourse of ethnic and linguistic standardization widely known as "Americanization" that had flourished during the war, as this report of one of her speeches suggests:

> Miss Cather told her audience that one of the things which retarded art in America was the indiscriminate Americanization work of overzealous patriots who implant into the foreign minds a distaste for all they have brought of value from their own country. "The Americanization committee worker who persuades an old Bohemian housewife that it is better for her to feed her family out of tin cans instead of cooking them a steaming goose for dinner is committing a crime against art" declared Miss Cather ... Laws which stifle personal liberty are forever a bar to the real development of art.[61]

For Cather, then, the cultural pluralism of the prairies contained at least two things worth preserving: a residue of preindustrial cultural practices that could serve as a point of resistance to the new (and national) economy of mass-produced commodities, and alternative modes of perception and expression that were essential to artistic creation.

Such claims would seem to bring Cather's regionalism into line with the arguments made for the genre's counterhegemonic potential, that it often refuses "to reproduce the national narrative of violence or the definitions of masculine and feminine, American and foreign, which such a narrative presents as our national interest," in the words of Marjorie Pryce and Judith Fetterley.[62] And yet, although her wartime essays focused on the friction caused by how the increased nationalism of wartime and the penetration of the state into new spaces of regional and domestic activity were received by German-Americans, these accounts usually served to consider what a practice of multiple loyalty would look like rather than to craft any kind of radical politics of resistance. A good example is Cather's article "Roll Call on the Prairies," which Cather wrote for the Red Cross in 1917, and which was much concerned with documenting German-American life on the Prairies after the US declaration of war. The article recounted the "Hooverizing" of domestic economy by farm housewives; so enthusiastic were they at following the advice from the Food Administration's Herbert Hoover on how to conserve foodstuffs essential for assisting the Allies and feeding US troops that one German-American farm housewife she spoke to confessed "I chust Hoovered and Hoovered so long I loss my appetite. I don't eat no more."[63] The imposition of federal management into domestic economy is represented as deeply intrusive in the article; it even registers at the level of somatic self-regulation, a Foucauldian moment of discipline that seems close to self-erasure. Moreover, this coercion of foodways by the state, as well as being ethno-centric, is also palpably metropolitan, as "diet and cookery, the foundation of life, were revolutionized (city people could never realize what this means in the country and in little towns)."[64] What Cather calls the "test of character" of Hooverizing is never openly resented in this piece, but the sternness of its coercive discipline on rural and ethnic-minority foodways is constantly registered. The piece also spoke of Cather's recollection of her "many German neighbors," during her Nebraska childhood, and how "the mothers and grandmothers told me such interesting things about farm-life and customs in the old country – beautiful things which I can never forget," even as they asserted their main reason for leaving Germany was to avoid its compulsory, and often demeaning, military service.[65] (What separates state overreach in Germany from conscription and "Hooverizing" in the United States remains unremarked in the essay, but the question looms large.) Superficially patriotic, these wartime essays nonetheless demonstrate an implicit, and often uneasy, questioning of exactly what obligations the state should expect of its citizens in wartime, and how the force of those obligations registered differently across lines of urban and rural, native-born and immigrant, and male and female.

When *One of Ours* appeared, it seemed in many ways to continue the sentiments of these wartime articles and her Nebraska speeches of 1921. It embedded a resistance to certain "national narratives." It lambasted the kind of harassment of German-Americans that had occurred in the Midwest in the war years; and it bewailed the basic conditions of the national corporate economy, which mass-produced "manufactured articles of poor quality; showy furniture that went to pieces, carpets and draperies that faded, clothes that made a handsome man look like a clown" that the Nebraskan farmers swap for "wheat and corn as good as could be grown anywhere in the world."[66] It also considered divided German-American loyalty, most obviously by thinly fictionalizing an account she read in a Nebraskan newspaper in 1917. As she recounted,

> Two rich German farmers who lived on their broad acres near Beatrice, Nebraska, did say bitter things when America entered the war. They were summoned before a magistrate in Lincoln, who fined them lightly and administered to them a rebuke which was so wise and temperate and fair-minded that I cut the printed report of it out of the newspaper and put it in my scrap-book. "No man," he said, "can ask you to cease from loving the country of your birth."[67]

Cather included this scene at the magistrate's in her novel, having the German-American August Yoeder play the part of the defendant, a scene that follows the language of this letter and the press clipping almost verbatim. This episode seems emblematic of a dynamic observed by Leigh Ann Duck, namely that

> regional identities have offered amelioration for precisely the damage that U.S. nationality threatens to inflict ... regionalism, as a cultural discourse, has often functioned as a supplement to U.S. nationalism; it serves to suggest that, at the local level, the United States maintains precisely the kind of the cultural particularities that the state ideology of liberalism disavows.[68]

The judiciary here is "temperate and fair-minded," exemplifying the pragmatic nonemotionality of a bloodless and abstract civic nationalism that recognizes – and even valorizes – the strength of cultural affinities that cut against national loyalty. Yet that judiciary sees no contradiction in enacting punitive, and paternalistic, justice – which chastises rather than suppresses – simultaneously with such a recognition. Cather was less interested in resistance to national narratives in *One of Ours*, then, than she was in correcting those who wanted to identify civic and cultural loyalty as the same thing, to an ultimate purpose of tracing a model of civic unity within a landscape of cultural differentiation. In effect, she crafted a model capable of celebrating German-American resistance to the war at the same time as "rebuking" it.

In doing so, Cather was enacting in fictional form a model being currently proposed by political theorists such as Walter Lippmann, who just after the American declaration of war had championed Harold Laski's call for "the necessary pluralism of modern sovereignty."[69] Noting that the "state is not absolute but plural," and that "allegiance in the modern world is necessarily experimental and federal," he identified the most pressing challenge not just for political science but for all types of "form or inquiry into human need and organization" as being to "invent the machinery, methods of thought, and educational practice by which such federal citizenship can be made workable." He posed the question

> How, for example, shall a man distribute his available energy between a league of nations, the government at Washington, his state government, his city, his neighborhood, his family, his church, his vocation? That he owes some loyalty to each, few will deny. That he cannot be effectively loyal to all at the same time is obvious.

Making such "federal citizenship" workable, he suggested, was the only way to accommodate "the issues raised by class, nationality, religion, and imperial expansion."

One of Ours sought to sensitively articulate the nature of "federal citizenship" for several foreign-born characters, from Yoeder's boorish anti-Americanism to the war-weariness of the Bohemian Ernest Havel. Yet the novel's main concern is tracking its protagonist, Claude Wheeler, in his journey from local, then national, to international forms of experience and political affiliation as he enlists as a member of the AEF. Constellating "federal" loyalty, then, between the cultural practices and affinities of region, nation, ethnicity, and state, a constellation that invariably dwelt on the tensions and conflicts such multiple affinities invariably produced, was at the heart of her interests in representing the war in Nebraska and beyond. And this process of constellation underpins some of the most critically contentious features of *One of Ours.*

*

After decades of being regarded as one of Cather's weakest novels, *One of Ours* is now increasingly read as one of the most important American novels of World War One. This reevaluation is often precisely because its discordant deployment of multiple and inconsistent generic conventions – a discordance that underpinned its earlier critical excoriation – is now seen to offer a rich testament to the historical struggles gripping its moment of production. As Steven Trout has demonstrated in his excellent book on Cather and her "memorial fictions" of World War One, Cather had been captivated by the letters home of her cousin, G.P. Cather, who served as a lieutenant in the AEF and was killed in one of its major initial engagements, at Cantigny in May 1918. She was particularly moved by what Trout calls the "sense of exuberant self-fulfillment" in G.P.'s letters, in contrast to the frustration and boredom Willa Cather knew he experienced in his life in Nebraska.[70] Inspired, she embarked on a bildungsroman based on his life that would take four years to research and write. Her protagonist Claude Wheeler is a Nebraskan farmer, disaffected by both the conditions of an encroaching modernity into the pioneer plains life and an unhappy marriage, but who finds his life's calling in the "great adventure" of serving in the AEF in World War One. Cather expended exhaustive research on the military details of the AEF in order to write the novel's combat scenes, including interviewing numerous war veterans in her New York apartment. This helped her write combat scenes lengthier than any other woman writer in America or England produced in fiction of the war.[71] Yet she was unable to reconcile the grim naturalism of her representations of the trenches with the spirit of heroic romance that elsewhere characterizes the novel, an aesthetic awkwardness that caused a critical furor on its initial release. Although the book received praise from many veterans, and went on to win the Pulitzer Prize in 1923, it received hostile reviews from several male writers and critics, including Sinclair Lewis and H.L. Mencken, who were keen to champion a new generation of war writers at the expense of what they saw as Cather's sentimentality and idealizations of combat. Mencken was especially harsh in his criticism of the novel's stylistic discontinuities; he felt *One of Ours* "divides itself very neatly into two halves, one of which deserves to rank almost with 'My Antonia' and the other of which drops precipitately to the level of a serial in the *Ladies' Home Journal*," with that division between good and bad corresponding exactly to the sections in Nebraska and the sections in France.[72] For more recent critics, however, these stylistic disjunctions are what make the novel interesting rather than bad. Steven Trout, for example, reads the tonal inconsistency of *One of Ours* as signifying the broad lack of consensus in American culture over the appropriate discourse to remember America's involvement in the conflict. For Guy Reynolds, the novel's often awkward "mixture of idealism and disillusion, fervor and pessimism, heightened rhetoric and flattened irony" is indicative of the novel's simultaneous lament over the failures of Progressivism in the war, and of Cather's desire to see it persevere. Claude's characterization bears the weight of this strain; he functions as "a Wilsonian idealist, an American progressive with dreams of a multicultural enlightened community," and his character often becomes little more than "a projection of the warring cultural forces of the time."[73] Seeing Cather as "caught . . . between an endorsement of Claude's visions and a savage undercutting of his illusions," Reynolds reads *One of Ours* as attempting "to maintain a progressive momentum against the weight of historical experience."[74]

It is true that disorienting stylistic shifts are characteristic of the book, and that these occur most noticeably when Claude shifts from his life as a Nebraskan farmer into his period of army service. Cather herself was worried about these shifts, noting in a letter to her publisher Alfred Knopf that "the relation of one part to another and the corresponding changes in tempo were the things I was most interested in throughout the story."[75] These "changes in tempo" and style corresponded to transitions between different scales of political geography, as Claude moves from local, to national, and then to international vantage points. And those shifts in scale closely correlate to the novel's navigations between abstract and the material, between dematerialized ideals and gritty or embodied particularity. In so doing, Cather meditates on what Lewis Mumford, in an influential 1926 manifesto for the importance of regional aesthetics, called the "process of abstraction" that characterized nationalizing and homogenizing economic and political forces – or what Harold Stearns termed "the problem of loyalty," which was to "break through the miasma of abstractions and concepts and imaginative entities" so typical of "federal entit[ies] at Washington" to find "visible and sensuous objects to which our affections can spontaneously cling."[76] And while such shuttling between the abstract and the concrete has often been seen as constitutive of Cather's mature style, *One of Ours* pushes those tensions to often unsustainable extremes in considering how these registers relate to coexisting (and sometimes competing) forms of imaginative geographies and their related types of political affinity.[77] It does so to reveal the advantages and the limits of these different kinds of imaginary, but also to think through what kind of citizenship might result from trying to hold them all together. In this sense, then, *One of Ours* is a bildungsroman that accounts for Claude's growth into a modern federated citizen, one capable of holding attachments to multiple political units in a way that is inevitably rife with self-contradiction. In being so, *One of Ours* fits with affirmative readings of regionalism's ability to represent emergent political phenomena, rather than being merely "a form of literary primitivism"; instead, it was uniquely suited to capture "the heterogeneous web of spatial dependencies characteristic of the modern moment," as Carrie Tirado Bramen avers.[78] Perhaps the best example to help explicate this knotty political and aesthetic feature of *One of Ours* comes in the opening passage of the novel's fourth book, the "Voyage of the Anchises," when Claude is sat on a stationary train waiting to roll in to Hoboken, where his unit will embark on their troop transport to France. It is there that the discordances and ironies that emerge from Claude's travels between not only different places but different forms of political perspective and affinity become very palpable.

At this moment, the narrative voice strays away from any single character for the first three paragraphs, naming Claude only in paragraph four. This is a notable departure for a novel tied closely to the interior lives of three or four main characters, and it is the only one of the five books that excludes Claude's name from its first sentence (two books have his name as their first word). It also shifts verb tense, moving from the usual verb tense of classical realism, the past tense, into the continuous present; the conductor "goes through the cars," as the train "is lying beside an arm of the sea that reaches far into the green shore" (*OOO* 267). The short chapter moves to an example of the powerful epiphany characteristic of Cather's fiction as the men watch boats being constructed in this green, and seemingly empty, landscape; although a few riveters are at work, "only by listening very closely can one hear the tap of their hammers. No orders are shouted, no thud of heavy machinery or scream of iron drills tears the air. These strange boats seem to be building themselves" (*OOO* 268). As Claude, in a reverie, regards them, he feels "these craft did not seem to be nailed together, – they seemed all of a piece, like sculpture. They reminded him of the houses not made with hands; they were like simple and great thoughts, like purposes forming slowly here in the silence beside an unruffled arm of the Atlantic" (*OOO* 268). And Claude's imagination takes hackneyed and bathetic flight as the narrative voice finally assumes his consciousness in the chapter's closing paragraphs: "When great passions and great aspirations stirred a country, shapes like these formed along its shores to be the sheath of its valor . . . They were the very impulse, they were the potential act, then were the 'going over,' the drawn arrow, the great unuttered cry, they were Fate, they were tomorrow!" (*OOO* 268–269).

This section seems to encapsulate many of the representational problems that political theorists at the time identified with the state – its ghostliness, for Randolph Bourne, or its abstraction, for Lippmann. In beginning by suddenly detaching us from Claude's perspective, readers are left disoriented by the question of the place of our individual – and perhaps *the* individual – in this organizational frame of American mobilization. Moreover, the boats are abstracted out of a historical temporal order – the continuous present tense operates here as what Benedict Anderson thought of as the "homogeneous, empty time" so characteristic of modern thinking about the nation, a temporality that stretches without differentiation both forward and backward. It seems as though the boats are always being built, and that they are detached from any causation that might account for them. They are also abstracted out of the materiality of their construction. This applies to the origins of the material that goes into their building, as they take shape in an empty landscape seemingly void of the transportation lines or materials that were essential to the huge shipbuilding program embarked on by the US government. They are also abstracted from the labor force that constructs them (the boats "seem to be building themselves"). Their affective power to the men is reliant on exactly this quirk of perspective, which disconnects them from any of the realities of how boats must be built and transported. The men thrill to this abstraction, for in it they read the power of the state, a power so often reliant on such abstract appeal.

Yet the novel quickly associates this power with the boats' ability to head off into a preposterous plurality of symbolic meanings, to assume a seemingly unbearable load of symbolic freight. They are the "sheath" of the nation's "valor," "the very impulse, they were the potential act, they were the 'going over,' the drawn arrow, the great unuttered cry, they were Fate, they were tomorrow!" In the next chapter, as the men leave New York harbor, they gaze on the Statue of Liberty, and as they pass the Staten Island Ferry, Cather rams her point home. On the ferry stands an "old clergyman, a famous speaker in his day," who recites Longfellow's "sail on, O Ship of State,/Humanity, with all its fears,/With all its hopes of future years,/Is hanging breathless on thy fate" (*OOO* 274). And Claude's own ship, the *Anchises*, links their mission to Aeneas's quest to found a new civilization. The multiple ships that appear in just seven short pages, then, stack up quickly as symbolic vehicles for the state, for the global future, for a past of the glorious establishment of classical civilizations, and as the symbol of a nation's military "valor." And yet, Cather's narrator drily punctures these metaphorical flights by noting that the *Anchises* is actually "an English boat, an old liner pulled off the Australian trade," indicative of the fact that the American army was "using everything that's got a bottom now," in the words of Claude's Captain (*OOO* 271). Later, we see Claude on his cabin bunk with rusty water pipes and unpainted joinings over his head; "even the carpenters who made her over for the service had not thought her worth the trouble, and had done their worst by her" (*OOO* 300).[79] Unremarked, but a fact that would have been obvious to many readers in 1922, was also the fact that America's government-funded boat-building program had recently been publicly exposed as one of the costliest and most wasteful episodes in America's prosecution of the conflict. As Marc Allen Eisner notes, the Emergency Fleet Corporation, which was established in April 1917 under the aegis of the US Shipping Board, was charged with building 15 million tons of new shipping. Given a $50 million appropriation, delays meant it delivered its first ship in December 1918, a month after the conflict was over. As John Maurice Clark observed, the "Shipping Board and Emergency Fleet Corporation ... spent 3,316 millions and were left with ships, plants, structures, and materials which were worth only a small fraction of their cost."[80] In 1920 and 1921, investigations, including a congressional investigation, exposed a picture of mismanagement, graft, and the colossal waste of taxpayer money in the Shipping Board's wartime activities, a story widely covered in the national papers.[81] Cather, therefore, opens a significant gap between the symbolic resonance of boats and the actuality of how the US state managed its shipping needs in the conflict. If boats were a supreme vehicle for symbolically figuring the idealistic potential of what a Progressive state could do, she suggests, the actual boats that transported American troops were often cramped and shoddily constructed; and the systems that produced them were a prime example of how state agencies could grossly mismanage the wartime economy.

This section, then, mobilizes both the attractions and the drawbacks of flights of rhetorical abstraction; as Lauren Berlant has observed, such language is a staple of the "national symbolic" of the nation-state, and commonly works as "both a mode of political domination and a utopian mode of hope."[82] The boats can be disconnected from individual lives, temporality, and materiality, and this allows them to become supple vehicles for a host of inspirational and idealistic metaphors. Moreover, this perspective gives Claude an exhilarating release from the small-minded materialism that tormented his life in Nebraska, epitomized by the ascetic, parsimonious, and unimaginative attitude of his brother Bayliss. But such abstraction risks devaluing the realities of labor – realities the first half of the novel is careful to enumerate, with its lengthy descriptions of Claude's work on the family farm. Indeed, it was clear that tracing the provenance of, and the labor-power producing, the commodities that the United States shipped to Europe was a key objective of Cather's regionalist approach to World War One; in "Roll Call on the Prairies," she declared "shiploads of food, shiploads of clothes – what do they mean, unless you know the fields that grew the grain and the hands that made the clothes?"[83] The abstracting perspective in the New Jersey boat episode erases that materiality, and thereby that "meaning," and also ignores the inefficiencies and corruption involved in the boats' construction – actualities that run directly counter to the abstracted principles of public-spirited civic nationalism that Claude dreamily indulges.

Not that such indulgence is unexpected; from the outset, Cather positions Claude as "a romantic caught in a nightmarish world of realism," as Susan Rosowski puts it.[84] Indeed, his chafing at the nuts-and-bolts practicality of his Nebraska home informs his dissatisfied and vague sense of restlessness, an emotion that forms the dramatic interest of the first half of the book; in a crucial argument with his best friend Ernest, he wonders whether a life of farming and marriage is enough for him, grousing that "if we've only got once to live, it seems like that there ought to be something – well, something splendid about life, sometimes" (*OOO* 52). His father worries that he is "one of those visionary fellows who make unnecessary difficulties for themselves and other people" (*OOO* 103). In her letters of the time, it was clear that Cather admired this aspect of her character's personality, while simultaneously describing Claude as often painfully naïve. This insight at least partially endorses an ironic reading of *One of Ours*, a well-established strategy in its recent reception. Critics such as David Stouck, Frederick T. Griffith, Jean Schwind, James Woodress, and Susan J. Rosowski have engaged early Cather critics such as Stanley Cooperman, who charged Cather with having swallowed whole the bellicose discourse of the "Great Crusade" in a novel blemished by unrealistic scenes of combat and packed with "sentimentality and intrusive rhetoric."[85] In contrast, these later critics see Cather as having established an ironic narratorial distance from Claude, a distance that casts Cather as considerably more critical of the propagandistic strategies and bombastic rhetoric of wartime America than critics like Cooperman believed.[86] Yet I would argue that the story is a little more complicated than a straightforward critique of wartime economic and cultural "Americanization" effected by a wholly ironic relation between narrator and character. Instead, it is the discursive disjunctions of the novel that deliver its ironies, disjunctions that result from Cather's reflection on what a "federal citizenship" might mean – a reflection that works not merely by identifying such constellated affinities but by reproducing the discursive forms each specific political and geographical unit characteristically employs. What this delivers in *One of Ours* is a federated affinity that juxtaposes two important discourses in particular. On the one hand, it reproduces the kind of thick materiality of the local so important to the discourse of local color, which is both culturally affecting and yet often devolves into a crude materialism. On the other, it indulges the airily abstract style of idealist progressivism deployed at the level of both the nation-state and the international order – a discourse both idealistically compelling and yet often blind to the material inequities perpetrated under the cover of its abstractions. The points of friction between these two discourses produce some of Cather's most compelling political commentary.

Cather's consideration of federal citizenship, therefore, is delivered through what we might call a "discursive federalism" that stages both the attractions and the drawbacks of these different scales of sovereignty through the clash of their characteristic aesthetic practices. And one of the most striking components of that discursive federalism is Cather's consideration of how American regions look different when articulated in those different discourses, and particularly when observed in the terms of American global military and economic expansion. For example, as Claude returns to Nebraska before his deployment overseas, he is struck by the way it has become a "harmonious whole," rather than the stultifying and unimaginative locale he had formerly perceived it as (*OOO* 255). Most notably, as both Steven Trout and Joseph Urgo have observed, this internationalism changes Claude's opinion of mass-produced American commodities. Whereas previously, in Nebraska, the narrator had tracked Claude's thoughts about such commodities being "manufactured articles of poor quality," while in France he welcomes the sight of American packaging crates, and, just a few pages later, stacks of tinned goods "with American trade names he knew so well; names which seemed doubly familiar and 'reliable' here, so far from home" (*OOO* 386). These goods, now, seem a testament to his country's "long arm," one that makes "the difference between life and death" to the French civilians who have relied on these tinned goods through the winter of 1917/18 (*OOO* 386). That Cather's narrator cannot resist placing "reliable" in quotation marks indicates her wish to explicitly flag Claude's transformation in attitude and discourse, his assumption of a language that until recently had been abhorrent to him; for "reliable" was such a heavily used term in period advertising that it had assumed the status of cliché. Here, Cather suggests that Claude's perspective on his own region only gains totality when it is placed in a transatlantic perspective, a perspective inseparable from US military and economic power. And his views on that power alter as well; rather than seeing the productive capacities of American manufacturing industry as connected to the mass production of cheaply made, low-quality goods, now its economies of scale are welcome for the number of foreign civilians in war-ravaged Allied countries they can assist – civilians who become real rather than nominal for Claude as he is billeted in rural France. American regions, then, only gain their full meaning in economic, military, and aesthetic terms when they are considered in these transnational contexts. And, specifically, their cloddish materialism, rather than being solely for the profit motive, is now repurposed as the material force backing up the ideals – and the distinctly American language – of global progressivism.[87]

Ultimately, the novel does not even try to smooth over these contradictions. Claude is miserable in Nebraska as his wife feeds him canned food; yet in France, such canned food is literally the lifesaver for a woman with whom he shares the most intensely emotional hour of his life. The cottonwoods and fruit orchards he so loves in France, and that form a cultural connection to his home in Nebraska, are in fact all being torn out in Nebraska, where arguments are made that they make bad shade trees, are bad for drainage, or are too much work when compared to the ability to drive into town and buy fruit. America's ability to successfully wage a war to save a culture, then, is actually reliant on its own destruction of regional cultures, an ambivalence that makes the novel both elegiac and full of the patriotic progressivism that reviewers like Mencken decried. And such a perspective is only possible once the transatlantic journey has been made, because the internationalist dimension of that progressivism would promise to save political and cultural phenomena overseas that had been obliterated at home. Constellating – or federating – loyalty involved these kinds of incompatibilities; one could not be against canned food in both the United States and France; one could not decry the internal combustion engine on the western front, even if you could lament its transformation of the Nebraska prairie. And such conflicts are made formally possible through jarring the discourse of local color against the language and ideas of both Wilsonian international progressivism and America as an exceptionalist republic of goods.[88]

This is nowhere clearer than in the first encounter Claude and his men have with the French on French soil, an encounter based around access to commodities. Claude meets several of the troops under his command roaming the streets of the port; after days of meager provisions on the *Anchises*, they are desperate to buy some cheese. With his faltering French, Claude helps them to find a cheese shop, where the men – ignoring the rationing regulations in place – clean out the stock, in the process being extortionately overcharged by the shopkeeper. Yet despite making a handsome profit, the shopkeeper despises the visiting troops, as revealed by one of the few occasions the novel moves its focalization away from Claude – and the only occasion it does so to inhabit the consciousness of a French citizen. Scornful of their ignorance in holding out their money to her – allowing her to select how much she takes from them in payment – she muses that "it was a joke to them; they didn't know what it meant in the world. Behind them were shiploads of money, and behind the ships . . . the situation was unfair . . . she liked them well enough, but she did not like to do business with them . . . fictitious values were distasteful to her, and made everything seem flimsy and unsafe" (*OOO* 325–326). To her, America seems a "legend of waste and prodigality," one "superfluous and disintegrating in a world of hard facts" (*OOO* 326). Her final reflection is worth quoting more fully:

> All this was not war, – any more than having money thrust at you by grown men who could not count, was business. It was an invasion, like the other. The first destroyed material possessions, and this threatened everybody's integrity. Distaste of such methods, deep, recoiling distrust of them, clouded the cheesewoman's brow as she threw her money into the drawer and turned the key on it. (*OOO* 327)

This section mobilizes several of the familiar tropes of local color: an idealization of small-scale, artisanal production; a resentment of intruding outsiders with intimidating financial resources; and a fear of immanent cultural erasure. Moreover, German militarism and American economic power are treated as equally perilous to the "world of hard facts" of French economic and cultural autonomy – both carry a deeply threatening disintegrative potential. The moment is rich in irony: it demonstrates Claude, heady with a sense of mission to save what he perceives to be a preindustrial, organic culture of France, as an unwitting agent in its cultural, rather than military, destruction. Moreover, at this moment, Cather produces the same critique of parochial localism as she made of characters in Nebraska: her characterization of the cheesewoman hints at the same small-minded materialism and a charmless inability to embrace idealistic principle and romantic adventure as we saw in her characterization of Bayliss. Yet, here, those attitudes underpin a cultural conservatism that both Claude and Cather seem to endorse. A local color moment, then, serves both to undercut the naivety of idealistic, international progressivism and to render through a moment of supercilious mockery exactly the kind of smallness, parochialism, and backwardness that critics of local color have long argued the genre delivers when representing "regional" subjects. Both discourses emerge from this moment with their flaws and their advantages made clear.

Regionalism, therefore, emerges as a supple aesthetic for thinking through "federal citizenship," a political form that, in turn, made visible how the literary form of regionalism – rather than being sealed off from global commitments and affinities – was in fact thoroughly informed by them. Cognizant of the abstracting and dematerializing perspective that often attended globalized processes of circulation and theorization, especially those associated with the new ambitions of a global progressivism sponsored by a vastly expanded American state, Cather's identification of material solidity with regional identity and aesthetics allowed her to represent "the fields that grew the grain and the hands that made the clothes." This allowed her to embed a critique of the material inequities, exploitations, and even imperialism that was frequently hidden beneath the airy rhetoric of Wilsonian international Progressivism. At the same time, *One of Ours* reveals the sterility of a pure materialism, what at one point a disheartened Claude calls "the débris of human life" that is "more worthless and ugly than the dead and decaying things in nature" (*OOO* 223). Far from obsolete, then, regionalism emerges in *One of Ours*, as it would remain in the modernist regionalist classics of the 1920s and 1930s, as a genre uniquely capable of considering the representational and political relation between region, nation, state, and globe.

Regionalism's ability to perform this role was not entirely new. As recent critics of late realism and local color have contended, from at least the late nineteenth century it had been a central American genre for mediating between local, national, and international spheres. Indeed, key practitioners and theorists of local color, such as W.D. Howells, had positioned it less as a genre of provincial limitation than as a world genre with unique capacities for the mediation of divergent ethnic and national experiences (capacities to be globally developed under American leadership). Such ambitions formed "an aesthetic counterpart to Woodrow Wilson's political vision of the United States as the mediating nation," in Nathaniel Cadle's terms.[89] Critics such as Cadle and Brad Evans have also seen local color as an aesthetic model deeply connected to the rise of the Progressive state, a state that had empowered "Americans to harness emerging modes of transnational circulation" through copyright reform, immigration control, and financial regulation – as well as American imperial expansion.[90] Yet what *was* new in Cather's vision of "federal citizenship" was the ability of the American state both to project military force overseas and to trammel regional cultural and political autonomy at home and abroad with unprecedented power. Under this insistent pressure toward centralized consolidation, the political and aesthetic investigations of federalism on display in *One of Ours* and *The Builders* showed the strain, in ways that contemporary reviewers identified as flaws but that now register as the political difficulty of maintaining multiple and fractious kinds of civic affinity (and skepticism) at this moment in American history. Ultimately, perhaps the most important implication of Cather's federated model, and the "strained regionalism" it generates, is the way it allows her to examine the effects of the state-industrial complex on multiple kinds of geography; while it allows the United States to have a decisive impact on the western front, it also produces corrosive effects on localized cultures, both in the United States and in France. In "Nebraska: The End of the First Cycle," she sought to position war idealism as a nationalizing force different in its moral economy from the nationalizing effects of mass manufacture and commodity capitalism, remarking that Nebraska – as everywhere else – was being despoiled by "farmer boys who wish to be spenders before they are earners, girls who try to look like the heroines of the cinema screen, a coming generation which tries to cheat its aesthetic sense by buying things instead of making anything."[91] Yet, during the war, she was taken by "The wave of generous idealism, of noble seriousness, which swept over the state of Nebraska," which showed "of what men and women are capable. Surely the materialism and showy extravagance of this hour are a passing phase!"[92] But *One of Ours* suggests that these forces may not be so separate after all, as much as Claude and even Cather might wish them to be so.

Vigilante Regionalism: Zane Grey's West and World War One

If *One of Ours* was marked by an ambivalence about the potential of an expanded state – and to a degree excited by its potential for an internationally transformative purpose – by the time of *The Professor's House* in 1925, Cather's perspective was quite different. By then, the balance she struck in *One of Ours* between the transformative energy that made the federal state an exhilarating prospect for idealists and its countervailing tendency to eradicate small-scale, local economies and cultures, had been completely transformed.

In the later novel, Washington, DC is represented as a city stifled by bureaucracy and red tape, where political action happens largely by virtue of cronyism and bribery. And its inability to conserve pockets of local cultural autonomy, which this novel newly figures as America's archeological heritage of Cliff Dwelling Native Americans, is less a result of its dynamic collaboration with the imperial capacities of an internationalizing corporate economy and more because of its helplessness in the face of those globalized economic forces. It is a savage account of the federal state's smallness and weakness – the glacial and opaque nature of its structures of governance, the petty vanity of its employees, the inadequacy of its budget to meet basic functions of archeological preservation. As the romantic hero Tom Outland fails to secure federal resources to protect the antiquities he has excavated from the Blue Mesa, his partner sells them to a German collector. If Cather's earlier novel evinced a mix of being enthralled by the power of the new federal state and concern over its power to homogenize and dominate, the 1925 novel seems more frustrated by the state's limits and pettiness, perhaps in protest at 1920s Republican retrenchment of Wilson's progressive ambitions. And it is surely no coincidence that its failure is achieved at the expense of German success; although this story is loosely based on Gustaf Nordenskiöld's excavations at Mesa Verde, Cather switches the nationality of the expropriative European archeologist from Norwegian to German. This is not just an echo of the well-worn wartime trope of aggressively acquisitive Prussian militarism (and an acquisitiveness, also, in collusion with Mexico; the German collector ships the "curios" out of Mexico to avoid problems with customs at an American port, a collusion that harkens back to the Zimmerman telegram). It is an echo of the widely articulated notion during the war – sometimes envious, sometimes critical, but always anxious – that German principles of state organization and capability far exceeded those of the United States. Steven Trout has made a compelling claim that the novel is haunted by the war, whether in its representation of the crisis in the academic discipline of history that erupted in the 1920s or in its consideration of the multiple, and always inadequate, ways to memorialize Tom Outland, killed flying for the Foreign Legion in 1915. But perhaps we could add to that melancholic list a sorrow at the loss of public support in the 1920s for many of the wartime progressive ambitions for the state, a melancholia mobilized in *The Professor's House* around the particularly Catherian theme of conservation. If the American state cannot preserve national treasures from acquisitive foreign invaders and a global marketplace, the novel suggests, surely it is not much of a state at all.

Such a representation of Washington, DC as Byzantine, ineffectual, dominated by insiders with interests largely detached from the people they are supposed to represent, and the polar opposite to the close-knit community and cultural density of America's regions was, by 1925, hardly unique. Indeed, Amanda Claybaugh has usefully tracked how the conventions of the modern Washington novel were laid down in the aftermath of the Civil War, in novels preoccupied by how to represent a federal state so newly vast and diffuse that it seemed to defy representation – and also by how to connect the various landscapes, architectures, and social groups of Washington to this new governmental structure and new forms of power.[93] This genre received a significant boost in the aftermath of World War One, at a moment when the federal state had expanded to far greater proportions than witnessed in the 1860s and 1870s. As Harrison Rhodes put it in 1918, "you felt that Washington was the country" – a feeling decidedly new.[94] Carol Kennicott ventures from Gopher Prairie to a wartime DC in Sinclair Lewis's *Main Street* to work for the Bureau of War Risk Insurance, for example. And Laurence Stallings' *Plumes*, discussed in detail in Chapter 5, has his excruciatingly wounded veteran Richard Plume entangled in a nightmare of medical and bureaucratic governmentality in Washington, DC that stands in definitional contrast to the sleepy, idealized pastoral of his rural home in the Upper South. Yet the most widely read novelist replaying this idea was Zane Grey, whose novel *30,000 on the Hoof* deals with a corrupt army commissioning agent swindling an Arizonan rancher out of the proceeds of the sale of his herd during the war. Traveling to Washington from his idyllic Arizonan canyon to try to secure justice, the rancher is fleeced by an unscrupulous law firm and told by his US Senator that his case is hopeless, as "the whole country is rampant with graft and crooked work. Your case is one in a thousand."[95] He later learns that two of his sons have been killed in battle. This rash of DC fiction presented it as disorienting, subject to huge influxes and exoduses of itinerant workers, corrupt, insincere, and overpriced – the synecdoche of a host of popular complaints about the federal state. Moreover, as all these examples make clear, Washington, DC also served as an important foil for regionalist fiction, as the antithesis to much of what regionalist ideology came to stand for in the 1920s. The novel of government and the regional novel, therefore, were closely intertwined in the decade; and if regionalist fiction had always gained definition by posing regional identity at a generative distance from financial and social elites, by the 1920s its distance from newly centralized political power became an increasingly prevalent part of that equation.

Published in 1940, one year after his death, *30,000 on the Hoof* repeated ideas about the federal government, America's regions, and World War One that Grey had been making for twenty years. Grey reacted strongly to the carnage of the war; in April 1917, he had recorded in his diary that "I hate war more than I hate anything else. The agony to women and children I cannot forgive."[96] He became deeply concerned by the war's effects on American society and identity, especially sexual and gendered identities, and returned compulsively to this topic in novel after novel. Moreover, this period coincided with the peak of his popularity; between 1915 and the mid-1920s, Grey always had a title in the annual list of top-ten selling works of fiction in the United States, and in 1918, his *The U.P. Trail* was the bestselling book in the country.[97] Beginning with *The Desert of Wheat* in 1919, he published a series of novels that featured often severely wounded veterans returning to a society whose moral (and especially sexual) degeneracy shocks them.[98] These veterans are often poorly served by rehabilitation and medical care programs, and face indifference to their service from their home communities. While these issues are usually subplots playing second fiddle to his predominant theme of men struggling for success in the wild landscapes of the American West, Grey felt so strongly about them that he turned two novels – *The Day of the Beast* (1922) and *The Call of the Canyon* (1924) – completely over to their exploration, with *The Day of the Beast* so idiosyncratic in its shrill and overheated ranting about the postwar degeneration of female sexual morality that it met with bewilderment from reviewers and among the lowest sales of any of his novels. As Grey said at the time, he believed the novelist had "an appalling responsibility in these modern days of materialism to dare to foster idealism and love of nature, chivalry in men and chastity in women."[99] *The Day of the Beast*'s protagonist, Daren Lane, spends much of the novel aghast: at his prewar job being taken by a woman, at the slangy talk of his sister, at the sexual morality of his former fiancée, and at the corruption and sensuality of his former commanding officer. All combine to produce a feeling of horror in him at "The physical, the sensual, the violent, the simian – these instincts, engendering the Day of the Beast, [that] had come to dominate the people he had fought for."[100] At the same time, Lane is a compulsive voyeur of such behavior, spending most of his time secretly observing the behaviors of the younger generation that shock him so profoundly, and thereby giving Grey's readers the simultaneous pleasures of scandalized moral judgment and vicarious titillation.[101] Even the *New York Times*, usually very hospitable to the kind of politics on display in the novel, could barely manage to be charitable, suggesting that "his desire to write something that would help the American people to realize the materialism, the selfishness, the absorption in ignoble pleasure seeking, the callousness into which they plunged on the close of the war and in which they are still immersed" had blinded him to "the artistic sins he was committing upon almost every page, which vitiate [the novel's] whole structure."[102]

Grey's rather remarkable novel-length polemic seems continuous with the conservatism, masculinism, and antimodernism that the Western has often been charged with, even though *The Day of the Beast* departs from his usual Western settings.[103] Accordingly, there would not be much merit in recovering Grey's often spectacularly padded and incoherent novels featuring returning veterans were it not that they occasionally attempted to think through some of the issues that preoccupied Cather, Glasgow, and many other authors of regional fiction at the time, namely the meanings of federal citizenship and the relation of American regions to a newly powerful federal state that had globalized those regions in unprecedented ways. Not that this happens in every postwar text of Grey's – far from it, in fact. Many of Grey's postwar Westerns cling to the common representation of the West as a dehistoricized, mythic space that resists the transformative energies of modernity: accordingly, the West often acts in basically escapist and therapeutic ways for masculinities damaged in the war, which for Grey becomes modernity's singularly apocalyptic event.[104] Consolidating a trope that had its most famous proponent in Teddy Roosevelt's life stories of Western masculine rejuvenation, in several of Grey's post–World War One novels, physically and mentally incapacitated veterans are restored to the (almost) full inhabitation of normative, imperial, white heterosexual masculinity through the natural splendor of the American West and the physical rigor it demands of its inhabitants. Indeed, this was a plotline that Grey only tweakingly repurposed from a prewar formula he had perfected as early as 1910.[105] As Richard Slotkin argues, through the agency of writers like Roosevelt and Frederick Jackson Turner, the West at the outset of the twentieth century was "becoming a set of symbols that constituted an explanation of history. Its signification as a mythic space began to outweigh its importance as a real place, with its own peculiar geography, politics, and cultures," and Grey in particular was attracted to representing it as "a tourist's West," with "no ordinary terrain, only scenic attractions" that existed "beyond Metropolitan power and outside history."[106] A restorative refuge from history, and specifically the history of mass conscription into a global war, the Southwestern desert in *The Shepherd of Guadeloupe* and *The Call of the Canyon*, or the Rogue River in *Rogue River Feud*, carry the therapeutic power to bring back to psychological and physical vitality veterans whom medical science has given up for dead.

Yet perhaps Grey's most interesting war novel was the one he published in its immediate aftermath, *The Desert of Wheat* (1919), a novel that seeks to keep history in the frame rather than banishing it.[107] In so doing, it explores the role of the West in modern and global terms, and how the new functions of the federal state in many ways imperil Western exceptionalism. The novel is an uneasy generic mix, borrowing conventions from the Western, from wartime propaganda narratives treating US involvement in the war as a "great crusade" against German barbarism, and from an emergent antiwar rhetoric protesting the dehumanization of soldiers in processes of mass conscription and industrial warfare that reached its apogee in the United States with Dos Passos's *Three Soldiers*. And it puts pressure on some key ideas that appear again and again in Grey's work – the regenerative role of righteous vigilante violence; the possibility of geographical and ideological seclusion; and the political and cultural exceptionalism of the West. As with both *One of Ours* and *The Builders*, it shows the strain of the attempt to accommodate disparate scales of political geography, and of trying to reconcile well-established traditions of regional representation with the new kinds of political and cultural formation emerging from the war. The key difference is that Grey's novel addresses these issues on the terrain of what constitutes legitimate violence.

Like *One of Ours*, the protagonist of *The Desert of Wheat* features a young, dissatisfied farmer, Kurt Dorn, experiencing disagreements with a cantankerous father – only in this case his father is German. The action takes place in eastern Washington in early 1917, and Dorn and other local farmers are aware that their role as wheat producers has suddenly assumed considerable global strategic and military significance. The novel was published at the height of the first red scare, and blows with the prevailing winds of fierce xenophobia and antiunion sentiment: Kurt Dorn struggles to save his crops from both a dry spell and the increasingly obstructive practices of the Industrial Workers of the World (IWW), who are bent on sabotaging the harvest. (Indeed, so worried was Grey about the labor unrest that year that he had counselled his wife to stockpile cash in a safety deposit box in case of "any disturbance or riot or untoward circumstances."[108]) The Dorns are indebted to a wealthy local rancher, and soon Dorn falls in love with the daughter of this rancher, Lenore Anderson. It transpires that the IWW are led and funded by German agents, who are in league with Kurt's father, a man embittered at the United States for taking up arms against the country of his birth. However, in one of the novel's climactic scenes, Kurt's father dies trying to save his crops from burning after the IWW throw phosphorus cakes into his most productive field, and recants his pro-German sentiments with his dying words. Kurt is ruined, and signs his ranch over to Anderson, but subsequently saves Lenore from a rapacious IWW agent, and then foils a plot to murder her father. Vigilantes then round up all the IWW members and other "suspicious characters" they can find, lynch their leader, and run them out of the state on boxcars. This far in, the novel would seem to follow what Slotkin identifies as the classic Grey formula, namely that a wealthy white woman of high birth is threatened by a devious villain "whose conspiracies enmesh her and threaten her inheritance," but who is saved by a wandering stranger in a resolution achieved "through the hero's use of some spectacular act of violence, which is morally redemptive because it rescues the 'White woman' (who then accepts the hero as lover and husband)."[109] Yet this plotline is fulfilled halfway through the book, and much that happens afterwards works to complicate this formulaic simplicity. Subsequently, Dorn and Lenore become engaged, and Anderson urges him to accept a deferment, arguing his skill at raising wheat is more useful to the war effort than serving as a soldier; but Dorn's morbid guilt about his own German "blood" drives him to enlist. During the war, Anderson's son, Jim, dies of pneumonia in a New York encampment after receiving poor medical care and housing, while Dorn is gravely injured repulsing a German assault in the trenches in France. He returns home a deeply traumatized amputee, and with doctors predicting his imminent death. Yet he is nursed back to physical, if not mental, health by Lenore, encouraged by the prospect of helping the war effort through farming wheat on Anderson's immense holdings.

As might be expected, Grey's work is far less nuanced than Cather's when it comes to exploring "federated" loyalties, primarily because he has a fully biologized understanding of national and ethnic identity. Germanness, then, is configured less as a series of cultural practices and traditions and more as a temperamental inheritance. "Blood" rather than culture is the operative term here, a discourse that essentialized difference and that had become the dominant language for discussing race in the nineteenth century.[110] Germans are arrogant, violent, and cruel, and Kurt

is horrified at the persistence in himself of these attributes, even considering suicide to rid himself of them at the moments of his deepest despair: "if
there was German blood in him, poisoning the very wells of his heart, he
could have spilled it, and so, whether living or dead, have repudiated the
taint" (*DOW* 145). We are also told that "only death changes the state of
a real German, physical, moral, and spiritual" (*DOW* 95). When returned
from the war, Kurt's traumatized dreams make him relive his rampage with
a bayonet during a German assault, which sees him mimicking the bayonet
thrusts he made to dispatch nine Germans. And during those dreams he
changes from "a man to a gorilla," shouting in German, as he "repeat[s] the
savage orgy of remurdering his Huns" (*DOW* 332). Such scenes replicate
the characterization of Germans as apes or beasts in wartime propaganda –
Harry Hopps' poster "Destroy This Mad Brute" is the most famous
example – but also the phylogenetic account of German identity so prevalent in Allied propaganda, which saw them as racially inclined to
moments of evolutionary "reversion" to savage behavior. In this vision,
German-Americanness can only ever be an internalized struggle to hold
oneself to behave as one's higher, more civilized, American self, rather than
functioning as any kind of cultural hybridity. As such, Kurt ends the novel
aware that unless he can repress his traumatized and violent dreams, during
which he physically reenacts his brutal killing of nine German soldiers, his
marriage is probably doomed. Accordingly, he trains himself to experience
these dreams "without an outward quiver," meaning "'Lenore will never
know – how my Huns come back to me,' he whispered" (*DOW* 349).
Heroic psychological repression of all things German is the only future for
a successful life in America for a German-American in the postwar period,
this portrayal suggests.

Culture, therefore, is effectively taken out of the picture of "federal
citizenship" in Grey's vision. What takes its place as the dominant issue in
configuring regional identity and its relation to national citizenship is the
question of what constitutes legitimate violence. Violence has long had
a central place in definitions of the state, most famously in Max Weber's
formulation that the state is "a human community that (successfully)
claims *the monopoly of the legitimate use of physical force* within a given
territory," a territory wherein "the state is considered the sole source of the
'right' to use violence."[111] Yet historians have suggested that such
a monopoly was not established in the United States until the 1940s, as
previously "a decentralized and hybrid system of private security firms,
vigilantism, and state policing institutions" had claimed such legitimacy.[112]
The West had a special place in that history of hybrid legitimacy, and the

genre of the Western regularly sought to portray the West's heroicized process of historical formation, the "winning of the West," as reliant on the legitimation of violence by nonstate actors in a territory where the state was as yet too weak to claim a monopoly on its use. In such territory, vigilante violence serves the purpose of heroically prefiguring the rules of due process and state-monopolized violence that will come once the "frontier" has been transformed and "civilized" into the normalized territory of the nation-state. Such a portrayal is at the heart of the action in Owen Wister's *The Virginian* (1902), a novel often ritually cited as the foundational text in establishing the features of the modern Western, and that turns on a long legal and moral explication of why a deadly episode of extralegal violence (the lynching of cattle rustlers) was, in the context of uniquely Western conditions, legitimate. The argument in *The Virginian*, one replicated in many subsequent Westerns, including *The Desert of Wheat*, is that the perpetrators of vigilante violence are engaged in what sociologists have called "crime-control vigilantism," a form of violence "directed against people believed to be committing acts proscribed by the formal legal system. Such acts harm private persons or property, but the perpetrators escape justice due to governmental inefficiency, corruption, or the leniency of the system of due process."[113] Of course, historians have long identified "crime-control vigilantism" with the securing of power by politically dominant racial, ethnic, or socioeconomic groups, and both the history of vigilantism in the West and its centrality to the genre of the Western bear the stamp of this. Yet the heroic gloss afforded vigilante violence in many Westerns is achieved by presenting it as securing "law and order" not in the absence of the state but in the prehistory of the state, inserting vigilantes as pioneering forefathers of the police, due process, judiciary, and penal systems of a "civilized" society that their extralegal actions ultimately make possible.[114]

In *The Virginian*, and in *The Desert of Wheat*, the perpetrators of such violence seek to legitimate their actions on these grounds, arguing that the state is too weak or embryonic to enforce its own laws. In so doing, they claim a democratic and republican mantle for their deadly extralegal punishments. In *The Desert of Wheat*, for example, a group of vigilantes meet to hold a facsimile of jury-trial democracy in taking two separate votes on what punishment to mete out to the IWW members sabotaging their crop harvests: one for the regular members, and one for the IWW leadership. Yet such action is also designated as specifically cultural, a form with particular ties to the West and that takes on particularly "Western" dimensions. When Anderson is planning this vigilantism, for example, he "chuckled with the delight he always felt in the Western appreciation of summary violence justly dealt" (*DOW* 172). And, when Glidden, the German IWW leader, is lynched to hang under a bridge, in full view of the boxcars carrying the IWW members being deported from Washington, he has a placard placed on his breast reading "last warning. 3–7–77. The figures were the ones used in the frontier days by vigilantes" (*DOW* 229). For Grey, then, some of Western culture's most significant forms, and some of its greatest claims to regional exceptionalism, are particular kinds of spectacular vigilante violence.[115] And these ideas about the local agency of vigilantism were current in the 1920s in other areas of American politics, too, most importantly in how a mass-membership, resurgent Ku Klux Klan understood it. According to Sean McCann, they perceived it as an occasionally necessary use of "limited violence . . . as an inherently local solution for an ailing social body" capable of "seal[ing] the borders of a contained and harmonious world."[116]

If *The Desert of Wheat* stopped with these portrayals, it would differ little from the manifold defenses of such vigilante policing of organized labor that appeared in the popular press at the time, and that constituted such an effective front in mobilizing popular opinion behind the often brutal suppression of the labor movement in 1919 and 1920. Yet the novel is noticeably equivocal in its support of this violence, a fact that pays testament to how widely such vigilantism was decried in the war years, most importantly by President Wilson, in a series of political arguments that Christopher Capozzola has argued "laid the groundwork for the legal and political dismantling of vigilantism in the twentieth century."[117] In responding to the lynching of IWW leader Frank Little in Butte, Montana, in August 1917, for example – a case Grey researched and used as the basis of Glidden's lynching – *The Outlook* condemned as inexcusable

> those who, in the spirit of the vigilance committees of frontier days, took the law into their own hands when frontier conditions do not prevail. Did they forget that the Government is simply the people, who have delegated to it alone the power to act in local as well as in National difficulties, and to crush opposition by force of arms if necessary?[118]

This editorial takes aim at exactly the two defenses of vigilantism that appear in *The Desert of Wheat* – firstly, that it is necessary as a heroic forerunner to truly effective state-controlled policing in America's western regions; and secondly, that as a deeply ingrained feature of a localized political culture – a folkway, in the parlance of the time – it possessed a legitimacy that could coexist with federal authority.

Grey was clearly troubled by these twin charges of anachronism and parochialism leveled at vigilantism. Indeed, this anxiety is initially manifest in a clear gap in *The Desert of Wheat* between the mythic West he felt most comfortable writing about and the historical West whose labor dynamics involved a substantial and largely unskilled laboring class. This class often worked seasonal and itinerant jobs in lumber, canning, and fruit and arable crop harvesting in what historian Carlos Schwantes has influentially called the "wageworker's frontier."[119] Grey's awareness of the existence of this class – which is usually absent in conventional Westerns, including his own – means he cannot disparage and demonize the IWW wholesale. When Dorn speaks to one of the IWW men, it transpires he is an honest and hardworking man who lost his early oil business due to the unscrupulous and aggressive business practices of Standard Oil, and subsequently owned a farm ruined by water theft on the part of a "corporation" (*DOW* 156). Such a characterization lends legitimacy to IWW claims about the abuses of labor by capital in the period, and thereby complicates any total correlation between labor unionism and the obstruction of the war effort. The West is not a place, therefore, where rugged individualistic masculinity will always triumph; especially not when pitted against large corporations now thoroughly national in their scope and effects. Moreover, this section also seems to swipe away a crucial plank in the popular exceptionalist understanding of the West, in depicting a region embedded in a wage economy replete with the kinds of exploitations and inequities experienced nationwide, rather than existing as a unique and in some ways premodern pioneer economy of individuated work. In consequence, rather than dealing summary justice to thieves, rustlers, or ethnic or racial aliens, the antiunion vigilante action in *The Desert of Wheat* risks sweeping up honest laborers fighting for exactly the kind of economic self-determination (and the masculine identity that entailed) that Grey revered in most of his more formulaic Western fiction.

The kinds of violence characteristic of the Western genre, first complicated in *The Desert of Wheat* by the thoroughly modern kinds of union-busting violence characteristic of labor unrest in the United States, are further troubled by new kinds of violence promulgated by federal organization. These new modes of violence are effected by bureaucratic and institutional complexities, and deployed on such colossal national and international scales, that they go way beyond the kinds of interpersonal confrontation at the heart of the Western formula. Indeed, this violence is so institutionalized, widespread, and depersonalized that it is completely detached from the simplistic moral calculus that was at the heart of the myth of "regenerative violence" that underpinned the vigilante traditions of the West and that Grey, as we have seen, was so enamored of. Dorn is visited by a shadowy operative from Washington, DC; although he begins by telling him he is from the Conservation Commission, after a while he informs Dorn that "My name's not Hall. Never mind my name. For you it's Uncle Sam" (*DOW* 93). With his intimate knowledge of sabotage activities in the Northwest, it is clear by the end of their conversation that the operative works for the fledgling Bureau of Investigation, the agency that undertook much of the Justice Department's (often covert) campaign to suppress antiwar dissent.[120] And his deliberate anonymity, his duplicity, and his detailed intelligence on labor subversion all suggest the bureaucratization of policing, its detachment from the direct, interpersonal confrontations of Anderson's vigilantes, and its reliance on new modalities of surveillance, salaried professionalism, and emotional and geographical distance quite distinct from the cultures of violence typical of the Western.

As well as the changes in modalities of policing enacted by new federal agencies tasked with quashing antigovernment protests and activities, the novel also suggests the growing anachronism of one of the West's most cherished political and gender icons, the cowboy. Midway through the book, we are given a description of Jake, a cowboy and Anderson's right-hand man; he is "a potential force. The least significant thing about his appearance was that swinging gun. He seemed cool and easy, with hard, keen eyes" (*DOW* 231). The "potential force" of the cowboy here can be narrowly interpreted as his latent capacity for intense violence, but in this moment Grey uses that as the capstone holding together the wide reso-nances of the cowboy's "potential force" in national and regional political, cultural, mythical, and sexual arenas. He is a figure of all that Grey deems right in moral, gender, and political terms, a rightness anchored in his ability to deliver swift and consequential "force." Yet when Anderson receives letters from his son, Jim, we learn that his best friend in camp, named Montana – also identified as a "fine big cowboy" – has been hit over the head with a pick handle in a tawdry camp brawl with his fellow soldiers and has been permanently incapacitated (*DOW* 253). Most impactful is Jim's own death, of pneumonia after being housed in unheated tents with few blankets in the midst of a bitter Eastern winter, and then moved to an inadequately staffed and poorly constructed army hospital. Legitimate violence in the West is being bureaucratized, which multiplies and obscures its lines of operation and action, tying it to shady centers of intelligence and policy in Washington rather than to the immediacy of a clearly wronged local party. And in the meaningless disabling of Jim's "fine" cowboy, we see the "force" of Western political-cultural myth being subsumed, negated, and ultimately dissipated by the superior force of a federal state. This is a force operative in a way similar to how Simone Weil used the term: it is "a kind of superviolence, a sweeping and swirling phenomenon that belongs to no one group or person, and that touches those who wield power as well as those who are its victims," a phenomenon so characteristic of the twentieth century's two world wars.[121] All of the cowboy's physical fineness, skill, and moral character count for nothing against this "force," which in its massive scale and complexity has become both amoral and unhitched from narratives of masculine or regional becoming. In addition, rather than protecting the interest of local social elites, as was usually the case with Western vigilantism, the "force" of total war is much more socially indiscriminate in its effects and victims, as the son of the wealthy rancher succumbs to its deadliness. In this portrayal, then, Grey aligns with the many modernists – including E.E. Cummings and T.S. Eliot – who elegized what Daniel Worden has called "cowboy masculinity" in the postwar period, a gender form whose "brand of self-made manhood [gave] way to a wounded manhood emblematic of masculinist modernist fiction."[122]

The Desert of Wheat has other continuities with classic modernist representations of twentieth-century violence, too. Specifically, the dichotomy between the kind of language and moral charge Grey affords to the vigilante violence in the book and the violence experienced and promulgated by men who become part of the national army is similar to the dichotomy between the "enchanted" and the "disenchanted" modes the critic Sarah Cole finds so characteristic of twentieth-century representations of violence. If enchanted violence, so important to the Western genre, "imbue[s] the violent experience with symbolic and cultural potency" and "relies primarily on metaphors of growth and germination; it steers as clear of the violated body as it can," disenchanted violence instead "refuse[s] that structure, [insisting] on the bare, forked existence of the violated being, bereft of symbol."[123] As she goes on to explain, nationalism and militarism both rely heavily on "enchanted" representations of violence-as-generative, and perhaps in consequence the most well-known of the World War One poets conspicuously resist this mode; for them, "violence is meant to linger in the imagination and from there to compel change, but it is not the germ of culture, the force of national uplift, or the sign of sublimity."[124] Tellingly, Jim's body, victim of the violence of institutional neglect, is lingered over in highly disenchanted terms; his father describes finding him "in one of the little rooms. No heat! It was winter there . . . Only a bed! . . .

Jim lay on the floor, dead! He'd fallen or pitched off the bed. He had on only his underclothes that he had on – when he left – home ... He was stiff – an' must have – been dead – a good while" (*DOW* 262). Moreover, his parents desperately – and unsuccessfully – grasp at the language of sublimity to explain the medical negligence that led to his death; Anderson seeks to console his wife by suggesting "The gigantic task of a Government to draft and prepare a great army and navy was something beyond the grasp of ordinary minds" (*DOW* 263). One key feature of the enchanted mode of death was also its centrality to narratives of martial agency and purpose, and Jim's death is detached from both. One is reminded here of Margot Norris's assertion that the truly transformative nature of twentieth-century violence was its new relationship to individual agency; for "the agency of killing – always already dispersed among politicians, strategists, and soldiers – becomes so extremely dispersed with the deployment of weapons of mass destruction as to become virtually unlocatable."[125] Indeed, "the building-in of technological agency becomes the building-out of human responsibility," and we might add that the building-in of *technocratic* agency greatly accelerates that process.[126] No single person can be blamed for Jim's death; it is a result of institutional rather than personal negligence. As might be expected, Anderson's attempt to frame his son's loss in the terms of sublimity to his wife is far from comforting; the sublimity of a faceless death at the hands of an uncaring and inefficient bureaucratic leviathan is far from the sublimity of a soldier actively sacrificing his life for a broader, glorious national future so central to militaristic "enchanted" violence. It is no surprise she soon dies of grief at her loss.

That violence cannot remain enchanted and mythic, the supreme regenerative action at the heart of both masculine and regional formation, is inevitable once Grey had taken the decision to reconnect a dehistoricized and archetypal vision of the West with the historical actualities of total war. Violence, it seems, is less amenable to the kinds of "federated" and at times conflicted plurality at work in Cather's vision, existing instead as a zero-sum game in which the overwhelming "superviolence" of nationalized "force" threatens to erase local cultures of violence and thereby local particularity in general. If Western exceptionalism lives by local cultures of "regenerative" vigilante violence, Grey suggests, perhaps it dies when violence becomes the purview of a thoroughly nationalized state at war. This idea is implied by the ending too. A common trope in the endings of Grey's Westerns is the retreat of a heterosexual couple to paradisal seclusion from the outside world in a fabulously beautiful and "pristine" Western space, a motif that famously concludes *Riders of the Purple Sage* with Jane Withersteen and Lassiter's enclosure in "Surprise Valley," but that is also found in the retreat to the cabin on the Rogue in *Rogue River Feud*, Carley and Glenn's retreat to Deep Lake Ranch in *The Call of the Canyon*, and a return to the Huett family home in Sycamore Canyon in *30,000 on the Hoof*. By contrast, the importance of Kurt and Lenore's home at the end of *The Desert of Wheat* is defined in specifically global terms. Anderson reads aloud an extended crop report printed in a local newspaper, detailing the enormous quantity of wheat to be shipped to the Allies in Europe from Canada and the United States in 1918, wheat that Anderson proclaims will "feed and save the world" (*DOW* 334). As Anderson lists US northwestern crop output predictions alongside estimates of boosted crop production from Alberta, Argentina, and Australia, US Western exceptionalism seems to fade away here to become just one location among many making important contributions to wartime agricultural mobilization.

In many ways, then, *The Desert of Wheat* comes to function as an anti-Western, raising some of its most cherished motifs and narrative situations – the regenerative, enchanted capacity of vigilante violence; the regional and gendered iconicity of the cowboy; the West as an exceptional region in terms of its labor economy and its relative isolation from the agency of a federal state – only to undermine their significance in a modern world of changing political organization. The West in *The Desert of Wheat* is a valuable resource for a nation at war – in terms of labor, foodstuffs, and conscripts – but ultimately these things are little different from how they exist elsewhere in the nation, and indeed the world. Accordingly, the novel's final pages conclude with an image of rhapsodic sublimity characteristic of Grey's fiction, but rather than a particular landscape, it is fields of wheat in darkness that preoccupy Kurt, as he is "uplifted high above the dark pale of the present with its war and pain and clouded mind to wheat – to the fertile fields of a golden age to come" (*DOW* 350). By substituting a commodity for a specific landscape in a vision of idealized futurity, Grey makes a similar gesture to Cather in identifying aggregated and immense agricultural productivity as the core feature of American regional participation in a global conflict, and a cornerstone of newly established American military and imperial power. Indeed, Kurt's delocalized vision is just the final way the novel effectively decenters the West's role in informing national identity, and questions the tenets of its exceptionalist myths; thoroughly enmeshed in national systems of production, distribution, conscription, and surveillance, even the sublimity of Western scenery is denuded as an exceptionalist claim in the novel's final scenes.

Unsurprisingly, as a popular author who had hit on a winning commercial formula, Grey did not persist with challenging the conventions on which his genre fiction rested; as he was finishing up *The Desert of Wheat*, he wrote of his intention to abandon his ambition to write "powerful psychological novels of love, passion, and tragedy" and instead direct his energies to "that which I have already written best – the beauty and color and mystery of great spaces, of the open, of Nature in her wild moods. The decision has been a relief."[127] And subsequent novels – *The Day of the Beast* aside – would indeed retreat to the idea of an exceptionalist Western landscape possessing the therapeutic and isolationist potential to rescue shattered veterans from the wounds of modern history. *The Desert of Wheat* stands as an odd outlier in its imagination of what political communities constituted through violence mean within a global rather than a continental frame of reference, when Western frontier narratives of vigilantism seem less important to national-state formation than the weaponization of an arable production that is ultimately delocalized. Dorn's "home" of eastern Washington will neither restore him to full health nor seclude him from the traumas of modern history; but it does promise a sublime union with a commodity whose production and global mobility will underpin American superpower in the years to come.

*

In 1934, in his famous memoir of the roaring twenties, *Exile's Return*, Malcom Cowley remarked that for the American writers who came of age in the 1920s, generational differences were far more significant than regional ones; for "regional traditions were dying out; all regions were being transformed into a great unified market for motorcars and Ivory soap and ready-to-wear clothes."[128] As we have seen, this was a period in which the relationship between regional and national identity was widely identified as undergoing dramatic change, change the war's political transformations did much to accelerate. For some contemporary observers, the war served as a final push in the direction of centralization and standardization in national economy and political power that had all but obliterated regional particularity. For others, the forms and rhetoric of national unity and identity deployed in the war had been so defined by civic abstraction that the affective richness of local particularity seemed increasingly essential – at least in the imagination of the national collective, and at most as a countervailing force to the culturally impoverishing consequences of a nationalized market and a centralized governance. And literature had a widely recognized centrality to these issues. Cather,

Glasgow, and Grey were not unique in seeing that regionalist literary genres were one of the primary modalities by which Americans understood regional identity and indeed social difference in general, and that this made the political and economic transformations and conflicts that roiled the war years over the issue of regionality inseparable from how, or indeed whether, those genres would continue to be used.

Whether it was the doddering traditions of local color writing or the still-emergent conventions of the Western, these three writers all saw regionalist generic conventions as essential vehicles for exploring the new political formations – especially the new conditions of national citizen-ship – emerging in wartime. Glasgow and Cather were attracted to the political and aesthetic messiness of federated forms of affiliation and obligation, which involved juxtaposing multiple and sometimes incompatible generic forms (local color, the domestic romance, the abstractions of a national imaginary, and the war novel, to name just a few) as indispensable imaginative registers for considering the nature of the new political subjectivities emerging in 1917, which were similarly characterized by multiplicity, incongruity, and strain. By contrast, Grey's identification of legitimate violence as the cornerstone of state sovereignty brooked little of this. Instead, he saw federal regimes of bureaucratized and depersonalized violence as supplanting the "temporary embodiment of popular sover-eignty" of vigilante violence extensively romanticized by the Western, and in the process erasing much of what made the West distinctive at all.[129] In one sense, these features of all three novelists would seem to confirm long-standing critical views of regionalism as a genre whose huge success relied on its unique ability as a mediating form, an ultimately reconciliatory literature with an unmatched ambition to represent and dissipate the social frictions of racial, ethnic, and class difference but also the differentials of political power and economy across scenes of the local, national, and global.[130] Yet it was true that the extraordinary speed of wartime centralization, and the power and expanse of the wartime state, placed a particularly distorting pressure on all these three fictions, which show how the acute strain placed on the act of mediation in the political sphere at this moment was inevitably reflected in the aesthetic one.

This mediating function was pulled between civic and cultural under-standings of nationalism; between abstract and symbolic national forms of community and Dewey's localized "vitality and depth of close and direct intercourse and attachment"; and between differently scaled sovereignties of violence and economies of production. In doing this work, these novels represented one of the most intensive and thoroughgoing attempts to imagine the contours of the new state – how its abstractions and depersonalizations registered in concrete and often painful ways on localized communities, or how its "compensatory" configurations closely enmeshed it with enormous, international corporate structures. They saw it as so many of the authors considered elsewhere in this book did: ghostly, abstract, compulsive, and with new forms of power that were hard to put into existing forms of representation. Yet they also saw it as having a transformative and even parasitical relation to regional resources in every sense, drawing on the productive capacities but also the imaginative conventions of the regional as part of its newly expanded parameters and increasingly global operation. In some regards, this was just a moment in a long-standing feature of an American political imaginary; as Lauren Berlant has observed of Hawthorne's nineteenth-century political vision, "there is no such thing as everyday life in the abstract state of the nation, and ... there is much more coherence at the level of symbolic nationalist discourse than in personal, local, sectional, and regional practices," meaning that the representational forms of a "utopian nation" can only ever include "affective objects that have been wrested from their historical, practical, and experiential contexts."[131] In many ways, these novels were stymied by this disconnection, but novels like *One of Ours* took on the task of tracking those "affective objects" as they move back and forth across both these registers: from symbolic ships to shabby and disease-ridden everyday ones; from the iconic abstraction of "French culture" to the everyday parochialism of the interior of a cheese shop; or from the everyday fields of agricultural labor and even injury to the "long arm" of American agricultural might. And the kind of "federal citizenship" that Lippmann discussed emerges in the novel as precisely an effect of this kind of movement. Accordingly, *One of Ours* functioned as more than the "memorial fiction" that Steven Trout has so compellingly claimed it as; it was as forward-looking as it was elegiac. In signaling the multiple kinds and crucially the multiple scales of political imaginary that would become ever more central to modern American citizenship, it set out insightful parameters for the regionalist literature that would characterize the postwar period on how regional lives in an imperial nation could be discussed and represented.

CHAPTER 4

U.S.A., *World War One, and the Petromodern State*

The New Deal revolution took the management of the economy out of the hands of the bankers. The faucets that control the flow of credit are all in Washington today. We are more and more governed, instead of by the oldfashioned politicians, by people who are adept at institutional manipulation. We haven't quite found the terms that describe them exactly. When we like our new rulers we call them public servants. When we are mad at them we call them bureaucrats, but it is the business of selfgovernment to see that they remain servants of the public instead of becoming its masters.

John Dos Passos, "England under a Labor Government: 1947"[1]

In 1950, John Dos Passos published "England under a Labor Government," an account of his experiences touring England in the summer of 1947. That government, already two years old, had already passed the National Health Service Act, laying the foundations for the provision of universal health care free at the point of use – as well as instituting a national insurance scheme providing for universal old-age pensions and unemployment benefit. It had nationalized the railways and the coal industries, and would go on to nationalize iron, steel, and electricity – transferring 20 percent of the British economy to government ownership.[2] It had made secondary education universally free in state schools; had begun the creation of the National Park system; and had ended British rule in India. Clement Attlee's administration continues to serve as a benchmark among the British left for what social-democratic reform can do; it has been described as accomplishing "more than any other peacetime government, arguably before or since," and representing "the culmination of the entire tradition of Britain's reform movement since the Great Reform Act."[3] But in Dos Passos's essay, England appeared a dreary and exhausted place, rendered "dim" and "provincial" by the ebbing of empire and the stifling bureaucracy of the new welfare state.[4] As he tries to buy a peach from an unlicensed fruit barrow, or to tour a boarded-up Chiswick House (following in the footsteps of his beloved Jefferson and Adams), a refrain emerges: he is prohibited by what phlegmatic Cockneys wearily call "regulytions." Young people are emigrating because there is no opportunity for the energetic and imaginative; and "this great highly trained, highly disciplined and civilized nation is in danger of dying of inanition because in the elaborate structure of the welfare state there is so little room left where individual initiative can take hold."[5] While he acknowledges that many of these reforms to improve working people's lives were akin to those he campaigned for in the 1920s and 1930s, this could not compensate for the fact that they had failed to "promote self-government, expand individual liberty and make for wider distribution of life's goods." Ultimately, "British socialism is turning out to be not so very different from the Russian brand," and had merely substituted bureaucrats for plutocrats as an oppressive governing caste.[6]

This essay does much to illuminate Dos Passos's political turnaround within the previous fifteen years; and it remains surprising to read such invective from a writer whose fiction in the 1920s and 1930s dwelt so frequently on the disastrous effects of doctors' bills on the lives of the working class, or the inequities that ensued when labor had no effective governmental representation. That political shift is central to how Dos Passos is treated in most literary histories, where he holds the dubious distinction of being one of the most dramatic changelings in American twentieth-century literature; his own critical heritage is disproportionally characterized by biographical work assessing his lengthy political trajectory from Communist Party darling in the early 1930s to Barry Goldwater supporter in 1964.[7] Yet Dos Passos always rejected the charge that his politics had dramatically changed throughout his life, claiming that "the basic tragedy my work tries to express seems to remain monotonously the same: man's struggle for life against the strangling institutions he himself creates."[8] Of course, this was disingenuous; as Donald Pizer notes, what had changed was his perception of "the nature of the principal threat to freedom – from 'organized money' to the power of the modern state."[9] Yet both Dos Passos and some of his critics have regularly identified an anti-institutionalism as the heart of his politics; he would belatedly – and frequently – assert that his early optimism about the Soviet Union was never based in an optimism about state centralization but rather in the hope that it "might develop into something like the New England town meeting," becoming a system of highly local direct democracy.[10] Dos Passos's most meticulous recent critic, Seth Moglen, accedes that Dos Passos had always been "suspicious of statist versions of socialism"; for some of Dos Passos's critics on the left, his politics was always essentially couched in an anti-institutional romanticism, which made him perennially "agin' the system" in a fashion that was "politically simple-minded," in the caustic judgment of Alfred Kazin.[11] Such anti-institutionalism informed Dos Passos's later prioritization of "selfgovernment" as the cornerstone of his political creed, and underpinned his arguments in the 1940s and 1950s that the greatest threat to this national tradition of individual sovereignty was not the large corporations that had preoccupied his early novels but instead a "bureaucratic despotism" that he associated with the federal military and the welfare state.[12] As the epigraph to this chapter suggests, the New Deal loomed large in that narrative; his account of its modes of governance as coercive and disempowering would be fully realized in his 1949 novel *The Grand Design*. Yet Dos Passos also regularly claimed that the purported federal overreach of the New Deal had been pioneered in World War One, a war he later identified as "the birth of Leviathan."[13] In 1956, he reminisced that "It's hard to remember in the middle fifties today that in those years [before World War One] what little military service there was in America was voluntary, that taxes were infinitesimal, that if you could scrape up the price of a ticket you could travel anywhere in the world except through Russia and Turkey, without saying boo to a bureaucrat."[14] He saw Wilson's wartime state as the blueprint to FDR's brain trust, claiming that "in [FDR's] third term, the consolidation of the federal government really was the rebirth of bureaucracy, which had shown its head under [Woodrow] Wilson and then faded away."[15]

While most scholarly attention has been devoted to Dos Passos's depiction of the growth of the coercive state in World War One – particularly its conscript military and its new security apparatus – this chapter instead explores his awareness of a different feature of this wartime "Leviathan," one that was arguably more significant to his long-term antistatist politics. This was a model of governmental and corporate collaboration named the "compensatory state" by historian Marc Allen Eisner, a model revived in the New Deal that ultimately became a durable template for modern US welfare state organization. As Eisner outlines, the "compensatory state" emerged as a result of American underpreparedness for involvement in a global war against the world's military superpower.[16] As the demands of a "total war" became apparent, small, ill-prepared, and often newly minted federal agencies turned to the superior structures of organization and governance of America's national corporations in order to fully mobilize America's industrial and manpower resources. What emerged was "compensatory state building," wherein "state capacity was expanded by appending the capacities of private-sector associations on to the state."[17] Relatively little scholarship has linked Dos Passos's accounts of World War One with his critiques of the New Deal–era welfare state, and yet the new state–corporate collaborations that typified the system of national governance that emerged from World War One, and particularly the new infrastructures this generated, are commonalities between the two periods that his fiction extensively registers. Moreover, these (infra) structural changes, which did so much to transform US economic and social life, underlie both the melancholia of Dos Passos's account of modern political subjectivities and the fictional forms he used to frame that account. The wartime innovations and transformations of modern state institutions, and their entwining with the capital, technological, and bureaucratic technologies of corporate America within what Leo Marx has called Large Scale Technological Systems, in many ways provided him with the fictional structures informing his two cataclysmic modern epics, the *U.S.A.* trilogy and the *District of Columbia* trilogy.[18] As Patrick Joyce notes, these systems were so large and complex, and so thoroughly blurred boundaries between state, corporation, material life, and individual, that they presented exceptional representational challenges; they were "as vague as [they were] powerful."[19]

As "England under a Labor Government" intimated, Dos Passos held an intense interest in meeting that challenge, in devising effective forms and terms to describe the actions, agencies, and actors of the contemporary state – both human and nonhuman – in seeking alternatives to the inadequacy of phrases such as "public servant" and "bureaucrat." Moreover, he saw that modern state–corporate collaboration – its bureaucracies, infrastructures, labor force, and modes of governance – was itself an innovative apparatus that the form of the modern novel must in some ways accommodate. This chapter tracks such ambitions within *U.S.A.*, a trilogy centered on one of the most important – and overlooked – World War One novels in the American canon: *1919*. Yet that importance arises from *1919*'s ambition to largely eschew representations of combat in order to trace how the innovations of the wartime state became a determinant of modern American social experience, both through new institutions of security and through new infrastructures of transport. In doing so, the chapter dwells on a political double bind Dos Passos had fully recognized by the time of the New Deal: that whereas the modern state had (to his mind) destroyed the political culture of "selfgovernment" and masculine republicanism he so venerated, its structural features had aesthetic implications indispensable to any modernist formal theory of the social novel.

U.S.A. does much of this work through the structural, affective, and political centrality to the novel of one of the major new infrastructures of the "compensatory state" to arise from the war: that related to the extraction, processing, and consumption of oil. U.S.A. is a particularly oily trilogy; its first book, *The 42nd Parallel*, finishes with several major characters connected to the oil industry congregating in Mexico around the time of the US military invasion of 1914, an invasion prosecuted in part to protect US oil interests.[20] The second novel, *1919*, takes the negotiations over how the victorious Allies would divide the world's oil resources at the Paris Peace Conference in 1919 as one of the main geopolitical forces shaping world history. One of U.S.A.'s major characters, Joe Williams, works as a sailor on a Standard Oil tanker; another, J. Ward Moorehouse, does public relations first for Southwestern Oil and then for Standard Oil. Many of the Texan family members of another major character, Anne Trent, have extensive investments in the oil industry. Minor characters work in oil fields, work as lobbyists for Standard Oil to the federal government, or are unsuccessful oil speculators. And petroleum is everywhere in the trilogy, as characters drive, fly, and motor-propel themselves through the roaring twenties. In his recent monograph on the ecopoetics of American modernism, Joshua Schuster posed the question "where is the oil in modernism?", noting the gap between petroleum's ubiquity in the modern era and its relative absence in modernist writing.[21] Dos Passos's trilogy presents itself as a compelling answer: indeed, one of its newsreel sections even has a tongue-in-cheek, self-referential moment about the sheer ubiquity of oil in the trilogy, presenting the ad copy "IMPROVED LUBRICATING SYSTEM THAT INSURES POSITIVE AND CONSTANT OILING OVER THE ENTIRE BEARING SURFACES."[22] We could see the novel itself as subject to "constant oiling," as oil seems to everywhere lubricate the contact between differential parts of the social machine – particularly contact between individuals, states, and corporations – as well as fueling multiple kinds of mobility and trajectories.

Counterintuitively, it is perhaps oil's prominent place in Dos Passos's trilogy that has evacuated it from sustained critical notice; it is usually itemized as just one of many features of twentieth-century US material culture and economy that Dos Passos so compulsively collates over his 1,300-page epic.[23] And this curious omission overlaps with the implications of what has become a truism of recent scholarship on oil and petroleum culture – if oil is ubiquitous and unavoidable, implicated in every facet of modern materiality and lived experience (from plastics to asphalt, agricultural fertilizer to clothing fabrics, and even printing ink), there is an extraordinary difficulty in finding "a point of view from which to frame the *everything* of oil," in the words of Stephanie LeMenager.[24] Indeed, if every novel could now be read as an oil novel, because every modern experience and representation is inevitably saturated and structured by the products and processes of oil, perhaps no novel is worth reading in these terms, so unavoidable is oil's sustaining presence.[25] Yet *U.S.A.*'s treatment of oil shows deep interconnections between energy history and cultural history, especially what happens culturally at the moments of transition between historically dominant energy regimes. The thirty-year time span of *U.S.A.* broadly corresponds to a major shift from an energy system of "coal capitalism" to "oil-electric-coal capitalism," to deploy Frederick Buell's terms; and Timothy Mitchell's account of the political dimensions of that shift, which foreclosed the kind of possibilities for workers' assertiveness and successful labor activism found in an earlier, more singular dependence on coal, clearly maps on to Dos Passos's despairing vision of the fate of the organized left in the United States across the trilogy (*USA* 277–280).[26] Yet Dos Passos's novel also maps the more everyday politics of how new infrastructures and materialities of oil begin to condition experiences of social connection and pleasure, often in ways that complicates what is often taken to be the book's more straightforward Thermidor narrative of the decline of the organized left after the revolutionary potential of 1919.

Dos Passos weaves the history of an emergent global oil system through the formal experimentalism and narrative multiplicity of *U.S.A.*, employing innovative literary structures of narrative progression and interpersonal encounters to make oil palpable, particularly its often habitually occluded infrastructures – both oil's materialization in the construction of asphalt roads and the huge extraction, refining, and transport systems delivering the combustible fuel that increasingly organized global sociality. Moreover, this habitual invisibility, as recent scholars have suggested, is something that seems to unite both oil and infrastructure; if oil experiences a kind of invisibility of ubiquity, then infrastructure disappears from view because it "lives – conceptually though not actually – outside the domain of private property" in the boring domain of the publicly owned that represents a political "minimum threshold, an earth-bound zone in which the large irresolutions of politics can for once be ignored and decisions safely left to the technocrats."[27] Defamiliarizing oil and its infrastructure emerges as a political preoccupation for Dos Passos, for two main reasons. The first was because the blend of public and private, state regulation and corporate ownership, that characterized oil infrastructure was becoming so characteristic of the "compensatory state" that emerged from World War One; and the second was the way that consuming oil was coming to dominate, in exhilarating but also limiting ways, an American political imaginary. *U.S.A.* tells a story of how oil became a central part of the American state; its identification as a national security resource; and how its consumption on roads and in the air was governed by an expanding set of state-funded or state-authored legislation, contracts, and infrastructure. In more individualized – and privatized – terms, oil appears as both liberating and devastating, capable of delivering both personal exhilaration and occasions of spectacular violence. It structures both social connection and personal experiences of freedom through motorized speed, and dramatizes the inherent and often violent contradiction between the highly managed, state-controlled systems of automobility that were emerging in the era and the privatized, atomized exhilaration of driving a motor car – an activity that was becoming increasingly central to the imaginary of the freedoms of liberal citizenship.[28]

This chapter explores how such a political imaginary develops in *U.S.A.*, and how the formal innovations of Dos Passos's text are entwined with the patterns of sociality and mobility of an age of "petromodernity," to use LeMenager's term.[29] Ultimately, *U.S.A.* rests on two, connected, features, the first primarily aesthetic and the second ideological: first, that despite Dos Passos's political misgivings about the erosions of individual sovereignty in the modern state, its structuring of social relations would inevitably inform the aesthetic practices of any novel committed to social mimesis. And, second, that modern subjectivity was largely inconceivable outside of a petromodern imaginary grounded in the promise of personal, and exhilarated, liberation – but was simultaneously wholly reliant on the state–corporate infrastructure of a global system of extracting, processing, distributing, and consuming oil that had assumed its mature complexion in the events of World War One. This simultaneity, which the trilogy often renders as an inherent tension arising from a version of freedom that is thoroughly produced and regulated by the state, is in several moments pushed to the limits of outright contradiction – moments that assume fatal consequences for Dos Passos's characters.

Dos Passos and World War One

World War One has always figured large in Dos Passos's writings and critical reception. He himself called it his "university," and Alfred Kazin claimed his career "would have been nothing" without it.[30] One of the

famous cadre of volunteer American ambulance drivers to serve in World
War One, Dos Passos enlisted first with the Norton-Harjes unit, entering
the fray on the Verdun sector of the western front in fall of 1917, before
transferring to the American Red Cross in November to see service in
Bassano, Italy. In his letters from early 1918 onward, he began to voice his
opposition to the war, and when one of these was intercepted by Red Cross
officers he faced the prospect of a dishonorable discharge. Despite traveling
to Paris in August 1918 to appeal to the Red Cross authorities, he was
drummed out of the organization, but not before he had volunteered to
help the wounded brought into Paris from the battle of Château-Thierry –
a job that involved him carrying buckets of amputated limbs away from the
operating tables. By the end of August 1918, he was back in the United
States.[31] Eager to join the US Army Medical Corps, he used family connections to smooth over the fallout from his run-in with the military
authorities, and was also able to gain a waiver for his terrible eyesight;
but by the time he was back in Europe, the war was over.

These experiences formed the basis of his first two books; the first was
a highly autobiographical debut novel, *One Man's Initiation: 1917*, which
follows the volunteer ambulance driver Martin Howe through his shock-
ing and disillusioning experiences on the western front. In a letter to
Arthur K. McComb written from training camp in late 1918, Dos Passos
had remarked that "You cant imagine the simple and sublime amiability of
the average American soldier – Here is clay for almost any moulding. Who
is to be the potter? That is the great question."[32] He also later recalled that
at this time he repeated the words "organization is death" to himself over
and over. These feelings informed Dos Passos's next novel, which garnered
fourteen rejections before being accepted by George H. Doran. Even after
his new publisher had insisted on extensive revisions, *Three Soldiers* generated substantial controversy on its appearance in 1921 for its depiction of
the US Army as a callous and often brutal (and brutalizing) institution.[33]
Dos Passos's AEF was riddled with petty and self-aggrandizing impositions
of authority on the part of officers, while drafted men lived tedious lives
only mitigated by occasional drunken womanizing; both groups demonstrated an almost total disengagement with the war's larger geopolitical
effects or significance. Coupled with a caustic depiction of the ethically
corrosive impact of wartime propaganda and religious rhetoric, the novel
showed an institution destroying the citizenship rights and compassionate
ethics it was supposedly fighting a Prussian autocracy to protect. This
institution causes one of his (initially idealistic) "Three Soldiers" to dodge
front-line service to languish in a menial job in a behind-the-lines supply

section; and another to murder his superior officer. The third, the aspiring musician and Harvard-educated John Andrews, deserts – just one of the many sensitive young male artists destroyed by the war that would appear in Dos Passos's fiction.

As the first "Lost Generation" portrayal of the war as an experience of senseless industrial slaughter and institutional tyranny, *Three Soldiers* drew ferocious criticism from those who had served in the AEF ("John Dos Passos Lies!" was a representative review title), and from prominent newspapers, including the *New York Times Book Review*, which ran Coningsby Dawson's review "Insulting the Army."[34] On the other hand, it was hailed by critics such as Frances Hackett at the *New Republic*, John Peale Bishop at *Vanity Fair*, and H.L. Mencken at *Smart Set* as the first authentic fictionalization of the war unencumbered by the Espionage and Sedition Acts of 1917 and 1918. As Steven Trout has shown, the controversy over the novel set the tone for debates in the early 1920s over what the dominant narrative of US involvement in the conflict would be, debates that were intensely polarizing. While outlets such as the publications of the American Legion, or novels such as Willa Cather's Pulitzer Prize–winning *One of Ours*, presented the war as politically necessary and/or personally formative for the soldiers involved, a younger group of male writers rose to prominence on claims that the war had rendered entire systems of representation and modes of citizenship deeply discredited.[35]

Yet *Three Soldiers* features relatively little depiction of combat. The Armistice is declared halfway through the book, and previous to this Andrews has been hospitalized with a minor wound during his first artillery barrage. A single, twelve-page chapter recounts the experiences of his comrade Chrisfield at the Meuse-Argonne offensive. The brevity of these explorations in *Three Soldiers* suggested that Dos Passos's main interests were elsewhere, and indeed in all his future work the war's significance becomes registered more in the social and institutional transformations it effects than in the experiential horrors of battlefield violence. This was first manifest in his seminal *Manhattan Transfer* of 1925, which chronicles New York life from the 1890s to the mid-1920s; the war is a key event for the novel, but the time span of American combat involvement is omitted entirely. The novel's chronology skips from 1914 to 1919 between sections two and three, leaving the close of the novel to consider the war's effects on American finance, on labor relations, and on its returning veterans. Chapter 1 of section three, "Rejoicing City That Dwelt Carelessly," depicts New York in the moment of mass demobilization in 1919, and provides a narrative that would remain a staple of Dos Passos's view of the war: that it had been an opportunity for colossal American corporate enrichment at the expense of millions of conscripts' lives and liberty. The prose poem at the beginning of the chapter – a device that would eventually inform the Camera Eye sections of *U.S.A.* – relates how "the harbor is packed with zebrastriped skunkstriped piebald steamboats, the Narrows are choked with bullion, they're piling gold sovereigns up to the ceilings in the Subtreasury. Dollars whine on the radio, all the cables tap out dollars."[36] The symbolism is hard to miss: the war's boon to US corporate interests – manifest in the huge transfer of gold reserves from European central banks – has been camouflaged by a nationalistic and idealistic rhetoric. Moreover, in a theme he pioneered in *One Man's Initiation* and would return to in *U.S.A.*, the obscene duplicity of that rhetoric has devalued contemporary language itself (the novel's highly autobiographical character and newspaperman Jimmy Herf ends the novel lamenting "If only I still had faith in words").[37] The contrast in war experience according to social class is dramatized in this chapter by the differences between Captain James Merivale, scion of a prominent New York family, and Joe O'Keeffe and Dutch Robinson, both working-class soldiers. Merivale returns smart, spotless, and decorated with the Distinguished Service Cross; he will soon take up a job in the finance industry secured for him by a friend he made during the war. O'Keeffe and Robinson return on a "snubnosed transport" that "sludges slowly through the Narrows in the rain"; O'Keeffe finds he is syphilitic, and Robinson is forced to turn to crime after failing to find work and going hungry.[38] They return soiled or infected by their experiences, and are superfluous to the postwar economy. At the end of the chapter, a crowd watches a boatload of "reds" being deported, an allusion to the deportation of 249 people aboard the *Buford* in December 1919, many of whom had been arrested during the Palmer Raids of the first red scare. *Manhattan Transfer* therefore unfolded a narrative about World War One that Dos Passos would return to and amplify in the *U.S.A.* trilogy – that US involvement in World War One had delivered the triumph of a business class that simultaneously secured spectacular profits from the conflict, decimated the American labor movement, and cemented a plutocracy. As he would summarize in his biography section of Thorstein Veblen in *The Big Money*, "Veblen still held to the hope that the workingclass would take over the machine of production before monopoly had pushed the western nations down into the dark again. War cut across all that: under the cover of the bunting of Woodrow Wilson's phrases the monopolies cracked down. American democracy was crushed" (*USA* 852).

U.S.A. also went on to criticize the growth of the security services during the war, and the abridgment of free speech caused by the Espionage and Sedition Acts; *1919* features numerous incidences of covert surveillance, brutality on the part of federal agents, paramilitary violence against leftist organizations, and finishes with Ben Compton being sent to federal prison for ten years for violating the Espionage Act. Yet as he moved into his *U.S.A.* trilogy, Dos Passos began to change the architectonics of his fictional form, and also the forces of narrative propulsion, to unfold a broader argument about the politics of American sociality and American subjective experience, and ultimately how the war had been decisive in shaping them.

U.S.A., World War One, and Form

As Dos Passos's novels became more ambitious in scope and broadened their focus to depict what Cecelia Tichi has called a widespread "mix of characters who form an aggregation but not a society," he began to drain his characters of the interiority that had characterized work such as *Three Soldiers*.[39] This feature of his writing regularly drew criticism from critics invested in traditional models of fictional realism, especially by the time of *U.S.A.*; Bernard De Voto spoke for many in faulting Dos Passos's "intention to reduce personality to a mere pulsation of behavior under the impersonal and implacable drive of circumstance," a rendering of character that risked depriving fiction of "its preeminent value – the exploration of individual human nature."[40] Along with the most prominent Marxist theorists of the 1920s and 1930s – Georg Lukács, Ernst Bloch, Walter Benjamin – Dos Passos became interested in fictions of totality, and shared Lukács's view that "the underlying unity, the totality [of global capitalism], all of whose parts are objectively interrelated, manifests itself most strikingly in the fact of crisis," although he differed sharply from Lukács's dismissive view of naturalism and montage.[41] Accordingly, the *U.S.A.* trilogy was his final step in largely ignoring the war's effects on individual psychological experience, especially the experience of combatants (of whom there is only one among the novel's twelve separate narrative characters), in order to prioritize a representation of how the contemporary connective tissues of sociality were both intricately related to the new economic and governmental structures that emerged from the war and were rendered most visible in the global political crisis of 1919.

Part of the formal brilliance of *U.S.A.* was the effort to find literary analogues to these socioeconomic phenomena. This was quickly identified as an elaboration of a leftist politics at the level of form as well as characterization and theme; it became the primary reason he was celebrated as *the* writer of the American left in the early 1930s. By the time of the *U.S.A.* trilogy, Dos Passos's critics on the left – in noticeable contrast to voices like De Voto's – would be enthusing that his innovative fictional models of sociality had managed to transcend the novel's previous commitment to individual, bourgeois, perception – and thereby had initiated the "collective novel," in the words of Mike Gold, capable of presenting a "collective emotion [that] is the new and inevitable hope of the world."[42] Matthew Josephson called *1919* a "Marxist epic," wherein "the hero ... is not a single person, but a great crowd"; and rather than "watching too many disconnected characters and scenes falling apart," the novel was able to interconnect its characters through the force of "the 'collective' character of the various world-historical developments which [drive] the characters of the Dos Passos epic before them."[43] As Barbara Foley has shown, the "collective novel" was an emergent form within international proletarian literature in the late 1920s and early 1930s, and prompted enthusiastic theoretical attention from around the world, attention that often centered on Dos Passos. In 1933, Matthew Josephson could report from the Soviet Union that Shakespeare was the only other foreign writer rivaling him for attention.[44]

Yet, as critics noted both then and now, the "'collective' character of the various world-historical developments" that propel the novel's characters are largely invisible to the characters themselves, who are often beset by atomized loneliness. Such readings recall Fredric Jameson's influential formulation of the shifting perceptions of social space under the emerging conditions of monopoly capital, which saw "a growing contradiction between lived experience and structure, or between a phenomenological description of the life of an individual and a more properly structural model of the conditions of existence," a gap and contradiction that it was the privileged place of what Jameson calls "cognitive art" to attempt to redress.[45] Indeed, Dos Passos identified this as an important feature of modern social experience, wherein "the shape of society is changing so fast that the descriptive and analytical part of the human mind has not been able to keep up with it," a formulation that helps explain why *U.S.A.* has often been seen as an important example of "cognitive art."[46] Foley, for example, in her classic *Radical Representations*, reads *U.S.A.* not merely as grounded in a Marxist view of history but also as promoting a Marxist interpretive *process* at the level of narrative structure, as "Readers who wish to understand the rationale for various characters' presence within a single narrative are . . . compelled to look beyond the 'text itself' – and usually to Marxist class analysis – in order to grasp the text's principle of coherence."[47] Similarly, Michael North sees atomization and isolation bedeviling working-class life in the trilogy, an isolation explored thematically but also imposed formally by the separate narrative sections of the twelve central characters. Yet he is drawn to moments when the trilogy seemingly "violates its own form" through moments of chance meeting, as "In a few cases . . . dislocations [and chance meetings] . . . seem to reveal something else entirely, a hidden order, a truth that is social."[48] Like Foley, he sees political force in these formally disruptive fleeting encounters, for "political insight, both for the characters within *U.S.A.* and the reader outside it, seems to arise from the chance juxtaposition of atomized experiences" that can "[expose] the force that drives the whole."[49]

North's prime example of such a chance meeting unwittingly revealing a previously obscure social macrostructure comes in *1919*, when Joe Williams and Richard Ellsworth Savage meet in Genoa. Both are fascinated by a Standard Oil tanker ablaze at night in the harbor, a blaze so fierce that "you could see the breakwater and the lighthouses and the town piling up the hills behind with red glitter in all the windows and the crowded ships in the harbor all lit up with the red flare" (*USA* 557). Separate narrative sections describe Joe and Dick's meeting, each focalized from their respective points of view. Moreover, this incident is the sole occasion when one of the trilogy's impressionistic Camera Eye sections, which Dos Passos identified as "a safety valve for my own subjective feelings," overlaps with not one but two characters' experience in the narrative sections, as it relates seeing the "ancient ducal city burning"[50] (*USA* 487). This is an unprecedented moment of triple overlap of perspective for the novel, as three separate narratives recount the same events. This singularity briefly and tellingly reverses Dos Passos's customary formal principles of social atomization and interior evacuation, and arguably lays bare some of the mechanisms whereby social connections were forged in the modern world.

What North's interpretation of this moment ignores, however, is that Dos Passos identifies one specific (though habitually occluded) agency and fuel as propelling, structuring, and literally illuminating these social interconnections: oil. Seeing this moment of social connection from a uniquely triple perspective makes this conjunction of characters seem less like coincidence and more like a glimpse of Jameson's "properly structural model of the conditions of existence." This happens because oil in this incident is defamiliarized and thereby rendered conspicuous; rather than being out of sight in storage or transportation, or being consumed in the "invisible" process of internal combustion, its accidental visibility colors the town and landscape anew, with "every façade that faced the sea . . . pink with the glow of the fire" (my ellipses, *USA* 525). Under this glow of spectacular, "external" combustion, we see the details of social reality and social connection uncannily emerge from the darkness, an emergence colored by the light of oil's flammable nature, wherein its capital and political value resides. Yet this sudden visibility of oil and its infrastructure only makes palpable its habitual, yet structuring, invisibility; the tanker is in Genoa to fuel the city and the Italian war effort, as many largely unnoticed tankers would be before and after this blazing aberration. Accordingly, few moments in *U.S.A.* make clearer the state–corporate mutuality that characterized the US war effort, and the interpellation of all of its characters into the systems of mobility and economy that this mutuality produced.

It is this combination of oil's habitual invisibility, its combustibility, and its structural necessity to modern social life and economy that makes it Dos Passos's commodity of choice in delimiting the emergent collaborations between big corporations and the expanding federal state that so frequently govern the lives of his characters. Oil often serves as the fuel for a personal freedom largely understood as mobility; and simultaneously as the instrument of increasing forms of state and corporate control. At the same time, its combustibility and volatility suggest the violence encoded into this system of social and material relations, the latent potential for chemical or social conflagration caused by the conditions of its extraction and production.

Oil and the Petrostate

Before reading these features of the modern politics of oil into *U.S.A.* further, a brief historical digression is necessary to underscore just how dramatically the political economy of oil had changed in these years. In November 1918, the soon-to-be British Foreign Secretary (and former Viceroy of India) Lord Curzon declared that the Allies had "floated to victory upon a wave of oil."[51] The Royal Navy had converted to oil (from coal) as its fuel between 1912 and 1914, in its most expensive building operation ever. Oil had significant strategic advantages: it made stokers obsolete and enabled faster ships with a bigger range that were easier to refuel, all of which gave Britain an edge over the (coal-powered) German fleet during the conflict.[52] The US Navy had also converted to oil before the war, allowing it to project naval power across the Pacific in unprecedented ways.[53] Moreover, it had an advantage the British did not: by 1917, the United States was producing 67 percent of the world's oil, and met 80 percent of the Allies' wartime oil requirements.[54] The war demonstrated the superiority of oil-powered navies, and that oil was vital in the manufacture of modern munitions (toluol, an essential ingredient in TNT, was extracted from oil). It also showed that the internal combustion engine – in trucks, tanks, submarines, ambulances, and motorcycles – was the future of military technology.[55] In consequence, the world's great military nation-states soon determined that reliable access to oil – both in its current production sites and in the areas of greatest geological promise – was a strategic imperative.

In fall 1917, Wilson established the Fuel Administration, and appointed the oil man Mark Requa as the head of its oil division. It liaised closely with Standard Oil of New Jersey – by far the biggest supplier of American oil – for military supplies, and set the pattern of cooperation between government and industry in resource management that would became the modus operandi of US oil policy during the war (in opposition to the hopes of both the secretary of the navy, Josephus Daniels, who had advocated for the navy to control all its own drilling and refining, and also sections of the organized labor movement in oil, who advocated for public ownership).[56] Indeed, this relationship epitomized the "compensatory state" model that historians such as Eisner have argued emerged during the US mobilization, as the inadequacies of an underdeveloped federal state caused the Wilson administration to turn to partnerships with the superior organizational capacities of private industry rather than commandeering or nationalizing their resources. Nationalization, which appealed to other nations, was an option "unavailable in the United States due to a combination of historical, institutional, ideological, and political factors. Most important, in this connection, was the severe disjunction between state and corporate development," especially in the field of bureaucratic systems capable of generating and archiving reliable information about the size and distribution of America's industrial plant.[57] The structure ultimately adopted in organizations such as the multiagency War Industries Board, which relied on governance by dollar-a-year men from America's large corporations and on preexisting corporate organizational and productive resources, assisted large expansions in major US corporations such as Dow Chemical, Du Pont, Bethlehem Steel, and Standard Oil of New Jersey. (The National Petroleum War Services Committee, which advised the Federal Fuel Administration, was headed by A.C. Bedford, Chair of the Board of Standard Oil of New Jersey.) These companies became major recipients of massive federal wartime expenditures, as they were tasked to undertake types of manufacturing or statistical production that were under nationalized control in other belligerent nations.[58] The closeness of this relationship blurred the line between state and corporation, and embedded self-interested, and enduring, corporate representational and informational systems at the heart of governmental organization and spending patterns. The limitations of the "compensatory state" model were obvious when the Federal Trade Commission (FTC) issued a report in April 1918 accusing oil producers and refiners of profiteering, and again raised the possibility of nationalizing the industry; instead, Requa acted quickly to prevent formal proceedings by the FTC.[59]

Toward the end of the war, the combatants scrambled to secure oil resources; and at the postwar peace negotiations, access to oil concessions, particularly those in Mesopotamia, became a central issue. Ultimately, Britain secured a mandate over Mesopotamia after agreeing to share 25 percent of all oil drilled there with France, a deal received with outrage in the United States, which saw it as old-fashioned imperialism.[60] US trade journals such as the *Oil and Gas Journal* published a number of editorials warning of "the British oil menace," and cautioned that without support from the government, US oil companies would never get access to the foreign oil concessions necessary for keeping prices stable for US consumers and ensuring consistent supplies for the military.[61] This fear that the European powers were securing vital strategic interests at America's expense was a factor in the US government's increasingly close postwar relationship with Standard Oil of New Jersey – despite having "busted" the Standard Oil trust only eight years earlier. In 1920, at Standard Oil's fiftieth anniversary celebrations, its president, Walter Teagle, declared that "the present policy of Standard Oil is to be interested in every producing area, no matter in what country it is situated"; and, by the end of the decade, America had secured a large stake in the Mesopotamian fields.[62] The fear that European powers were securing oil interests increasingly framed as militarily "strategic" at America's expense informed the US government's increasingly close postwar relationship with the large oil corporations. As well as rejecting tariffs on foreign oil imports, a policy urged by small, independent US producers, Warren G. Harding's administration became increasingly involved in pushing for US firms' access to concessions worldwide, often with the rationale that reliable supplies were needed for the navy against a backdrop of domestic production scarcity.[63]

By 1934, US companies had gained oil concessions in the Netherlands East Indies, Venezuela, Iraq, Bahrain, Saudi Arabia, and Kuwait; and Standard Oil's adept manipulation of local political forces protesting the British mandate over Iraq had gained it a piece of the Mesopotamia concession.[64] Historians are divided over whether this expansion of Western financial and military power into the Middle East was primarily driven by governments or by corporations. Some see it as an imperialist development, as Western nation-states sought control of vast oil reserves increasingly important to their militaries and domestic economies. Others, such as Timothy Mitchell, have recently argued that companies such as Standard Oil sought these concessions in order to pursue a policy of "managed scarcity," essentially securing these monopolized Middle Eastern concessions only to delay the building of infrastructure and thereby restrict production and keep oil prices (and profits) high. And these corporations secured the necessary military backing of nation-states for the management of those concessions by successfully presenting them to policymakers and the broader public as national "strategic" interests. But, either way, oil companies and states cooperated ever more closely in an increasingly globalized industry that relied on a handful of major players exercising a combination of concentrated military and financial power, a power that, as Mitchell has shown, produced a new politics often inimical to democratized political agency.

Such developments were set against the backdrop of booming domestic demand; the number of automobiles registered in the United States surged from 3.4 million in 1916 to 23.1 million in 1929, with oil consumption rising from 1.03 million barrels a day in 1919 to 2.58 million in 1929.[65] Gas stations became a ubiquitous feature of the American landscape; over 140,000 drive-in stations were built in the 1920s alone.[66] Prominent military figures such as John Pershing publicly argued for the national security imperative of improving America's road network; and a young Dwight Eisenhower participated in a Transcontinental Motor Convoy in 1919 designed to bring national attention to the poor ability of the nation's road infrastructure to support large-scale motorized military transportation. (The convoy took sixty-two days to traverse the country.[67]) Such efforts were influential in securing federal matched funding to assist individual states in pursuing an ambitious program of nationally integrated roadbuilding in the 1920s.[68] The burgeoning road network, however, was mostly funded by gas taxes, whose use was often reserved solely for roadbuilding programs. As Christopher W. Wells has shown, between 1902 and 1927 road expenditure leapt from 2 percent of state expenditure to 27 percent in a system whereby increased road use by motor vehicles led to increased gas-tax revenue, which led to increased spending on roads and thereby further increases in road use – a system "designed explicitly to stimulate near-constant growth in American demand for gasoline."[69] The size and expenditures of the state and oil consumption, then, grew symbiotically together in this period in ways that profoundly shaped both.

Oil and *U.S.A.*

These economic, political, and cultural histories of oil are central to the *U.S.A.* trilogy in three interlocking ways. Firstly, they inform some of the trilogy's most explicit political statements about the expanding American security state and its coeval development with the increasingly globalized ambitions of large, US-based oil corporations. Secondly, oil is central to the characters' mobility and networks of sociality; in a novel marked by social atomization, incidents concerning oil or the oil industry serve as contexts for several of its characters to encounter one another, suggesting that oil is a defining factor in the modern structure of social experience and interpersonal connection. And these connections are specifically multinational; for, as LeMenager observes, "no oil culture can exist without the self-consciousness of the world energy markets and foreign wars that oil sustains, and so ... there can be no 'American' oil novel. Or no national oil novel per se."[70] Accordingly, social encounters orchestrated around the oil industry occur in *U.S.A.* in Mexico, Italy, France, and Egypt, as well as in the United States. Moreover, an expanding road network and the expanding system of federally orchestrated airfields essential for the national airmail system pioneered in the war frequently provide mobility and connection for characters bereft of earlier forms of sociality such as family, religion, or ethnic community. Thirdly, the consumption of oil and especially petroleum becomes an important modality of pleasure in the age of what Dos Passos himself called the "great automotive boom" – especially the pleasures of driving or flying; but it also becomes characters' primary experience of risk and (often catastrophic) accident (*USA* 812). Taken together, Dos Passos's novel suggests that the acquisition and regulation of oil, and the construction of an infrastructure supporting an ever-enlarging oil economy, have emerged as an enormous new function of the federal state at the same time that individuals' understandings of both individuated pleasure and its frequent corollary of freedom from the state were becoming inextricable from petroleum consumption.

1919 dwells most explicitly on the geopolitical dimensions of this emergent petromodern state. Dos Passos had already suggested the necessity of looking at the broader infrastructural effects of the war by locating his characters within the enormous auxiliary agencies of the wartime state rather than within the military itself; Joe Williams works in the Merchant Marine, Eveline Hutchins and Dick Savage work for the Red Cross, Anne Trent works for the Near East Relief, and Moorehouse, Savage, and Janey are attached to the American delegation at Versailles. Throughout the Parisian sections of *1919*, Dos Passos uncovers oil as an increasingly important infrastructural element of national security and economy: he dwells on the strategic importance of oil to the negotiations at Versailles, and its status as a commodity that although extracted, distributed, and sold by giant international corporations is subject to aggressive state acquisition and regulation. (During a tedious press conference organized by Moorehouse during the negotiations, "[w]hen somebody spoke the word oil everybody sat up in their chairs" [*USA* 752].) The biographical sections of the novel are where the state–corporate expansions of World War One are protested most forcefully; the section on Randolph Bourne several times recurs to his phrase that "war is the health of the state," and reports how he was "shadowed by the espionage service and the counter-espionage service" for his antiwar articles at the *Seven Arts* after "the rainbowtinted future of reformed democracy went pop like a pricked soap-bubble" (*USA* 449). Similarly, the section on the House of Morgan repeats the phrase "war and panics on the stock exchange, bankruptcies, war-loans, good growing weather for the House of Morgan" (*USA* 645). Perhaps the two climactic sections of *1919* are the biographical portraits of "Meester Veelson" and "The Body of an American," both of which indict Wilson for the terrifying grandiosity of his idealism. "Meester Veelson" describes how during the war "Wilson became the state (war is the health of the state), Washington his Versailles, manned the socialized government with dollar a year men out of the great corporations and ran the big parade/of men munitions groceries mules and trucks to France" (*USA* 567). And, during the peace conference,

Clemenceau,
Lloyd George,
Woodrow Wilson.
Three old men shuffling the pack,
dealing out the cards:
the Rhineland, Danzig, the Polish corridor, the Ruhr, self
   determination of small nations, the Saar, League of
   Nations, mandates, the Mespot, Freedom of the Seas,
   Transjordania, Shantung, Fiume and the Island of Yap:
machine gun fire and arson
starvation, lice, cholera, typhus;
oil was trumps.   (*USA* 570)

The significance of oil at the negotiation table is also registered in the narrative sections, particularly by Edgar Robbins, Moorehouse's assistant, and the Standard Oil engineer Rasmussen, who are concerned that the United States is being elbowed out of access to global oil reserves. Robbins fumes that "while we sit here wrangling under schoolmaster Wilson, John Bull's putting his hands on all the world's future supplies of oil. . . . They've got Persia and the messpot and now I'll be damned if they don't want Baku" (*USA* 615). In a conversation with Robbins about "Emperor Petroleum," Savage blandly suggests Americans have "plenty of oil at home," but Robbins replies "You can never have plenty of anything . . . You're a young fellow, do you ever have plenty of tail? Well, neither Standard Oil or the Royal Dutch-Shell can ever have plenty of crude oil" (*USA* 664). Robbins suggests here the economics of the marginal revolution, a seminal change in economic theory in the late nineteenth century that (among other things) argued that the value of a commodity was configured less as the labor hours that produced it, or its scarcity, and more by the consumer's belief in the satisfaction it could offer. In an economy where wants became more important than needs, resources became viewed in libidinal rather than instrumental terms, and endlessly expanding desire was key to the liberal economic dream of continuous and limitless growth that typified the 1920s. Robbins' suggestion that insatiable sexual appetite is the most fitting corollary for an oil economy similarly detaches energy resources from the realm of necessity and places them in the realm of desire, foreshadowing how economic models of inexhaustibly proliferating consumer desire would underpin the hubris of the era's liberal economic dreams of continuous growth.

By *The Big Money*, this infinitely elastic demand is enmeshed with the global American security perimeter that limitless access to energy resources necessitates; and these intertwined forces become embodied in the shady figure of Senator Bowie C. Planet. Planet meets Charley Anderson in Washington, DC to discuss military contracts for the Askew-Merritt airplane starter he has designed; Planet is also later involved in negotiations for government concessions for new airfields. Fat, unctuous, and corrupt, Planet first appears in *The 42nd Parallel* as Judge Planet, an "unlucky oil speculator" whose law firm had been involved with what Planet alludes to as "that Colorado trouble" (*USA* 235). This is probably a reference to the Ludlow Massacre of April 1914, when the Colorado National Guard and corporation militia killed a number of striking coal workers and their families, including women and children (*USA* 235). In a meeting with J. Ward Moorehouse in the earlier novel, Planet enthuses that the war is "America's great opportunity," as "whoever wins, Europe will be economically ruined" (*USA* 237). By the final novel, and as his name suggests, his career has ascended in connection with the politics and the economies of planetary violence and military expansion, as he becomes the deal-broker between Charley and the military for government contracts for his aviation technology. He is also involved in the awarding of government contracts for new airfields, a nod to how government subsidies for such construction as a way of facilitating a new infrastructure for the national airmail system were instrumental in the development of the country's civil aviation network.[71]

Planet exemplifies a feature that Stephanie LeMenager has noted about the era of petromodernity, the way that it became inextricable from experiences of embodiment – whether through petrochemical cosmetics, the way human energy was conceptualized, or the way it often produced "abject impurity" within corporeal experience, an affect scrambling divisions between "me/not me, inside/outside, alive/dead."[72] Planet's physically oleaginous nature provides just such abject impurity – in the first few pages of his reintroduction in *The Big Money* he is described solely as "the fat senator" with a voice that "played smoothly in and out of the folds of his chin" (*USA* 946). He takes Charley and Andy Merritt to his home in a "great black Lincoln," a home that "was a continuation of his car, big and dark and faintly gleaming and soundless," commodities that become extensions of his own morbid body but also connote the black and "gleaming" surface of oil (*USA* 947). Moreover, he is identified as homosexual – Dick Savage tells Charley Anderson that Planet "never has women to dinner ... He's got a funny reputation" (*USA* 948). Seth Moglen's suggestion that homophobia in the *U.S.A.* trilogy can be primarily under-stood as a form of "libidinal pessimism" endemic to Dos Passos's views of sexuality is helpful here. Moglen argues that a "psychically underlying, culturally pervasive, melancholic structure of homophobia" is a force that tragically undermines the American labor movement in *U.S.A.*, given Dos Passos's presentation of "American radicalism [having] drawn much of its libidinal intensity from homoerotically charged male bonds"; conse-quently, men in the novel renounce homosocial radical collaboration due to homophobic fears.[73] Planet therefore draws in multiple political trajec-tories – grieving for the failure of radical male homosocial bonding under the sign of homophobia; the complicity of the state in stamping out radical working-class movements, often with murderous violence; the global ambitions and expansions of a mutually dependent federal military and the oil industry; and the way these historical forces become naturalized at the level of bodily experience.

As well as the moralizing of the biography sections, or the outspokenly political characterizations of Planet or Robbins, Dos Passos also establishes a number of more formally based indications of the way the new oil economy structures characters' social and subjective experience. These begin in *The 42nd Parallel,* whose central section focuses on Mexico at a key moment of US involvement in its oil industry. This novel hosts the first moment where one character who has their own narrative section encounters another such character, as Eleanor Stoddard, who at this point has her own decoration business, is introduced to J. Ward Moorehouse, whose house in Great Neck she is contracted to redecorate. Stoddard is first introduced to Moorehouse, a public relations executive Svengali, after he has just "been playing golf and . . . talking about Tampico and oilwells" (*USA* 245). This refers to the so-called Tampico affair and the growing US involvement in the Mexican Civil War, as the government sought to protect US oil interests in Mexico. Soon, oil in Tampico provides the context where the characters Mac, Moorehouse, and Janey Williams first meet. In *1919,* Dick Savage's first meeting with Moorehouse and Eleanor Stoddard comes on the same evening he discusses US oil policy with Robbins (*USA* 664).

As with the Genoa section of *1919,* therefore, oil is often the social context facilitating moments when these focalizing characters overlap into one another's narrative sections, a device Donald Pizer has called "interlacing," a technique he finds "is Dos Passos's most immediate and dramatic means of establishing connections."[74] If, as North suggested, such "interlacing" moments of "chance juxtaposition of atomized experiences" expose "the force that drives the whole," then that force can be read not merely as global capitalism but more precisely as a new governmental and corporate infrastructure devoted to the global extraction and American consumption of oil that was one of modern capitalism's defining structural features.[75] Therefore, in contrast to other oil novels of the period, such as Upton Sinclair's *Oil!* (1927) and John Joseph Mathews' *Sundown* (1934), which observe classic realist principles in following a single protagonist's engagements with the environmental devastation and political corruption inherent in the oil industry's expanding role in American life, Dos Passos's multiple characters with their separate narrative sections facilitate a more complex limning of the patterns of sociability inherent to petromodern society. And a major part of that complexity is how "interlacing" orchestrates the oscillation between oil's invisibility and its visibility, and thereby attends not only to the infrastructure of an expanding "compensatory state" deeply reliant on the globalizing oil industry but to how that infrastructure habitually passes from notice. As Bruce Robbins has observed, "it is not rare for modernism's structural experiments to refer, if that is the right verb, to infrastructure, finding ways to denaturalize and revalue our taken-for-granted conveniences," and here Dos Passos's structural experiment does exactly that.[76]

U.S.A., therefore, uses such "interlacing" to suggest at the level of narrative form that social connections are increasingly facilitated by the infrastructures of oil. Yet, in addition, Dos Passos is frequently drawn to a representational mode Buell finds characteristic of "oil culture" more generally, namely an oscillation between "exuberance and catastrophe," a mode that "materialized as historically specific forms of capitalist triumph and oppression, of environmental domination and destruction, and of human liberation and psychic and bodily oppression."[77] This dichotomized outcome is starkly presented in the final section of *U.S.A.*, as the narrative perspective splits between two characters with polarized relationships to a modern petro-state. One, "Vag," has been brutally forced out of town by "cops and deputies" (presumably under vagrancy laws), and is aching from "the punch in the jaw, the slam on the head with the nightstick, the wrist grabbed and twisted behind the back, the big knee brought up sharp into the crotch." He waits to hitch a ride "at the edge of the hissing speeding string of cars where the reek of ether and lead and gas melts into the silent grassy smell of the earth" (*USA* 1239). The other character is a passenger flying overhead on a transcontinental flight, a flight depicted as a moment of sublime "exuberance" in its ocular mastery of an American landscape, as they pass "tightbaled clouds to westward

[that] burst and scatter in tatters over the strawcolored hills. Indigo mountains jut rimrock" (*USA* 1240). The passenger "thinks contracts, profits, vacationtrips, mighty continent between Atlantic and Pacific, power . . . the macadamed pike, the concrete skyway; trains, planes: history the billiondollar speedup" (my ellipses, *USA* 1240). For Vag, the nexus of state and petroleum is an experience of police brutality and pollution as he stands at the margins of America's transport network, inhaling lead and carbon monoxide; he feels excluded from the "speed" that "ads promised" (*USA* 1240). For the transcontinental passenger, in contrast, the experience of that network is one of smoothness and surfeit, "sitting pretty" in a "soft seat" as the plane makes a "smooth spiral" toward an airfield similar to the Miami airport we earlier saw Senator Planet investing in. The passenger vomits up his steak dinner, but this is "no matter, silver in the pocket, greenbacks in the wallet, drafts, certified checks, plenty restaurants in L.A." (*USA* 1240). This is a familiar dichotomy of leftist caricature, of course – decadent fat cat businessman and hungry worker – but what makes it revisionary is their differential access to speed and the networks that host it.[78] This moment recalls Enda Duffy's two foundational claims in *The Speed Handbook*, namely that "speed is the single new pleasure invented by modernity" and that "the experience of speed is political," claims that derive from the radical novelty of motorized speed, which for the first time allowed "individual people . . . to feel modernity in their bones: to feel its power as a physical sensation."[79] Yet, here, the somatic politics of speed register in parallel but opposed experiences of nausea; the nausea of hunger and inhaling fumes by the roadside for Vag, and of motion sickness for the airline passenger. This closing moment suggests enormous differentiation between the beneficiaries and the bystanders of the "billiondollar speedup," in the literal gap of thousands of feet and hundreds of miles per hour between those with the means to experience speed's "power as a physical sensation" and those without; but it also suggests that even its beneficiaries cannot escape that speedup's deleterious physical effects. Exuberance and catastrophe are experienced differentially according to class, but few can avoid oil's sickening and damaging ramifications entirely.

Dos Passos stresses this point most frequently, however, by rendering the oscillation between "exuberance and catastrophe" a *narrative* form within multiple characters' lives. Specifically, petroleum-delivered speed forms the novel's central imaginary of both exhilarated liberation and catastrophic risk. *The Big Money* often depicts the exuberance (and sensual richness) Charley Anderson experiences flying or driving; in one flight from New York to Washington, "The Askew-Merritt starter worked like a dream. The motor sounded smooth and quiet as a sewingmachine," and when they are airborne, "Even at two thousand feet he could feel the warm steam of spring from the plowed land. Flying low over the farms he could see the white fluff of orchards in bloom" (*USA* 944). Later, in driving from Virginia to Florida:

> Driving down was a circus. The weather was good. As they went further south there began to be a green fuzz of spring on the woods. There were flowers in the pinebarrens. Birds were singing. The car ran like a dream. Charley kept her at sixty on the concrete roads, driving carefully, enjoying the driving, the good fourwheel brakes, the easy whir of the motor under the hood. (*USA* 1070)

Yet Charley dies from injuries sustained in a car crash after racing against a train, a crash that also injures the young woman he was driving with; earlier, his friend Bill Cermak dies in a plane crash. In *1919*, one scene features Eveline Hutchins "driving home with Dirk" and enjoying "the glare of his headlights, the strong leap forward of the car on the pickup, the purr of the motor, his arm around her, the great force pressing her against him when they went around curves" – only for the trip to end with the car "smashed up" and Dirk "bleeding from a gash in his forehead and ... holding his arm against his body as if he were cold" (*USA* 460–461). Anne Trent dies in a plane crash after meeting a French flying ace, having a night of carousing in Montmartre, and driving recklessly through the streets of Paris before going up at daybreak against the advice of the pilot's mechanic. As Duffy points out, catastrophic risk was often the necessary corollary to the exhilaration of driving, whose thrills were both enhanced by the danger it entailed and were often described in explicitly sexual terms. *U.S.A.* certainly confirms the idea that petroculture had thoroughly permeated the discourse and experience of sexuality; in a scene between former Ziegfeld Follies chorine Margo Dowling and millionaire Yale halfback Tad Whittlesea, for example, as they borrow Tad's father's yacht for a romantic tryst in Florida, Tad boasts that "it's a diesel" – to which Margo replies "aren't we all?" (*USA* 994). And even as a youth, Anne Trent understands that motor cars assist her own sexual objectification, a process she wishes she could somehow observe; on the morning of her Commencement, "sitting at the wheel in a fluffy white dress ... she had thought how much she'd like to be able to see herself sitting there in the not too hot June morning in the lustrous black shiny car among the shiny brass and nickel fixtures under the shiny paleblue big Texas sky" (*USA* 577). Yet as well as frequently emphasizing the way, as Duffy suggests, that driving had invaded "the domain of ... sexual lives and [the] very sense of what constituted human energy itself," the many crashes that often conclude *U.S.A.*'s exhilarated moments of driving or flying always reintroduce the social aspect of these activities through the extreme antisociality of violence.[80] Dos Passos therefore encourages us to see a petroculture as fueling not just new experiences of pleasure but also immense bodily damage; this culture is often one that lethally accelerates bodies along and often off the networks of sociality that had been constructed for motor cars and airplanes under the aegis of the state, producing excesses of speed that turn social connection into catastrophic collision.[81] Even as driving was becoming increasingly central to an American political imaginary of the freedoms of liberal citizenship, as Sarah Frohardt-Lane's research shows, the trilogy often turns its most euphoric and thrilling moments of personal liberation and individual control into social and personal catastrophes.

Ultimately, this dynamic allows the reframing of two frequent criticisms of *U.S.A.* across its reception history, namely its defeatism and its anachronism. Dos Passos's refusal to limn feasible options for a more just, equitable, and personally enriching society within the text's narrative trajectories or characterizations was the main reason his communist critics reacted so negatively to the final volume of the trilogy. More recently, Michael Denning has argued that *U.S.A.* has evaporated from the canon less because of Dos Passos's personal political trajectory and more because its mourning for a "Lincoln republic" of small farmers and producers completely fails to account for the racialized and gendered restrictions inherent in the history of US citizenship. This has rendered the text inaccessibly anachronistic for contemporary readers. To explore further, it is worth revisiting Dos Passos's most widely cited formulation of the position of the writer, his 1935 contribution to the American Writers' Congress entitled "The Writer as Technician." Dos Passos likened contemporary writers to technicians, skilled workers whose principal function was "discovery, originality, invention."[82] However, these functions were only accomplishable if writer-technicians could "secure enough freedom from interference from the managers of the society in which he lives to be able to do his work."[83] He concluded that "the dilemma that faces honest technicians all over the world to-day is how to combat the imperial and bureaucratic tendencies of the groups whose aims they believe in, without giving aid and comfort to the enemy."[84] And, indeed, maverick "technicians" such as Steinmetz, the Wright Brothers, Frank Lloyd Wright, and Edison come to feature as heroes in *U.S.A.*'s biographical sections.

Yet perhaps the fatalism – and the anachronism – of *U.S.A.* comes when we realize not only that Dos Passos glosses over how these technicians are embedded within bureaucratic and state–corporate networks of fuel production and distribution, or blinks at their reliance on the transport networks that enable their inventions to function; but that he as a writer-technician shares that unavoidable complicity in his inability to imagine modalities of freedom outside of those networks. Despite his dream of a relative autonomy for artisanal and/or artistic "technicians" in his essay, and in *U.S.A.*'s biographical sections, *U.S.A.*'s narrative sections show a grimmer awareness that when such "technicians" are reinserted in the dense social fabric and networks of day-to-day life such autonomy becomes impossible, even as the allure of it operates as a powerful ideological force. The principal figure here is Charley Anderson, and the novel frequently adopts a tone of liberated exhilaration rather than its usual caustic irony in the moments when he is designing aircraft, or driving on well-paved roads, or flying the machines he has designed. These moments become the novel's acme of individual freedom and liberation, both at the level of imagination/invention and at the kinetic level of self-determined speed and direction. This understanding of driving has been explored by historians of automobility in the twentieth century: for Cotten Seiler, automobility was ultimately a deeply compensatory activity that delivered the experience of freedom and autonomy to modern subjects who had largely relinquished such feelings in increasingly bureaucratized or Taylorized workplaces.[85] Yet driving also necessitated "the construction of an apparatus, consisting of legal, technical, medical, cultural, economic, political, ethical, and architectural/spatial elements, that would simultaneously enable and constrain, cultivate and regulate, *govern* and *license* it."[86] Accordingly, "driving . . . enables an affirmative performance of energy, speed, and motion even as it emplaces the subject in social relations and environments not of her making and decreasingly malleable by democratic, collective will."[87] Driving, then, delivers the thrills of self-determination and agency often by obscuring the thoroughly managed and social contexts that enable it.

U.S.A. indulges the illusion of driving as modernity's quintessential compensatory, liberating, and autonomous activity. But it also breaks it with frequent moments of shattering collision that reintroduce the social contexts of shared infrastructures that make driving possible, including the crashes that Charley is involved with and that kill both his best friend and later himself. This recalls Charles Taylor's decrial of the "dark side of individualism" in contemporary life, a prevalent form of subjectivity that involves "a centering on the self, which both flattens and narrows our lives, makes them poorer in meaning, and less concerned with others or society."[88] Indeed, the novel's breathless representations of individual freedom figured as motorized speed are frequently inextricable from an indifference to the welfare of others, or a refusal to see transport networks as a truly social space. For example, Anne Trent is thrilled at being driven at dangerous speed through the streets of Paris by the French pilot she meets on a drunken evening in Montmartre; she had "never seen such speeding," and is especially exhilarated by his "game of running full speed toward a gendarme and swerving just enough at the right moment." But when she asks him if this isn't too dangerous, he replies "It does not mattair . . . they are . . . ow do you call it? . . . bloody cows" (*USA* 711). *U.S.A.* is ultimately an ambivalent text that dramatizes the thrill – somatic and political – of an anarchistic, individualized "selfgovernment" whose possibilities (in the absence of a viable leftist politics) are figured in the activity of driving or flying at speed. Yet just as there is no technician without a sponsoring corporation, or no internal combustion engine without an oil industry, there is no road without asphalt from the oil industry or the enormous, interlocking system of government and corporate collaboration in funding, construction contracts, and the application of eminent domain statutes. And, increasingly, there was no driving without driving licenses, speed limits, mandatory driving education and insurance, and traffic police. It is this that ultimately renders acts of exhilarating freedom, in a society so closely interconnected and mutually reliant, as fatally antisocial; what looks like exhilarated liberty to Dos Passos's speeding characters is in fact mutual endangerment. Moreover, Dos Passos himself, the "writer as technician," frequently cannot think of freedom or liberation outside of the terms of mobility or technocratic innovation, and demonstrates his awareness of those limits by returning again and again to scenes of the exhilaration of motorized speed that fleetingly feel like freedom but end with brutal crashes. Such analysis prefigures contemporary analyses of the deleteriousness of our current politics of oil; on the one hand, it begins to suggest an environment in which thinking outside of oil in political or material terms has become nigh-on impossible. And on the other, *U.S.A.* demonstrates the consolidation of a disastrous ideology informing oil dependency in the United States, namely the emerging hegemony of "an appearance of privatized command over space and life," a chronically antisocial "petroprivatism" that imagined American life as a series of "singular, heroic, entrepreneurial projects ... only made possible through petroleum products."[89]

U.S.A. stands as one of the indispensable works of US World War One fiction, but largely because it affords so little space to representing combat across its 1,240 pages. By placing *1919* as the middle volume, Dos Passos suggested the war's centrality to the reordering of the global economic order, and to the transformation in how Americans experienced mobility and social interaction. In the burgeoning federal state of 1917–1919, he saw the birth of a government–corporate collaboration in building a "compensatory state" that would become an unavoidable part of national experience – and that helped established a petroculture that would shape most aspects of American subjectivities and lives. The form of *U.S.A.* follows the shape of those corporate–governmental networks that under-pin contemporary life: the huge auxiliary services associated with the US government in World War One, or the way that the infrastructures of oil extraction and petroleum consumption put in place the modalities of how Americans would come into contact with each other and with others across the globe.[90] The brilliance of *U.S.A.* is the way it makes this argument largely in formal terms – through the relation of chapter "inter-lacing" to the oil industry, and through the repeated pattern of exhilarated individual will in the act of driving literally and fatally colliding with the obligations of mutual interconnectedness.

This feature alone should reclaim *U.S.A.* from its consignment as a 1930s period piece, a melancholic paean to a Lincoln Republic of small producers that only made sense in a masculinist, nativist moment of left-wing anguish in the 1930s. Yet there are other reasons too. *U.S.A.* makes visible the often-occluded networks that connect modern societies together in the processes of resource extraction and use, as well as suggests some of the subjectivities that an era of petromodernity might condition. It dispels the common historical narrative that the federal state receded in the 1920s in the face of postwar anti-collectivism and Republican "normalcy," a hiatus bookended by the federalizing impulses of Wilsonian war collectivism and the New Deal. Instead, Dos Passos suggests, the state assumes substantial material, economic, and regulatory form in the enormous transport and fuel net-works that developed in the 1920s and increasingly structured American experiences of sociality, pleasure, and what it was to feel free. It is an early text in asking, for the era of petromodernity, what kinds of liberty are possible in an era of ever-denser social connection, and whether certain technological-romantic appeals to freedom might in fact be recklessly and dangerously antisocial. And, well before the dramatic extension of the

US military footprint overseas to secure oil resources for the United States that occurred after World War Two, it asks us to consider the implications of an increasingly globalized American security perimeter designed in part to protect reliable access to overseas oil for America's military and civilian institutions. Perhaps for these reasons, then, it might be worth reading anew.

CHAPTER 5

Fictions of Rehabilitation
Narratives of Disabled Veterans' Health Care in the World War One Era

In August 1917, *McClure's* magazine published "Efficiency: A Play in One Act," by Perley Poore Sheehan and Robert H. Davis. Set in Kaiser Wilhelm II's private quarters, the drama portrays an encounter between the kaiser and one of his chief scientists; the latter unveils a breakthrough that could win the Central Powers the war. This is "241," a badly wounded German soldier – and their 241st test subject – who is now "fifty per cent. human and fifty per cent. machine," with prosthetic hands, left leg, right forearm and elbow, eye, ear, and teeth.[1] The scientist boasts that "After countless experiments, we can now take a soldier, no matter how badly wounded, and return him to the trenches – a super-soldier – no longer a bungling, mortal man – but a beautiful, efficient machine!"[2] The soldier has supernatural strength and sensory perception – is able to hear at extraordinary distances, is gifted with telescopic sight and night vision, and has teeth that can bite through wire. Hailed as a "triumph over matter . . . the fragment of a soldier reconstructed under the magic touch of Science," "241" has been transformed from "a shattered, bleeding wreck of no value to his country" into "an efficient man."[3] The scientist promises "the restoration of five army corps now immobilized because of missing arms and legs, deafened ears and blinded eyes," and with it, victory in the war.[4] Troubled and fascinated by this "super-soldier," the kaiser requests a private conversation with him. Once alone, "241" accuses the kaiser, and his scientists, of having developed technologies that might increase military efficiency but have increased "human – grief."[5] Invoking God as the supreme arbiter of "efficiency," "241" then throttles the kaiser, describing himself as the "hope – of – the – people." As the scientist rushes back in and the final curtain falls, "241" raises his hands to the heavens and intones, "EF – FI – CIEN – CY!"[6]

Taken as an example of popular US wartime literature, "Efficiency" was fairly unremarkable in characterizing Germans as vain, autocratic, and arrogant, or as willing to sacrifice basic precepts of civilizational humanism to wartime utility. (Indeed, this was why Teddy Roosevelt liked it, praising the play for how it had shown "in a dramatic manner how the Prussianized militaristic autocracy of the Hohenzollerns has turned Germany into an inhuman machine for the destruction of what is highest and best in mankind," one willing to use "every resource of a materialistic science to aid in the wide-spread application of their brutal, treacherous, and merciless world-ethic."[7]) Much anti-German US and British propaganda took this line, and often linked characterizations of German inhumanity to German scientific prowess. Whether in the historical record of the German military's pioneering use of chemical weapons or flamethrowers or in the propaganda science fiction that was such an important part of the cultural landscape of the time, German scientific rationalism was regularly depicted as a threat to social ethics of compassion and sympathy, the politics of liberal democracy, and civilizational achievements in art and culture. Yet the play also participated in a broader conversation about contemporary medicine's ability to rehabilitate the war wounded – a conversation that carried as much force at home as it did when confronting America's wartime enemies. That debate pondered – often anxiously – the ethical and political consequences of rehabilitative medicine's improved ability to return injured men to the battlefront and the workplace, and indeed whether rehabilitation and modern prosthetics might in fact be able to improve on the "natural" body. In the United States, this conversation often assumed typically Progressive dimensions, as some doctors and public health officials expressed an overweening confidence in the capacity of newly institutionalized and professionalized fields to redress long-standing and stubborn social problems. As John M. Kinder observes, "to its most fervent disciples, rehabilitation marked the start of a new historical epoch, one in which disability itself would soon disappear."[8] And such faith in rehabilitation was inseparable from the Progressive emphasis on efficiency, as its "proponents aimed to rid the nation of 'war's waste,' a turn of phrase that referred to the human remains of war as well as to the economic cost that the nation had to endure after the battle was over."[9] A belief in the medical efficacy and fiscal efficiency of rehabilitation became central to the US government's institutionalization of veterans' care during and after World War One, wherein "the magic touch of Science" promised a new contract between wounded citizen-soldier and state under the stamp of the rehabilitation movement. In its positive aspect, this contract promised massive governmental investment in medical and vocational programs to restore wounded men to the "full" citizenship of workplace autonomy and breadwinning, marital domesticity. But it was also a promise hemmed by fears over the potential for state coercion and eroded individual agency embedded within that movement's ethos and institutions. "Efficiency's" nod to Mary Shelley's *Frankenstein* – recently floated as the very first bioethical text – vividly dramatizes the weight of those fears.[10]

"Efficiency," therefore, appeared in a US political landscape wherein wholesale changes were being enacted to the state's involvement in veterans' health care, changes that transformed not only the meaning of being a disabled veteran but the entire nature of male, martial citizenship. Moreover, the new US rehabilitation program was intent not merely on reconstructing soldiers but on the "reconstruction of the public," in the words of one of rehabilitation's adherents, to the new civic ideas that underpinned it. This chapter explores the nature of those changes and the discursive effort at such "reconstruction," particularly the government's promotion of what Beth Linker has called an "ethic of rehabilitation," which stressed both the supreme efficacy of modern rehabilitative medicine and the obligation of wounded veterans to subject themselves to its practices – and the part that literature played in both advancing and questioning elements of that ethic. Indeed, the substantial amount of fiction and poetry that dealt with returning disabled veterans, some written by those veterans themselves, often offered an important counterdiscourse to this "ethic of rehabilitation," and in doing so, offered a public voice invested in shaping the new health care institutions that emerged from the war. These writers treated Progressive rehabilitative rhetoric – which, at its most extreme, promised that modern medicine could make wounded veterans at least as physically capable as they were before their wounding – with frequent skepticism. Authors such as Laurence Stallings, William March, and Ernest Hemingway deflated this meliorist optimism by dwelling on the stubborn and tormenting materiality of the wounded veteran body in pain. Moreover, they constructed a view of pain that saw it as more than merely an unfortunate byproduct of the rehabilitative process, or a barrier that willpower could inevitably surmount; instead, they represented it as centering both the epistemology and the abrogated civic status of wounded veterans. Conversely, authors more aligned with the sentimental tradition, such as Edna Ferber, rejected the rehabilitative ethic's vision of care as occurring in depersonalized, professionalized, and institutional settings to favor more traditional, domestic accounts of wives, sweethearts, and mothers being the best agents in successful recovery. And both sets of writers, as in "Efficiency," worried over the implications of veterans being subject to new levels of embodied entanglement with the state, as advances in prostheses and orthopedic surgery involved disabled vets in unprecedented situations of ongoing state care, often with limited options for refusal. Yet this fiction was not uniformly a Jeffersonian complaint about overreaching government, which saw familial and local modalities of caring for wounded veterans as superior to an overempowered federal medical bureaucracy. Instead, it often sought to intervene in the practice of institution-building at a moment when federal health care and rehabilitative medicine were at one of their most plastic moments.

The Ethic of Rehabilitation and World War One

Confidence in the powers of rehabilitative medicine shaped the Wilson administration's attitude to its long-term responsibilities toward injured World War One veterans as the United States entered the war in early 1917. From the outset, they recognized those responsibilities would be substantial; the record of three years of war in Europe meant the US government well understood that mobilizing an AEF for the western front would mean planning for how to reincorporate hundreds of thousands of disabled veterans back into American society. By summer of 1915 alone, over two million combatants had been permanently disabled in the war. Improvements in various fields – antiseptic surgery, battlefield triage, evacuation procedures, and surgical technique – meant that many battlefield wounds that would have proven fatal in earlier conflicts were now survivable.[11] Such conditions meant that over 930,000 US service personnel had applied for disability benefits by 1923, and over 200,000 returned from the war as permanently disabled.[12]

To tackle this issue, Wilson's government devised the War Risk Insurance Act (WRIA) of 1917. This had two core components; a faith in rehabilitation underpinned both. First, the WRIA sought to break decisively with the pension system the US government had in place as its primary mechanism for supporting Civil War veterans, a system that by 1917 was a byword for bloated government spending and political clientelism. This pension system was (in)famous as one of the world's most lavish state welfare systems; by 1915, the United States had spent more on Civil War pensions than it had on prosecuting the war itself.[13] Subject to increasingly generous eligibility expansions throughout the Gilded Age, the pension system was exploited by the Republican Party to reward one of the most influential lobbying groups of the period, the Grand Army of the Republic, who carried significant political power in the so-called pension belt of the mid-Atlantic and Midwestern states.[14] By 1900, 74 percent of all Union veterans received benefits, and over half of the federal budget went on these pensions.[15] In consequence, it became a frequent target of Progressive reformers keen to reduce budgetary "waste" and eliminate political crony-ism. Accordingly, the WRIA transferred some of this financial burden to the soldiers themselves, linking disability pensions to subsidized insurance premiums taken from their wages.

Second, the new policy embedded the assumption that disabled veterans were obligated to undergo rehabilitative medical treatment and reintegrate into the workforce. As John Kinder observes, rehabilitation was "an integrated program of physical and social reform combining orthopedics, vocational training, psychological counseling, and industrial discipline" that became the cornerstone of how the US government framed its obligations to the disabled veterans of World War One.[16] To put this program in place the government built and expanded hospitals capable of providing rehabilitative care, and extensively refitted Walter Reed (in Washington, DC) and Letterman General (in San Francisco) as its two flagship institutions.[17] By 1930, fifty-eight specialized and general hospitals had been built and placed under the control of the US Veterans Bureau.[18] As both Linker and Kinder observe, this program's "ethic of rehabilitation" was grounded in the hope that "medicine can cure disability and, more important, solve the social problems brought about by a war that funda-mentally disrupts the lives of its citizens."[19] As one hopeful promoter of rehabilitation put it, this would fundamentally redress the civic and financial losses of "pensioning off" veterans – losses borne by both indivi-dual veterans and the public purse – by substituting the chance for full workplace, marital, and civic participation. For if "In past times, govern-ments have found it cheaper to entomb such men in institutions for incurables and in soldiers' homes – to pay them their pensions and forget about them . . . The present idea is that the country owes them more than their pensions; it owes them the fullest possible return to a normal life."[20]

Yet institutionalizing veterans' obligation to undergo rehabilitation also meant "the meaning of what it meant to be both a U.S soldier and a male citizen changed dramatically."[21] Men no longer qualified as heroic simply by receiving a battlefield wound; now, full masculinity was only achievable through a successful return to the workplace, ideally in work that sup-ported a wife and family who stayed at home. Enforced retirement and subsistence on a pension – being a "home slacker," in the parlance of the time – was increasingly seen as infantilizing or feminizing, and certainly as incompatible with full citizenship. The government assumed full respon-sibility for paying for disabled veterans' medical care, providing them with a federalized health care system that continues to this day. Indeed, they were the only social group to see realized the Progressive dream of universal, state-provided health care, as ambitions for more expansive state involvement in health insurance ran aground – stymied by coordinated campaigns by the insurance industry and the American Medical Association to cast such schemes as un-American. (From 1917 onward, this became a hugely effective tactic, as health care reform was linked by these groups to cautionary tales of first Prussian, and then Bolshevik, state overreach.[22]) But in return, the WRIA made rehabilitation mandatory, refusing honorable discharges for servicemen who rejected it.[23] As one proselytizer for rehabilitation put it at the time, "parents, wives, sisters, and brothers of these war disabled boys" might be excused for "sympathize-[ing] with them for past and present discomforts and embarrassments and mak[ing] heroes of them for a time if you must and will." But their ultimate duty was to "discharge your obligations conscientiously by making them, if that is necessary, take advantage of the opportunities afforded by the Government to become self-sustaining, happy citizens of the civilized world they helped to preserve."[24] Under this new ethic, being "self-sustaining" and being a full citizen were now indivisible.

Such arguments took place in a cultural field that did much to promote the "ethic of rehabilitation." Singular examples include the work of Anna Coleman Ladd, an American sculptor who led the American Red Cross's Studio for Portrait Masks in Paris from late 1917 onward; Ladd's team sculpted incredibly lifelike prosthetic tin masks for French soldiers with severe facial injury. Ladd would claim that through the efficacy of these masks, "many of these soldiers have returned back to wife, children or family, slipping back into their former places in society, able to work and derive a bit of happiness out of life"; and the American Red Cross produced a film extolling her work in 1918.[25] More prominent was Hollywood's support of the "rehabilitation ethic," most famously in King Vidor's war movie *The Big Parade* (1925), at the time the highest-grossing movie in history, and which, in the words of Timothy Barnard, broke new ground in Hollywood by creating "a new kind of problematic yet appealing male star portrayed as both romantically desirable and physically disabled."[26] Yet much of the promulgation of the ethic of rehabilitation took place through the kind of public information apparatus of state-funded magazines and publicity bureaus that characterized Wilsonian progressivism. Magazine articles promoting government rehabilitation efforts regularly appeared in the *Ladies' Home Journal*, the *World's Work*, the *Literary Digest*, *Illustrated World*, *Popular Science Monthly*, the *Red Cross Magazine*,

Scientific American, and *Survey*, with many being ghostwritten by the Office of the Surgeon General (OSG).[27] As David Kennedy observes, Progressive modalities for reform hinged on the belief that "social change should come about primarily through education and the appeal to people's enlightened, better selves," a belief that conceived of government "publicity" less as the insidious tool of the state than as an alternative to its most direct methods.[28] And such publicity was frequently housed in government-sponsored magazines that scramble the common methodologies for dividing up the periodical literature of the era's cultural field – whether the content-driven divisions between highbrow, middlebrow, and lowbrow, or the economic divisions between pulp, slick, and little magazine. This meant that titles routinely dismissed as two-dimensional "propaganda" in fact often had a surprising amount of generic and ideological heterogeneity.

This was certainly the case in the most focused and sustained public platform for the rehabilitative ethic, namely the (OSG's) own journal, *Carry On: A Magazine on the Reconstruction of Disabled Soldiers and Sailors*. For ten issues between June 1918 and July 1919, *Carry On* presented a mix of essays, speeches, feature articles, photographs of rehabilitated veterans, fiction, cartoons, and even comic sketches (which frequently drew on traditions of ethnic/racial humor). This mix was "popular in [its] make-up," providing "ideas to the general public as well as the [medical] profession," in the words of the OSG.[29] As Beth Linker has discussed, the magazine was profusely illustrated with cartoons and photographs in order to appeal to illiterate disabled veterans, or those whose first language was not English. And in general, its material envisaged veterans enacting a smooth transition from war disability to home-front industrial workplace and heteronormative romantic and marital success, through the agency of rehabilitative medicine and vocational training. As such, it is the fullest cultural artifact for examining how Linker's "ethic of rehabilitation" became a discourse, an interconnected set of representational, professional, and political practices that consolidated emergent knowledge and belief in the fields of the medical, civic, and social understandings of war injury.

Carry On was no small magazine, although it was a niche one. It published pieces by Woodrow Wilson, Theodore Roosevelt, Samuel Gompers, Charles M. Schwab, and John Galsworthy. From its March 1919 issue onward, the magazine carried as its frontispiece what it called the "Creed of the Disabled": "Once more to be useful – to see pity in the eyes of my friends replaced with commendation – to work, produce, provide, and to feel that I have a place in the world – seeking no favors and given none – a MAN among MEN in spite of this physical handicap."[30] Most of *Carry On*'s pieces contributed to the objectives of this creed: to reject what it characterized as the culture of dependency embedded in the Civil War pension system, and to link full male citizenship and heteronormativity to a full reintegration into the workplace, earning a wage that could support a family and a wife at home. It was full of pieces on what disability scholars term "supercrips," individuals lauded for "triumphing" over disabilities to win extraordinary success. Theodore Roosevelt's journey from "frail" asthmatic child to the "rough life" of his cowpunching, military, and presidential adulthood was enlisted as one such example.[31] So too was the case of Michael Dowling, who lost both legs, his left arm, and fingers of his right hand to frostbite after being caught in a Minnesota blizzard at age fourteen. As the article on him exclaimed, his subsequent life gave proof that "from his neck up a man may be worth $100,000 a year," charting his ascendancy to the positions of bank president, Speaker of the Minnesota House of Representatives, and married father of three.[32] In tandem with this kind of supercrip hagiography, the more extreme of the magazine's editorializing suggested that successful reintegration to the workplace was largely a matter of individual willpower. As editorial team member Herbert Kaufman put it, due to advances in medical technology and the decline in demand for unskilled labor, "the only hopeless cripple is a deliberate shirker."[33] Yet just as important to the magazine as this kind of high-handed exhortation to wounded veterans about their ongoing rehabilitative obligations to their communities were its attempts at "reconstructing the public," in the words of Assistant Editor Arthur H. Samuels.[34] Conceived as an effort to bring "reconstruction and its significance into the American home and American industry," this broader public campaign aimed to efface sentimental discourses of charitable and feminized obligation toward wounded soldiers, and also to discourage well-entrenched practices of discriminatory hiring that tended to exclude disabled men from the industrial workplace.[35] Targeted as much at mothers, wives, and employers as it was at disabled veterans, the magazine boldly imagined itself as in the vanguard of a wide-scale social transformation of attitudes toward war disability and male martial citizenship under the sign of rehabilitation.

Yet even in the pages of *Carry On*, not all authors were ready to entertain such wholesale transformations in the social understanding of disability. In particular, some were loath to abandon sentimental narratives about the potential of feminized, affective care to restore wounded American men.

The lead piece in the October–November 1918 issue, for example, was Edna Ferber's illustrated short story "Long Distance" – quite a coup for the magazine, given that Ferber could legendarily name her own price for her stories from America's large circulation slick magazines at this point in her career, and had just revived her well-known self-made heroine Emma McChesney for a war story in *Metropolitan* magazine.[36] "Long Distance" is set in an American rehabilitation hospital in England, and focuses on the incapacitated Chet Ball, an AEF veteran and brawny Chicagoan whose prewar work was fixing overhead power lines. Having been shelled in battle, his wounded leg has been "mended by one of those miracles of modern war surgery," but he is uncured from "the other thing – they put ... down under the broad general head of shell shock."[37] His chief symptom is memory loss. Chet is put to work at occupational therapy; having made "everything from pottery jars to bead chains; from baskets to rugs," the story opens with him painting a small toy chicken on wheels.[38] And, while "slowly the tortured nerves healed" through this therapy, it does not succeed in restoring his memory, specifically the memory of his devoted fiancée back in Chicago. At the end of the story, as he is read a letter from her by a caring and attentive nurse, he is snapped back to himself by his fiancée recounting their first meeting – when she slapped him for catcalling her from atop a utility pole. In the closing scene of the story, and "between anger and amusement," Chet puts the toy chicken "down on the table none too gently and stood up, yawning a little," exclaiming "That's a hell of a job for a he-man."[39]

While the story clearly praises "the miracles of modern war surgery," it endorses well-entrenched ideas about the gendering of disability and therapy that *Carry On* elsewhere worked hard to overturn. The story mocks occupational therapy as infantilizing and effeminizing – for example, observing that "everything about [Chet], from the big blunt-fingered hands that held the ridiculous chick, to the great muscular pillar of his neck, was in direct opposition to his task, his surroundings, and his attitude."[40] "He-men," it suggests, do not make toy chickens. Such condescension was in sharp contrast to the regular featuring of occupational therapy in the magazine, which was identified as "cheer-up work" with considerable value as the first stage in long-term rehabilitation programs and as a way of lifting ward morale; in 1919, 1,200 women were employed in American reconstruction hospitals as occupational therapists.[41] Other pieces praised it as a way of increasing dexterity and strength in wounded or paralyzed limbs and digits, and as a way of training men in craft vocational skills useful for postdischarge careers.[42] Similarly, the magazine took a stern attitude to the place of feminized "sentiment" in the practice of rehabilitation, often characterizing female compassion and sympathy as hindering wounded soldiers' ability to return to the workforce (see Figure 5.1).

Many of *Carry On*'s pieces outlined women's obligations in the rehabilitation process in similar terms, cautioning them against "too much sympathy of the wrong kind," and asserting that their primary role in the rehabilitative process was not to provide therapy or even compassion.[43] Instead, they could best help a disabled soldier by not only "cheering him during the first stages [of rehabilitation], but in encouraging him to follow patiently and exactly the detail of his training."[44] Indeed, if sentimentality can be loosely identified, in June Howard's phrase, as a moment readers can recognize when "a trope from the immense repertory of sympathy and domesticity has been deployed," post–World War One rehabilitative rhetoric was rigorously unsentimental.[45] The governmental rehabilitation program was critical of domestically based therapy, which its leaders saw as fostering the kind of dependency and mollycoddling characteristic of the Civil War system – a system that, they asserted, encouraged pension-dependent men to languish, unproductively and at subsistence levels, in the family home.[46] The government's rehabilitation program both discouraged excessive sympathy among disabled veterans' wives and mothers and trained its female physical therapists in "scientific charity," which had "little room for 'emotion, sensitivity, and personal connection.'"[47] Accordingly, this created "a complex web in which domestic womanhood was seen as both the enemy and the modus operandi of reconstruction"; while marriage and breadwinning to support a domestic sphere was the long-term goal for wounded veterans undergoing rehabilitation, *Carry On* and similar government organs suggested the affective dynamics of that sphere hindered the efficacy of rehabilitation itself.[48]

Yet writers of popular fiction were less keen to relinquish narratives of the curative agency of women in domestic settings (a staple trope of sentimental fiction) in favor of state institutions whose female employees were encouraged to avoid "sentimental" relationships with their male patients. Instead, fiction writers frequently characterized emotion, sensitivity, and personal connection from sweethearts, mothers, wives, or fiancées as carrying an unparalleled therapeutic value. "Long Distance" is one such example, where the textual reminder of the first physical contact Chet and his fiancée had is enough to fully "restore" him from the amnesias and,

Figure 5.1 Briggs, "When a Feller Needs a Friend," *Carry On* (June 1918), 19

implicitly, the traumas of shell shock. Moreover, Ferber mischievously inserts her own shorthand to signal the story's sentimental coordinates, observing that "a description of [Chet's] surroundings would sound like Pages 3 to 17 of a novel by Mrs. Humphrey Ward," a widely read English author of wartime sentimental and patriotic fiction.[49] Similarly, Zane Grey's fiction – discussed at length in Chapter 4 – regularly disparaged the poor standard of care in veterans' hospitals, and praised instead the therapeutic value of Western landscapes and heterosexual love. Indeed, his work drew on the escalating public scandal during the Harding administration about the ineffectiveness and corruption within the newly fledged system of government-run veterans' medical care. This filled newspapers with stories of impoverished disabled veterans dying in squalid conditions, disgraceful standards at Veteran's Bureau hospitals, fraud and profiteering by the Veterans' Bureau top administrators, and thousands of letters from veterans going unanswered by the Veterans' Bureau.[50] In the *Day of the Beast* (1922), for example, disabled veterans are crowded into shabby hospitals, and beg on the streets, to the shame of what one character calls a "selfish and weak administration."[51] One veteran, with lungs damaged by a gas attack at the front, struggles unsuccessfully to obtain government funds to relocate to a "dry climate, where doctors assured him he might get well," and dies of a hemorrhage in a waiting room of a government office while petitioning for help.[52] In contrast, novels such as *The Call of the Canyon*, *The Shepherd of Guadeloupe*, and *Rogue River Feud* show veterans healed from seemingly incurable wartime injuries by a combination of the therapeutic value of beautiful and rugged Western spaces and the restorative power of romantic love.[53] And in Sinclair Lewis's story "Things" (1919), the cross-class love story concludes as the bourgeois Theo Duke nurses her childhood sweetheart, the working-class Stacy Lindstrom, back to health from seemingly fatal injuries sustained on the western front. As the two meet for the first time since Stacy's wounding, Theo reflects that "Even Red Cross efficiency was nothing in the presence of her first contact with raw living life – most rawly living when crawling out from the slime of death."[54] And ever the writer for arch self-reflexivity, Lewis even has Theo muse that "I've canned the word ... 'sentiment' entirely. But if I hadn't, Stace wouldn't be a bad one to write little poems about."[55] Domestic sentiment, in this story, thereby triumphs roundly over both the discursive registers and the therapeutic efficacy (and "efficiency") of state rehabilitation. In many cases, then, American writers tasked both the new institutions of rehabilitation and the rhetoric of desentimentalization that accompanied them to accommodate the therapeutic efficacy of older locations and languages of domestic sentimentality by depicting the power of the sentimental to heal disabled veterans and subsequently to return them to vocational and marital success.

To chart this is just to see writers of fiction as protecting the kinds of domestic space and agency that had always undergirded fiction's patterns of consumption and marketplace success. It also registered their uncertainty over the affective and narrative coordinates involved in new state-run systems of care and rehabilitation. Literary critics such as Jennifer Haytock, Mark Van Wienen, and Celia Malone Kingsbury have examined how popular wartime US writing during the war frequently identified domestic space as a key location of female agency; fiction and poetry regularly portrayed women's actions to conserve food, knit clothing, or devote money and labor to war charities as capable of reducing geographical and gendered separations between home front and war front. Moreover, as Kingsbury notes, even when therapeutic care was portrayed in more institutional rather than domestic settings, popular writers regularly tied women's nursing to the marriage plot, thus folding rehabilitative care back into the registers of the sentimental and domestic.[56] As Bruce Robbins has argued, the welfare institutions of modern social democracy could only come into being "by taking over some of the functions and responsibilities that used to be seen as natural to the individual and the family."[57] And while Robbins brilliantly charts how the fictional genre of the upward mobility story helped set the discursive ground for that process of transfer, the texts I am examining acted in more cautionary ways to complicate the effort to "rehabilitate the public" that *Carry On* hoped to achieve on the issue of the proper location and emotional register of rehabilitative care. Perhaps, they suggested, sentimentality had an affective and discursive armory that government rehabilitation would do well to deploy.

Rehabilitation and Veterans' Fiction

Popular wartime fiction, therefore, was deeply invested in integrating the sentimental to the professional, thereby endorsing long-standing traditions of the proper locations and affective registers of therapeutic care that had close and mutually nourishing relationships to its own narrative conventions. Yet veterans' fiction had quite different reactions to the ambitious promises of rehabilitative rhetoric and its related institutional practices. Particularly, that fiction homed in on the new rehabilitation program's promise to restore full male citizenship for disabled men. They also questioned rehabilitative rhetoric's account of willpower and discipline triumphing over the purported plasticity of embodied materiality by forcefully identifying the stubbornness of injuries that refused to heal. This strategy was notably deployed by veterans who had suffered injury themselves, and who often spotlighted the most glaring lacuna in rehabilitative rhetoric, namely pain.

The egregiousness of pain's absence from rehabilitative rhetoric preoccupies Ernest Hemingway's major story of rehabilitation "In Another Country," which deals with Nick Adams' time in a rehabilitation hospital in Milan as he tries to recover from a leg injury. This is a story closely informed by Hemingway's own experiences of medical care in Italy after his leg was badly wounded by shellfire and machine-gun rounds while he was delivering chocolate and cigarettes to front-line troops near Fossalta as part of his work with the American Red Cross.[58] In the story, the rhetoric of the medical personnel is at constant, jarring, distance from what we infer to be Nick's embodied experience of rehabilitation, first indicated in his darkly ironic remembrance of the hospital pavilions where "we met every afternoon and were all very polite and interested in what was the matter, and sat in the machines that were to make so much difference."[59] The ambiguity here allows for the sentence to both mimic rehabilitative rhetoric's confident technophilia but also to suggest that the outcomes of rehabilitation were more various and perhaps even disadvantageous than such rhetoric envisioned; exactly *what* kind of difference, and to what object, the machines made is tellingly vague. Moreover, the conditional "were to make" is a substantial diminution of agency from the firmer "made," suggesting that the meliorist medical hopes for the machines were not ultimately achieved. Nick goes on to observe that "The machines were new then and it was we who were to prove them," a swipe at a technophilic discourse that sees patients' primary function as validating the machines, rather than vice versa.[60] As the patients undergo these novel therapies, the doctors in attendance constantly reassure them of the inevitability of their full rehabilitation; Nick's doctor assures him that "You will be able to play football again better than ever."[61] Yet Nick's "knee did not bend and the leg dropped straight from the knee to the ankle without a calf, and the machine was to bend the knee and make it move as riding a tricycle. But it did not bend yet, and instead the machine lurched when it came to the bending part. The doctor said: "That will all pass. You are a fortunate young man."[62] Any detail of the physical sensation this machine causes is forcefully suppressed here by the narrative's focus on the movement of the machine and its smothering continuity with the doctor's voice, yet the pain Nick doubtless experiences in this moment, and which the story fails to narrate, resonates loudly through this glaring omission. More interested in its own techniques than in the experience of the patients undergoing them, rehabilitative medicine emerges here as so enamored of its own rhetoric that it has become indifferent to the embodied experiences it produces. Specifically, rehabilitative medicine's exclusion of pain from its meliorist language, the story suggests, could sometimes be a brutal discursive strategy that facilitated the inflicting of it.

Alongside making palpable the omission of pain from the languages of rehabilitation, a tactic Hemingway's signature prose style was so well suited to accomplish, other veterans' fiction sought instead to spectacularize pain as their mode of rejoinder. This can be seen in William March's novel *Company K* (1933). March served in the Fifth Marines and fought at Belleau Wood, Saint-Mihiel, and the Meuse-Argonne, the three fiercest engagements of the AEF's campaign in Europe, and received the Croix de Guerre, Distinguished Service Cross, and the Navy Cross for Valor.[63] *Company K* is a novel composed of 113 first-person monologues, each delivered by a different member of the company. The novel's time span tracks the company through induction, training, transport, combat, demobilization, and the longer term of how the company's surviving members remember their service. Its final section has several narratives from demobilized combatants relating their stories of reintegrating into civic society. While, for some, this process is smooth and relatively uneventful, this is not so for the veterans physically or psychologically damaged by the war. In Private Walter Webster's monologue, for example, he forces his fiancée to go through with marrying him against her will, even though she is repelled by his badly burned face; in the final scene, their wedding night, she tells him "if you touch me, I'll vomit."[64] Private Leslie Jourdan, although successful in business and happily married, no longer plays the piano, even though his distinguished teacher had predicted he would be "the great virtuoso of [his] day"; for "nothing remains of my left hand except an elongated thumb and two ragged teats of boneless flesh."[65] Other narrators suffer from prolonged post-traumatic stress and experience debilitating flashbacks, as did March himself.[66]

Perhaps the most harrowing monologue by March's disabled veterans, however, belongs to Theodore Irvine. Suffering from a flesh wound in his foot, one that seemed "unimportant . . . at first," Irvine's wound becomes incurably infected and necessitates a foot amputation.[67] In a moment before the development of antibiotics (which essentially ended postoperative gangrene), bone necrosis and continuing infection result in multiple amputations over the course of six years – yet always the doctors were "sawing behind" the "rot [that] crept upward toward [his] thigh."[68] For Irvine, this unhealed wound means that "for ten years I have been like a side of beef on a butcher's block," unable "to remember, now, what freedom from pain is like."[69] March's lingering focus on damaged, and in several cases painfully unhealed, flesh is in stark contrast to the representational choices of *Carry On*, which tended to hide amputated limbs within flowing clothing in its many photographs of veterans making a successful return to manual labor. As Beth Linker points out, this was partly in deference to conventions of propriety at the time, which shied from presenting photographs of limb stumps to the public; but it also stressed the agency of willpower (and Progressive representation) in triumphing over embodied damage.[70] Yet, for March, as in Elaine Scarry's classic analysis, intense pain becomes an omnipresent and all-conditioning force. Irvine's torturing sensory awareness of his own body greatly attenuates his civic, sexual, and vocational agency or interest, in a rebuke to the rehabilitative ethic's positioning of pain as an obstacle that the right kind of willpower could surmount. Not so much a barrier to his civic reintegration, capable of being "overcome," his pain-wracked body often sets the terms and preoccupations of his political subjectivity in ways not so neatly separated from his "real" self. Yet, for Irvine, pain does not – as Scarry claims – annihilate "the objects of complex thought and emotion [nor] the objects of the most elemental acts of perception."[71] Instead, Irvine is as perceptive and articulate about the social and medical discourses of pain that work to exclude him from various forms of community as he is about the physical and psychological dimensions of his own pain. In particular, as Santanu Das has pointed out, pain is often understood as carrying an absolute incommensurability, stretching the limits of empathy or understanding within the medical professionals and loved ones surrounding the patient who are not experiencing pain themselves, and in consequence often fostering feelings of shame or bewilderment among those carers and bystanders.[72] As Irvine states, "My mother and my wife cannot bear the sight of my suffering any more. Even the doctors cannot bear it: they leave overdoses of morphine near me, a mute hint which I shall not take."[73]

Irvine's narrative is an example of how the politics of injury – what it does to subjects' ability to make choices, forge social and intimate relationships, and fully participate within various kinds of community, including the civic community that is the location of citizenship – is at the forefront of many veterans' fictions. As March's account makes clear, those politics were as much located in social understanding of bodies in pain as they were inherent to the injured body; the social configuration of pain as disabling was often just as civically exclusionary as its sensory dimensions. Irvine's doctors can conceive of no other future than death for the body in extreme pain, a choice that Irvine rejects. As Alyson Patsavas observes, such medical and social understandings of extreme pain are part of an "over-determined relationship between disability, pain, and the (supposed) desire to die," an ableism that understands "chronic pain [as] a fate worse than death."[74] It is no accident, therefore, that pain was a word rarely found within *Carry On*'s cheerful accounts of disabled civic enfranchisement – indeed, a concordance analysis shows only ten uses of the word across its entire run. And partly in consequence, pain's insistence, intransigence, and enormous political valence was wielded as a rebuke to such meliorist rehabilitative rhetoric in the fictions of several veterans – many of them disabled – who wrote about the process of coming home, and about the difficulties of reintegration. If the rehabilitative ethic saw the convergence of the prowess of medical science and individual willpower as wielding almost unlimited agency over the wounded body, the foregrounding of pain in veterans' fiction was a corrective reminder of the realities of embodied materiality, and the civic consequences that reality entailed.

Probably the most famous and influential veteran to write on this theme was Laurence Stallings. Like March, he was a veteran of the US Marine Corps Fifth Regiment, where he served as a second lieutenant. At the battle of Belleau Wood on June 26, 1918, while assaulting a German machine-gun nest, he was badly wounded by a machine-gun bullet that tore away his right kneecap.[75] Surgeons saved his leg, but his bones failed to knit properly, and he suffered near-constant pain.[76] In subsequent years, he underwent multiple operations, and had lengthy stays at Walter Reed, but after a bad fall in 1922 his right leg was amputated. Stallings' life's work was deeply conditioned by this experience; he co-wrote the antiwar play *What Price Glory?* with Maxwell Anderson in 1924, which became a smash Broadway hit. He also wrote the screenplay to King Vidor's *The Big Parade*, one of the most successful films of the silent era and still one of the indispensable films treating World War One; its portrayal of an amputee veteran as a romantic lead represented a pathbreaking representation of disability within the Hollywood tradition.[77] In the 1930s, he arranged the images and wrote the captions for the provocatively titled

The First World War: A Photographic History (1933). Replete with grim photographs of the suffering the war inflicted on civilians and combatants alike, this became an influential document in the pacifist culture of the 1930s.[78] Its tone was set by captions that often undercut belligerent, nationalist rhetoric through their jarring and darkly ironic contrast to the photographs they introduced ("Harvest," for example, captioned a photo of a field full of combatant corpses; "Field of Honor" appears below a photo of several dead horses around a destroyed supply train).[79] Yet his most prolonged and significant meditation on the process of wounded veterans returning home came in his only novel, *Plumes* (1924), a semi-autobiographical and harrowing treatment of a veteran negotiating the financial, marital, and physical hardships of rehabilitation. Set primarily in Washington, DC, the novel relentlessly literalizes the question of how the disabled body can negotiate civic space; the pain and difficulty its protagonist has in navigating the governmental buildings of DC becomes the primary mechanism for considering the relation between veterans' disability and citizenship.

The novel concerns Richard Plume, a white Georgian (like Stallings) whose male family history includes veterans of many American wars. Although, as Richard points out, "not one of them ... had anything worth going to war about," "not one of them, in so far as he could manage it, failed to be in the first wave."[80] Most of these Plume ancestors returned home wounded; and despite this recurrent, generational legacy of debilitating injury, as each subsequent war begins Plume men cannot resist the glamor of service. Noah Plume suffers from a bullet wound to the hip and the loss of seven toes in the Revolutionary War. His son, George Washington Plume, suffers an amputation in the War of 1812. His son, Old Hickory Plume, has his arm amputated following injuries suffered in the Mexican–American War. His son (and Richard's father), Zachary Taylor Plume, is denied the chance to serve due to the absence of any war during his young manhood; and his "chief regret was that he had never known the drumming pulse and blanched cheek of the man who feels the hot blast of enemy fire" (*PL* 23). Richard's knee is badly wounded by a machine-gun bullet in France, but the heroism or otherwise of Richard's actions is largely discounted as irrelevant by the novel through its technique of almost entirely eschewing combat scenes. Instead, it is mainly concerned with Richard's return to the United States, his medical treatment at Walter Reed, his profound disillusionment with the war, and his attempts to find work and provide for his newly wed wife, Esme, and their infant son. The devastating allure of martial nationalism and martial heroism is the bluntest of the novel's political messages; indeed, Noah

Plume's decision to extol the nobility of his military service to his sons, and to downplay the pain of amputation without anesthetic, "founded a tradition" that "[drenched] his descendants in blood" (*PL* 13).

Richard's life in Washington, DC unfolds against a backdrop of near-constant pain, as Stallings reminds us on almost every page. Moreover, this pain is not just a barrier to successful rehabilitation and full civic reintegration but is often a function of the rehabilitation program itself. At several times in the novel, Richard's protracted medical care – at one point, the novel ironically mentions the "customary twenty or thirty surgical operations required in such instances" – is contrasted to the amputations his ancestors received (*PL* 83). Indeed, "in another war, Richard would have had the surgeon's louts brace him while he drained the brandy flask and awaited the stroke of the merciful knife and the quick and mad pressure of the amputating iron" (*PL* 71). While amputation is more than once described as quick, painful, decisive, and indeed "merciful," the practice of what military historian Sanders Marble has called "maximalist" medicine at Walter Reed is portrayed as protracted, ineffective, and torturous. This "maximalist" approach was adopted by the army in 1918, whose official definition of rehabilitation announced that "Physical reconstruction is the completest form of medical and surgical treatment carried to the point where maximum functional restoration, mental and physical, may be secured."[81] For Richard Plume, this maximalism means that one should "trust no surgeon . . . to amputate anything he can work on," even if those surgeries are ineffective in eliminating pain or restoring greater mobility (*PL* 240). The physical exhaustion of multiple surgeries, lengthy stays in hospital, unhealed wounds, and the constant pain from the cumbersome brace Richard wears to support his injured knee present maximalist rehabilitation as far from a smooth process to "maximal functional restoration." Instead, maximalist medicine in *Plumes* becomes an extended, torturous bodily entanglement with an army medical system too enamored by the promises of its rehabilitative ideals to fully acknowledge the protracted agony this overweening confidence could inflict on its patients.

Indeed, rehabilitation is represented as both an embodied and a discursive system that Richard confronts at every turn. The iron brace designed to support his damaged knee, Richard is assured by "the orthopedic men at Walter Reed," is "the key to unlock the world denied him nearly three years" (*PL* 95). When he first puts it on, the slogan "this brace would carry a man to his work" appears in the narrative, in a voice seemingly unattributed to either Richard's interior narration or the third-person narrator, and which we thereby attribute to a discursive rehabilitative system rather than any individual speaker (*PL* 96). The personified agency attributed to this device in this phrase is amplified to absurdity soon after, when the brace is described as a "magic carpet which was to bear the lame prince from the tower" (*PL* 96). A devastating irony is soon revealed as we learn "within her heart, Esme had been crushed by those first, staggering, bear-like steps" (*PL* 96), and soon, the brace is causing "jangling whole discords of pain" and its supporting chamois ring "seemed rimmed with fire" (*PL* 106). Rehabilitation overinvests the brace with an agency it cannot deliver; and it does so through an intrusive and buttonholing rhetoric that intrudes on Richard and Esme's daily language and life in ways similar to the brace itself. Moreover, the rehabilitation program brackets the pain that Richard, in his daily life, finds to be the brace's singular distinguishing feature. Rather than making Richard a "man," completely reintegrated into normative workplace and domestic masculinity, its torturing cumbersomeness makes him both animal ("bear-like") and effeminized (his wife chides him that he is "through with these little courtesies ... your leg means much more to us both" when he offers to take out the trash, *PL* 192). The brace cannot "carry" him anywhere, and as well as its cumbersomeness and painfulness, the novel frequently stresses its inert heaviness, its inorganic and ill-fitting distance from organic fluidity and capability. Such descriptions reject the "technofetishism" that often "tends to transfer agency ... from human actors to human artefacts" in writing that not only deals with prostheses but expands material prosthetics into more ambitious, expansive metaphorical uses.[82] Rather than an enabling extension of his body, the brace is rather a painful and unwieldy superfluity, which Richard removes at any given opportunity.

Pain reaches its most central place in the novel, however, when Richard is hospitalized following a bad fall. He thinks about pain as a "centrifugal force that had its center in the body of Richard Plume," where even a movement of a "thousandths of an inch" can cause him to be "arrested by an iron barb that transfixed his right knee and carried a terrible message along the flank of his hip, across the hip to the center of his back and over the left shoulder and into the skull, exploding a star-shell in the base of his brain" (*PL* 241). In contrast to rehabilitative medicine carrying him forward to a more successful future, and outward into the social world, therefore, the pain it cannot cure draws him backwards to the originary moment of this pain (the "star-shell" he watched as he lay injured on the battlefield) and inward to his own interior agony. Once stabilized, he wonders if he could devise "some unit of measurement for pain; some method by which one might accurately measure the kilowatt hours of flow in each waking hour" (*PL* 249). Of course, pain can never be translated into the language of rationalist objectivity; its absolute incommensurability and interiority forecloses it forever from quantitative evaluation. Plume's consideration of it as an energy force, with measurable "flow," ironically gestures at the limits of rehabilitation's rationalist and efficiency-focused approach. The absurdity of his rumination is that pain is nontranslatable, nonconvertible, and unquantifiable, and therefore highly resistant to any kind of objective measurement. And while literary critics such as Tim Armstrong have discussed the centrality of metaphors of the electrified body to the modernist literary imagination – the "body electric" of electro-vitalism readable in Whitman, but also Ezra Pound, Theodore Dreiser, D.H. Lawrence, William Carlos Williams, Dora Marsden (and we could add Jean Toomer) – this imagination is usually social, as the body plugs into communal networks of desire, politics, and information.[83] In contrast, in metaphorizing pain as electricity here, Stallings imagines a closed-circuit body, alive with the intensity and energy of electricity but with no outlet, relay, or network beyond itself – and thus highly resistant to the rehabili-tative goal of transforming physical energy into remunerative labor.

Finally, Richard's pain only subsides once he finally receives an amputa-tion. On seeing him after the operation, his wife notes that "his face was peaceful," and "his mother had said that with the loss of the leg had gone the discontent, and the poison it had been secreting into his blood-stream" (*PL* 333). The language choice is deliberately ambiguous here: Richard's "discontent" is both physical and political, an unease with both the policy of "maximalist medicine" and the physical torment it delivers. The severance of his leg is also, in an important way, a blissful severance from a torturous, embodied intimacy with the state, materialized through its policy of maximal rehabilitation. Imagined here as a cruel, protracted, intrusive, and overambitious program enacted on a recalcitrant body whose pain it largely ignores, rehabilitation stands in stark contrast to the amputate-and-pension system that served his forefathers. Their embodied relationship to the state quickly over, Richard's ancestors could comfor-tably physically remove themselves from the institutions of government and "romance about [their] wounds," as his father-in-law puts it, safe in a domestic space of nostalgia where governmental intrusion was restricted to a monthly check (*PL* 81). Severing relations with both the diseased leg and with the institutions that failed so painfully to rehabilitate it, Plume's reversion to this earlier model of governmental welfare is typified as a blessed release. Pain, then, operates in *Plumes* as the counterweight to the technophilia of the rehabilitative ethic's faith in the agency of prosthetic devices, and its aligned rationalist ambitions to imagine the wounded body as a machine subject to strict laws of efficiency. Indeed, elsewhere Stallings explicitly faulted magazines like *Carry On* for this approach, pouring scorn on what he called the "uplift magazines" that started to appear while he was in "an amputation ward," and that "were at pains to uplift soldiers who shed a leg or two for the cause of Liberty Bonds."[84]

Laurence Stallings' *Plumes* and Adjunct Agency

Pain in *Plumes* is therefore effectively the medium among which all other events take place, coloring and shaping all moments of Richard's life. And, indeed, Richard's (and Stallings') standpoint epistemology of pain delivers a complex account of its shaping of perception and quotidian experience, as well as its intersectional relationship to other aspects of his subjectivity – including, most obviously, gender and race.[85] This civic and epistemological exploration of pain is what, in part, makes *Plumes* more complex than a novel of despair and retreat, one that valorizes the "simpler" medical techniques of yesteryear while raging against the new languages and institutions of rehabilitation. Instead, the novel holds a broader ambition to trace the nature of an agential disabled citizenship in 1920s America; if the war was disillusioning, and rehabilitation misguided, nonetheless Richard remains optimistic about the possibilities of an empowered state and curious about his role within it. In this, the novel reveals ambitions to reform institutions of government care, rather than to retreat from them forever. The most obvious mechanism for exploring this issue is Plume's desire to live in Washington, DC. While the Plume family have relatives in the small-town South willing to help support them – and even as Richard has a teaching job waiting for him there – he initially refuses to move back and "romance about his wounds," intent on remaining in Washington. As he explains to his son, "before I creep home for good I'm going to find out why this thing happened to me and see to it that . . . you will keep those two little kneecaps of yours all through life" (*PL* 79). From the outset, Richard's reason for staying in Washington is framed as an exercise in civic education, an attempt to find out "why this thing has battered us all," as he seeks not only to understand the causes and effects of America's entry into World War One and the peace negotiations that followed but, in a broader sense, to triangulate his position as a disabled veteran in a postwar civic order (*PL* 163). As Lauren Berlant has noted of the genre of the pilgrimage-to-Washington narrative, "Washington tests the very capacity of anyone who visits there: this test is a test of citizenship competence."[86] Yet *Plumes* twists this convention by establishing such a "test" as testing both Richard *and* Washington: the novel narrates the story of Richard's own evolving civic competence and understanding but also tests how competently the city manages to extend the ideals of citizenship embedded in federal law into the quotidian experience of civic belonging for disabled people. Stallings limns an abrogated, intensely embodied, and painful experience of citizenship for disabled veterans, but one that nonetheless has significant possibilities for agency within a modernized republican tradition that venerates civic service within a state apparatus identified as the indispensable actor in Progressive reform.

That Richard's relation to citizenship is completely changed from his prewar identity is established early in *Plumes*, which begins with a striking tableau of Richard's naked, unwounded body showering under a standpipe in Paris before his unit departs for the front. Both the local charwomen and his commanding officer are erotically captivated by this sight, "struck by the boy's physique, which at that time was a beautiful thing. Flat hips, and shoulders of a Rodin mold, with a shock of burnished hair topping a wild, happy face" (*PL* 4). Just after this, Richard breaks a black Senegalese soldier's thumb in a fight over Richard's insistence that Senegalese troops stay out of his unit's railway carriage because they are black. He is also heckled by one of the charwomen that "Eh Monsieur ... vous êtes plus grande" (*PL* 7). This vignette serves to identify Richard as what Rosemarie Garland-Thomson has called a "normate" body, "male, white, perfect in health and physical attributes, a standard that almost everyone fails to meet but nevertheless informs our assumptions about the body and how it should function in the world."[87] Replete with gendered, heterosexual, and racial privilege, his is a body whose racial and sexual power is on unabashed display. This is evinced by these twinned acts of segregationist racial violence and sexual exhibitionism, which both assert an identity-based right to dominate public space. Indeed, Richard even expects his naked body to serve as an emblem of military, but also racial, rank to the Senegalese soldiers, assuming "that his glistening shoulders asserted by Nordic magnificence the Sam Browne and Golden Bars of their vested rank" (*PL* 6). This assumption suggests that Richard imagines his sculpturesque, naked, male white body contains all the necessary cultural information to convey to all those around him his absolute centrality to, and mastery of, social and civic space; and historically speaking this assumption was absolutely correct.

This opening vignette frames the remainder of the narrative as one of loss, the loss of the social and civic privileges that adhere to this type of body – constructing a "story of national injustice on grounds of a defamed white manhood," as Jonathan Vincent puts it.[88] (Indeed, this was recognized by the novel's earliest reviewers; as one tellingly and bluntly put it, "Plumes is the story of what the war did to a young Anglo-Saxon and his wife," written by a "well bred normal young American."[89]) These "normal" (or "normate") privileges are not just the birthright of a white, middle-class American heterosexual male but are also connected to a kind of martial citizenship Kimberly Jensen has identified as a powerful model of exclusionary citizenship in the period, when "political authority, which . . . included leadership, office holding, and the vote, was tied by many Americans to [a] militarized civic role."[90] Plume experiences his losses of privilege in gendered and racial terms, as he is "reduced" to the second-class citizenship status of women and African Americans. As already noted, he finds his inability to do certain kinds of domestic tasks – like taking down the trash – as feminizing. And he recoils at being placed in a racially unsegregated ward at Walter Reed, which was one of the few military institutions of the time that did not strictly segregate according to race.[91] When he is returned to Walter Reed, on the one hand he is happy to see a familiar face in the "South Carolina mulatto" Lieutenant Jackson, whose damaged lungs force him to be hospitalized every winter for emphysema. Yet despite his outward friendliness, and even as Jackson coaches Plume in beadwork as the two do occupational therapy together (Jackson uses his "racial consciousness" to produce beadwork designs "savage in their effectiveness"), Plume's racist antipathy persists (*PL* 263–264). As the narrator reflects, "Even in the midst of Jackson's aid he longed to be away from the Negro. The prejudice of color was unreasoningly deep in him" (*PL* 264–265). During this convalescence, he vows to keep Esme away from "the vulgarities of the life he must lead," which presumably include the "vulgarity" of this unsegregated ward (*PL* 263). As we shall see, the attenuation of Plume's sense of citizenship is expressed in primarily spatial terms in *Plumes*. And one of the most pointed senses of spatial disfranchisement he experiences is a new inability to choose racially "uncontaminated" living spaces, spaces that can confirm the "inegalitarian ascriptive" traditions of American citizenship that so often restricted full civic belonging to white Americans only.[92] As well as living in unsegregated hospital wards, he and his family are forced into squalid, cramped accommodation in Washington, DC, similar to the apartments that housed many of the new African American migrants then coming to the city in the Great

Migration; and Esme is sexually harassed at the local market by an Italian greengrocer (*PL* 117). During a conversation about the Civil War, Esme ruminates on their family situation as one akin to racial bondage, likening the "Two of us cooped up here ... [to] Slaves ourselves ... You crippled and broken ... I broken with you" (*PL* 197). If, as many scholars have observed, African Americans and the disabled have often been discursively linked within a politics of abrogated citizenship – as "disability has historically served as a justification to deny the privileges of citizenship to ... African Americans" – *Plumes* demonstrates that this is a two-way connection, as disabled bodies are couched within a framework and a spatial logic of racial inferiority as part of their exclusion from full rights.[93]

While living in unsegregated spaces is one of the main ways Plume comes to understand the new and diminished citizenship he now occupies as a disabled person, the physical hardship he experiences in navigating the civic monumentality and bureaucratic architecture of Washington, DC is another. Stallings wrote about this transformed experience of urban space in an essay entitled "The Whole Art of a Wooden Leg," a wry piece that criticized the way disability was customarily treated in rehabilitation magazines like *Carry On*; while such magazines were heavily reliant on "supercrip" narratives of amputees overcoming their disability to succeed in business, they never treated "the bits of daily deftness that diffuse into and color the complexion of life."[94] That is, he felt these stories ignored how amputation changed the quotidian experience of mobility in a contemporary urban environment, and urged accounts that described "crutchful Theseus, entraining, not to slay the Minotaur but to catch the Bronx express."[95] Couched in a darkly ironic tone, the essay begins to fill that gap by offering tips on how amputees with prostheses can safely ride elevators, attend crowded theaters and football games, and cross busy traffic intersections. The latter is depicted as akin to a blood sport, in affording amputees "all the thrills of those gentlemen who play polo and thus arouse their atrophied senses of self-preservation. His heart is beating fast, a joyous tom-tom of fear and exhilaration, as the switch of a fender brushes his coat."[96] The experience of daily life in the city for people with prosthetic legs is often one of discomfort and danger, the essay suggests, and requires the acquisition of a whole new set of sensory and motile skills – a crip "daily deftness" that remakes the city from an alternative, disabled perspective. This is the experience that Plume faces, but this time without the comic overlay of Stallings' irony. The novel is full of both the motile techniques of "daily deftness" Richard develops to ensure his mobility and descriptions of the pain he experiences as the social environment fails to accommodate his injury. He is in agony when catching a crowded bus, due to his inability to find a seat where he can get his leg brace comfortable; and he is accused of sexually molesting a young woman when his braced leg rubs against hers. Standing at work, and then taking the journey home, is so exhausting that by the time he arrives, he has to take the stairs to their apartment one at a time, with his wife's help. And, later, in walking home because they cannot afford a taxi after watching a play, he falls on thick ice on a sidewalk and shatters his knee. If, as Emily Russell has argued, "national calls to liberty include a belief in freedom from excessive demands of the body," meaning "the fullest access to citizenship depends on mastery of the physical," then Plume's body's "excessive demands" remove him from full access to citizenship.[97] Indeed, at one point he bleakly acknowledges "I am cerebral from now on," excluded from embodied pleasures such as running or walking in the woods (*PL* 79). But this exclusion is enacted not solely by Plume's body, but by its interaction with the built environment and transportation systems of Washington; he is disabled less by his leg than by the way the design of the city's architecture and transport systems refuse to accommodate this damaged body. This bars him "from full citizenship because [his body does] not conform with architectural, attitudinal, educational, occupational, and legal conventions based on assumptions that bodies appear and perform in certain ways," as Garland-Thomson puts it.[98]

This point about how built environments abrogate citizenship for disabled veterans is emphasized by the embodied difficulty Plume experiences in navigating specifically *governmental* spaces and architecture, and also by the physical pain he experiences when visiting several prominent memorials to key moments in the history of the nation-state. The job he finds such discomfort in commuting to and from is at the Department of Agriculture, a building with halls that seem, to him, like "wide, dark steppes," expansive and gloomy spaces that are painful for him to move around (*PL* 107). He limps around a chaotic Veterans' Bureau, an institution held in extreme "contempt and loathing" by the other veterans he meets, during a frustrating and lengthy visit to try to secure a pension for a wounded veteran whose case has been lost in a disorganized maze of bureaucracy (*PL* 291). And the family visit Mount Vernon and Arlington Cemetery, where he feels similar discomfort even as he conducts lengthy political discussions with Esme and his co-worker and friend, Gary, who was also debilitated in the war. That the men struggle to physically inhabit the architecture that governs and memorializes the modern American nation-state signals the embodied unease these men face in occupying civic membership of that state. Civic belonging in *Plumes*, therefore, is a relentlessly embodied concept that is consistently outlined in relation to a series of state institutions – the Department of Agriculture, the Capitol, the Veterans' Bureau – which in abstract or rhetorical terms nominally serve disabled veterans but whose architectural and design practices effectively exclude or marginalize them from quotidian access, and thus, in a broader sense, from full citizenship. This is emphasized when Plume attends Harding's inauguration in 1921, as he struggles to find a comfortable place in the crowd; his "knee was on fire" and he frets "shifting his weight from bad knee to aching arch and back again ceaselessly" (*PL* 222–223).

Moreover, during this episode, the novel emphasizes the limitations that disability effects on full citizenship by co-opting Woodrow Wilson as a disabled war veteran. We learn that Esme "looked upon the President's long illness exactly as though it had been passed lying in a cot at Walter Reed hospital with a wound chevron on the coat sleeve hanging above the bed" (*PL* 216). This perspective was common at the time. Following Wilson's catastrophic stroke of October 1919, which left him paralyzed and partially blind, the Disabled American Veterans of the World War elected Wilson an honorary member for life, describing him as just as much a "casualty of the war as any doughboy wounded on the battlefields of France."[99] And on Wilson's death in 1924, the genteel poet M.A. De Wolfe Howe elegized him as "the known soldier," "mortally stricken in the long-drawn fray."[100] Significantly, *Plumes*' focus on Wilson at Harding's inauguration, the moment when Wilson transitioned from being president of the United States to becoming a private citizen, frames this change not as one from a position of executive power to one of civic normality but as a move from life to death. As the family watches him emerge from his car to enter the capitol, they see him as follows: "Dragging his leg with the skipping oscillations of the paralytic, his long, invulnerable jaw set in a speechless cast, Wilson shuffled through the portal and out of life" (*PL* 220). On the one hand, this follows the widespread "sacral" tradition of literary representations of US presidents that Sean McCann has identified, a tradition with Lincoln as its most powerful avatar and that "by joining oratory to sacrifice ... suggested that the president transcended a political realm characterized at its most essential by conquest and force when, by assuming a willingness to suffer and die, he transcended the role of commander-in-chief to assume that of national poet."[101] Indeed, an adoring Esme calls him "the greatest man in the world," and that "next to Jesus Christ, the Son of God, he had best impressed the ideals of human brotherhood into permanent literary form" (*PL* 216, 221). Yet this moment is *not* his death, which would come in 1924 (and which the novel clearly foreshadows), but rather a civic death as he is "shuffled out of life" not only by the loss of his executive power but by the disablement caused by his impairment. Such civic death, here, is equated with silencing, a silencing of particular significance as this "portal" between one political role and another transforms the world's most famous and consequential orator – a man whose innovations in public speech did so much to transform the institution of the presidency and the nature of American political language – into a "speechless" figure.[102] If Wilson had framed the awesome expansion of executive power that characterized his presidency as a fully nationalized "instrument of democratic community," which positioned him as "the simultaneous expression and servant of a popular will," then his silencing, here, suggests the power of embodied impairment to exclude, as it removes even him from participation in the "national voice."[103] As much is suggested by the bitter empathy Gary and Richard express for Wilson's physical pain and impending marginalization as they claim him as one of their own – a man with "the pain of the world revolving about his axis of personal agony," as Gary puts it (*PL* 221).

The novel's framing of disabled citizenship as a form of civic death, enacted through Gary and Richard's decentered relation to moments of civic ritual, is also established when Richard, his young son Dickie, Gary, and Esme visit Arlington Cemetery, which is preparing for the funeral of the Unknown Soldier.[104] During the visit, Gary and Dickie peer into the open grave, and Dickie becomes frightened by the prospect that this will be his grave as a casualty of America's future wars. Critics usually focus on this aspect of the scene as the novel's most powerful antiwar statement, its fiercest riposte to a culture of male martial nationalism that has ensnared every generation of Plume men in a history of death and injury and stands ready to enroll Dickie, its youngest member, in the wars to come.[105] Yet it is also clear that this moment is one where Gary ponders his own civic death, and sees the tomb as a reminder of his own interment and permanent separation from a full and enfranchised American life as a result of his war disability. As critics such as John Kinder have noted, World War One veterans – both disabled and not – frequently had antagonistic relationships to traditional forms of memorialization like monuments or statuary, which "tend to inhibit public recognition of disabled veterans' ongoing struggles."[106] Indeed, in contrast to the considerable annual publicity accompanying the Armistice Day memorial service to the nation's Unknown Soldier was the fact that by the early 1930s "the forgotten disabled doughboy had become something of a stereotype in American popular culture."[107] As early as 1922, the American Legion editorialized about the "regiments of the forgotten," disabled doughboys shuttered in insane asylums and poor quality hospitals "whose only duty has been to keep out of sight."[108] In 1933, the National Commander of the Legion used his address at the graveside of the Unknown Solider to highlight the neglect of disabled veterans, venturing that "We say that the Unknown Soldier, if he could speak, would ask our government to show compassion and mercy upon the comrade who may have fought by his side" and "who now is unable to care for himself, and who asks the government to protect and administer to him in his time of greatest need."[109] Around the same time the popular lyricist Billy Rose used the same trope of the Unknown Solider speaking in rebuke from the grave, and asking

> 'Are my buddies taken care of?
> Was their victory so sweet?
> Is that big reward you offered
> Selling pencils on the street?
>
> 'Did they really win the freedom
> They battled to achieve?
> Do you still respect that Croix de Guerre
> Above that empty sleeve?[110]

Wounded veterans and their champions, therefore, often found the hyper-visibility of the Unknown Soldier an effective foil to dramatize their own stories of material hardship and civic invisibility in a postwar order that often failed to recognize and adequately support them. The true "unknown soldiers," these claims implied, were those still alive and struggling for existence at the margins of American life, and Gary's bitterness at the grave's edge is replete with this kind of identification.

Such searing scenes of marginalization, bureaucratic failure, and painful civic exclusion through pain would seem to cast *Plumes* as exactly the kind of disillusioned and disenchanted "lost generation" text that it has, in fact, often been taken for, whose sole politics consists in a rejection of institutional politics *tout court*.[111] Indeed, Jonathan Vincent has recently argued that *Plumes'* politics is one of retreat, as Richard "longs finally for the simpler certitudes of nineteenth century agrarianism, for retreat to the 'woods and sleepy towns' as refuge from the racial, urban polyglot."[112] Yet this picture is complicated by *Plumes'* insight that the state is constituted by multiple separate institutions, with often overlapping or conflicted programs and agendas, making the state a haphazard and uneasily aggregated force rather than any kind of monolithic and unidirectional one. As Harold Laski noted of wartime Washington, each government department was "dominated by the eager determination to assert its own personality," and contained "its own rules, its own filing systems, its own special method of hierarchical control"; as such, "you search in vain for unity of purpose; government nowhere seeks nor displays it."[113] Accordingly, even as Richard and Gary launch scathing critiques of US foreign, military, and rehabilitative policy, and experience painful modalities of marginalization that decenter them from the martial male citizenship they enjoyed before their wounding, they work to construct forms of civic agency within other institutions of the state. They do this primarily in their jobs at the Department of Agriculture, and their enthusiasm for this work is the clearest example of their investment in the efficacy of the Progressive state and their sense of capability within it. As Gary puts it,

> if you consider Washington in terms of the White House, Capitol, State, War and Navy and all that rigmarole, you get it in a bad light. You'll conceive of your government in terms of political tricksters, country jesters, drooly-mouthed orators, social posturers, Messiahs, correspondents. The only government amounting to a whoop is in the background . . . We – you and I . . . are the real government. If we say that such-and-such will eradicate spore-bearing bacilli . . . By God, no farmer will tell us we are about to propagandize him. He'll listen to the remedy. If old Dr. Kibbe in there warns wheat growers that a certain rust will kill their profits, you don't hear some cross-roads diplomats crying referendum. You see, we'll be in the minority for a hundred years or so. We're the infants just yet. Take us a hundred years to overthrow the work of Hamilton and Jefferson. (*PL* 124)

Elsewhere, he boasts that Kibbe's expertise "is responsible for certain thousands of acres of winter wheat that has meant life to certain thousands of farmer folk" (*PL* 156). These statements are endorsements of the Progressive faith in the ability of professionalized expertise, housed in state institutions, to deliver rationalized, reformist progress. (Indeed, Gary's critique of both Hamilton and Jefferson, his regular critiques of political appointees, and his call for an enlarged civil service clearly echo similar policy positions in Herbert Croly's Progressive manifesto, *The Promise of American Life*.) Such an endorsement also affords Gary and Richard a place in a modernized iteration of the republican tradition of citizenship in the United States, a powerful ideal often posed against the liberal tradition as one of the two dominant modalities of citizenship in US history, and which Rogers M. Smith has articulated as valuing "a public morality of civic virtue, of services and sacrifices [performed] on behalf of the common good – even if this means the abandonment of many personal aspirations and 'liberal' private pursuits."[114] For Gary and Richard, that enfranchising "public morality of civic virtue" takes place first within the military and then within their work at the Department of Agriculture. That Gary's enthusiasm for a governmentality of scientific expertise in his work at the Department of Agriculture stands in contrast to the novel's hostility to those same principles at work in the WRIA rehabilitation program only indicates the way the novel imagines the state as a self-contradictory, messy amalgam of often insular institutions with little unidirectional or consistent method or politics. Moreover, that the men find a home in this relatively "forgotten" portion of the state – what Gary calls "background" government, their poorly paid appointments at the precarious whim of political appointees – clearly overlaps with the pre-carity of their relation to citizenship as well.

Moreover, once Richard leaves this job, his next one is working on a magazine with remarkable similarities to *Carry On*, entitled the *Wounded Doughboy*. Not government-funded, it is nonetheless "devoted to sending wounded men back to the land," and is filled with "tables of information for mutilated men who contemplated being farmers" and "photographs of Canadian and Australian and French and Italian farmers standing in the midst of ripe wheat and cornlands, steel arms and legs akimbo with prosperity" (*PL* 270). This was a clear echo of a similar focus in *Carry On*, which sought to promote agricultural labor for wounded veterans as a way of avoiding the more unpredictable labor markets of urban, industrial work, and which in consequence often featured photographs similar to the one Stallings describes here (see Figure 5.2). In order to write for the paper, Richard needs to take additional steps in his civic education, spending "days in the alcoves of the Congressional library" trying to "grasp the significance of the thousand schemes politicians and patri-ots had devised for reclaiming the disabled man for the land" (*PL* 288–289). While often deflating the relentless optimism and boosterish tone of magazines such as *Carry On*, then, Stallings' refiguration of it in the *Wounded Doughboy* makes clear his sense that press coverage of public policy concerning disabled doughboys was important, as was journalistic advocacy for their welfare. Moreover, it is here that Richard and Stallings' vocational choices for exercising a decentered republican citizenship overlap, as Stallings himself worked at the *Washington Times* and the *New York World* throughout the immediate postwar period.

If we return to "The Whole Art of a Wooden Leg," we see, essentially, a manifesto for a disabled citizenship aesthetics that articulates both the abrogations and the power of such decentered citizenship. The title alone

Figure 5.2 "Back Home," *Carry On* (June 1918), 5

has a punning duality, for on the one hand the essay is a call for a more representative and accurate artistic depiction of the day-to-day experience of being an amputee, one that faults current literature on this topic – what he calls the "five-foot shelf of ambulatory Iliads" – for failing to provide quotidian details of life with what he calls the "unsatisfactory adjunct to locomotion."[115] In these terms, a new "whole art" would enlarge the sphere of disabled representation to cover – as he goes on to do, at length – the discomfort facing amputees in their navigation of everyday social and built environments. But the designation of "whole art" also takes the process of learning to live with an amputation as akin to an art, as a set of methods and techniques for how to cross a road or place your body in a crowd, for example, which take ingenuity, practice, and embodied skill in order to be fully effectual. The "whole art" of a wooden leg, therefore, is both aesthetic and motile, a set of representational and embodied techniques. And the combination of enlarged representation and special, embodied knowledge that this "whole art" contains makes it a signal claim for a position of "entitlement, obligation, and belonging" that disability scholars have outlined as the key coordinates of an enlarged conception of citizenship, beyond strict legal codifications.[116]

If this essay was the manifesto, *Plumes* is the novel that delivers on it, as Stallings shows the embodied difficulties of disability simultaneously with Gary and Richard's work to reconfigure their political subjectivities into ones of "adjunct" civic agency (to paraphrase Stallings). They do this partly by doing work for the government that aids technocratic programs of agricultural reform, and partly through journalism that closely monitors and seeks to shape the legislative process surrounding veterans' welfare. Through being framed as an experience of partiality and loss, this civic agency becomes more informed and critical, and thus stands in definitional contrast to what Lauren Berlant has influentially called "infantile citizenship" – a model that "frequently seems a bad thing, a political subjectivity based on the suppression of critical knowledge and a resulting contraction of citizenship to something smaller than agency: patriotic inclination, default social membership, or simple possession of a normal national character."[117] Instead, Gary and Richard occupy something similar to what Emily Russell has called "savvy citizenship" in *Plumes*, as the men are fiercely critical of Wilson's foreign policy even as they hold out hope for an expansion of the technocratic managerial state in matters of economic, agricultural, and educational policy (at one point Richard wistfully observes that "perhaps there'll be a Secretary of Education in the Cabinet some day" (*PL* 130).[118] This decentered, but perceptive and engaged, model of agency and therefore citizenship is different from both the "disillusioned" and disengaged political subjectivity so often connected to the lost generation *and* the narrative of citizenship promulgated in magazines like *Carry On*, which often sought the diminution or even erasure of disability as the precondition for full male citizenship. Instead, *Plumes* suggests, although the American state was characterized by a grossly inadequate set of practices for reenfranchising its disabled veterans, the best way for veterans to address this was through close engagement with – and perhaps even working within – the very institutions that constituted that state, especially in the "background" pockets of hospitability that allowed them to do meaningful, republican civic work.

Of course, the novel does not deliver this message with any kind of triumphal or pat kind of narrative reversal or resolution; the scenes of embodied discomfort, and the resultant civic marginalization and figural death that Richard experiences, are never bracketed or presented as a character-building set of obstacles gloriously overcome. The adjunct agency he finds is always partial, and usually painful. Yet it works within a broader context of the multiple fictional reactions to the rehabilitative ethic that I have been considering in this chapter. Few of these various fictions resolutely rejected the new rehabilitation program; more commonly, they urged more complex accounts of how and where care took place, and sought more embodied, experiential accounts of what it meant to suffer injury and receive medical treatment. Indeed, these fictions were not merely critiques or rejections of rehabilitative institutions but attempts to provide those institutions with more supple and sophisticated ways of understanding the experience of being a patient within an institution, or how, in fact, the work of those institutions could be distributed across other social locations. This explanation accounts for the fact that a story like "Long Distance" can appear in *Carry On*, and why disabled veterans like Stallings could produce a searing indictment of the rehabilitation program while simultaneously expressing cheery confidence in the ability of the government to enact positive, technocratic agricultural reform. (And, indeed, there is some evidence that the institutions themselves were aware of this fictional input; excerpts from *Plumes* dealing with occupational therapy, for example, were included in the *American Journal of Physical Medicine and Rehabilitation* in 1925; and it was one of very few novels reviewed in the *Medical Journal and Record* that year.[119]) The fiction of rehabilitation is an attempt to understand a new state institution and also an attempt to shape it, and often presents a rich and complex example of how authors often characterized as in recoil from the Progressive state in fact sought to mold its new practices.

Conclusion

Nine years after the publication of *Plumes*, Laurence Stallings was again at the center of a debate over how to represent the Great War, and how that project related to the politics of the welfare state. In a famous exchange on the pages of the *New Republic*, New Dealer Archibald MacLeish and communist fellow-traveler Malcolm Cowley debated the merits of Stallings' recently published photo collection *The First World War*. This exchange occurred against the backdrop abroad of Hitler's recent rise to near-absolute dictatorial power in Germany, and at home against the first year of FDR's presidency, with its unprecedented peacetime federal interventions – including the passing of the National Industrial Recovery Act, the creation of the Civilian Conservation Corps and the Federal Emergency Relief Administration, and the birth of the Tennessee Valley Authority. Stallings' bleak and provocative title – commonly regarded as the first use in print of the term "the first world war" – oriented much of the discussion. MacLeish, who had served as an artillery officer in the war, argued that Stallings, in the service of an understandable but overly dogmatic antiwar agenda, had failed to present the "human war" of "parades, speeches, brass bands, bistros, boredom, terror, anguish, heroism, endurance, humor, death," a version of the war amply present in *Plumes* and Stallings' hit play *What Price Glory?* Instead, MacLeish charged Stallings with having depicted "a very impersonal and terrifying war" largely geared to forestalling another worldwide conflict rather than representing accurately the last one.[1]

In contrast, Cowley, who had driven ambulances on the western front in World War One, was more supportive of Stallings' vision and its contribution to the nascent 1930s peace movement. Admonishing MacLeish that "it is time for us to admit ... that all of us fought in vain," he suggested "it is time to inscribe at the entrance to every veteran's graveyard and over the tombs of all the unknown soldiers, They died bravely, they died in vain."[2] Mired in the Great Depression, Cowley suggested not only that if soldiers had fought "for Liberty, Democracy and the fourteen points, they fought for abstractions now more deeply buried than all the dead at the Argonne," but that capitalist oppression in America would have looked little different if Germany had won; for "Would it matter now if we were paying tribute to the Allgemeine Electrizitats Gessellschaft instead of General Electric? – to Fritz Thyssen instead of Mellen and Morgan?"[3] Against this historical landscape, the only salient question for artists representing World War One, for Cowley, was "what are you doing to prevent [another World] war before it is too late?"[4]

It was readily apparent that this debate was as much about the merits of the long arc of the liberal-democratic Progressive tradition (and the pragmatist philosophy that informed it) whose major achievement in the United States would be the welfare state then taking shape, as it was about how one should responsibly remember World War One. The two did not really differ on the political narrative of the postwar world; MacLeish concurred with Cowley that fighting the war had delivered no discernable political, social, or economic benefit to the United States. But he did disagree on the nature of political agency, suggesting that the particularities of individual experience within the war mattered – a heterogeneity disproving blanket assessments, like Cowley's, that the war had a singular experiential meaning. He concluded by wondering whether "is it perhaps conceivable that to die generously and in loyalty to the believed-in cause is not, regardless of the success of that cause, to die in vain?"[5] For Cowley, this was little but sentimental, bourgeois subjectivism, deploying liberal bromides that had kept a plutocratic order in place, flimsily posed against the "objective" collectivist perspective of Marxism and the absolute necessity of a robust antimilitarist commitment. Yet MacLeish's liberal individualism found an unlikely ally, and its fullest political extrapolation, in an essay by Kenneth Burke, who reflected on the *New Republic* exchange in his "War, Response, and Contradiction." Noting that "feelings of horror, repugnance, hatred" are themselves "extremely militaristic attitudes," he wondered "if, by picturing only the hideous side of war, we [might] lay the aesthetic groundwork above which a new stimulus to 'heroism' can be constructed," a stimulus that could ultimately serve to whip up enthusiasm for war rather than dispel it. In contrast, he wondered whether MacLeish's preferred option – presenting a "picture of war as thoroughly human" – might instead "serve conversely as the soundest deterrent to war?"[6] Burke went on to suggest that representing such a "human war" might "really serve to promote, not warlike zest, but a *cultural* approach toward the question of human happiness, a sense of critical appraisal, and incidentally, a realization that the purposes of humanity might be best attained through the machinery of peace."[7] Representations that thought about the multiplicity of experiences in war, that captured not only its horrors and heroisms but also its banality, including its presence within the politics of quotidian experience, might therefore be more of a cultural bulwark for the peacetime liberal progressive state than an indictment of it.

MacLeish was correct to suggest that this kind of "human war" – multifaceted, complex, and irreducible to singular political or emotional interpretations – was the kind of war Stallings had presented in *Plumes*, just as it was the kind of war found in Stevens' "Lettres d'un Soldat," Willa Cather's *One of Ours*, and even Dos Passos's *U.S.A.* And Burke was right to suggest that a sense of "critical appraisal" was the political upshot of this approach, a sensibility that might simultaneously neutralize some of the absolutist and emotional appeals of militarism while also making suggestions for how literary work might provide a "cultural approach" to progressive governance, what Burke called "the machinery of peace." A majority of the works considered in this book undertook a similar line in representing the war – they were equivocal, often self-contradictory, experimental, and marked by neither a sense of disillusioned withdrawal nor a recourse to radicalism as the proper political response to the war's unprecedented effects on American society and institutions. Frequently, those works wondered whether the wartime state would bequeath powers and capacities that might assist the "machinery of peace," even as they quailed at the effects of that power in the intensities of the wartime moment, both in France and at home. Nor was such equivocation a sign of political quietude or of fuzzy political thinking; it was a foretaste of the structural contradictions of the liberal capitalist welfare state itself that would become so palpable in the 1930s. Indeed, Burke would class the awareness of such contradiction – which, in his example, preserved elements of plutocratic injustice and violence within the shell of gradualist reform – as the curse of liberalism; for liberals (and even communists) within that system were "half the time advocating reforms when they know that reforms interfere with fundamental change."[8]

Most of the authors in this study agreed that liberal statehood was characterized by multiple such inconsistencies, inconsistencies that were arguably the determining feature of modern American citizenship. For example, Dos Passos, as well as the editors of the *Little Review* and many writers deploying the form of the wartime letter, highlighted how the freedoms of American liberal democracy were rarely freedoms from the state, but rather had often been essentially produced by the state. Most of the writers in this study also resisted a politics of exteriorizing the state, of seeing it as always faceless and elsewhere; instead, they often sought to locate individual agency (and responsibility) for the production and actions of the state within the lives of "ordinary" characters. Authors such as Stallings and Dos Passos were highly attuned to the compensatory nature of statist innovation, its propensity to develop institutions to ameliorate the damage or losses its own processes had inflicted elsewhere. The vision of the state these authors presented was not only authoritarian and centralized but deeply embedded in the texture of daily life, dispersed in its relations of power, and mixed in its effects. It was this vision of the state that would resurface in the New Deal, and in many ways remains in place today. As MacLeish, Cowley, and Burke understood, World War One had defined the experience of citizenship for their generation, a generation who would build and arbitrate the mature welfare state in the United States under an administration that had learned its statecraft in the Progressive experiments of World War One. And as writers, they understood that the literary culture of that war had a long legacy for forging the social compact of the welfare state, and for rendering that state available to the cultural imagination.

To observe this is in part to echo Perry Anderson's idea that the audacious experiments of modernism are inseparable from a moment of radical technological and political contingency. For Anderson, modernist aesthetics were enabled by a unique historical juncture when a host of possible futures were available for how the technologies of the second industrial revolution and its close interrelation with state organization and power might shape people's lives. While Anderson ignores US modernism entirely in his essay, his contention that modernism arose in "the space between a still usable classical past, a still indeterminate technical present, and a still unpredictable political future" holds true for many of the writers considered in this book.[9] What the state would become in the United States – whether its dominant characteristic would be the new and ambitious state-run provision of social welfare, or rather the authoritarianism of the Wilson era, or rather instead a fluid and constantly negotiated compact between citizens, corporations, and central government – was far from clear. Aligned with this contingency was the fact that the state was a growing presence in some novel places in the 1920s, particularly the increasingly sophisticated alchemy of new technologies and state innovation within the conjoint project of infrastructure, a project that, as several recent

literary critics have begun to explore, scrambles any easy binaries
between coercive versus progressive effects.[10]

This particular contingency, and the new nature of how and where
the state would be encountered, prompts a number of political and
cultural observations. For one, they undermine the still common idea
that the 1920s represented an interregnum of recoil against the
Progressive state, a decade poised between the two statist pinnacles of
World War One and the Great Depression. The large-scale technological systems of the Post Office, the Veterans' Bureau, or the gasoline
and automobile industries embedded the state at intimate levels of
everyday life for Americans in novel ways throughout that decade,
ways that had deep connections to the war. This was the understanding
of American political life that Walter Lippmann would memorably
define in 1929, as he outlined a situation where "as machine technology
makes social relations complex, it dissolves the habits of obedience and
dependence ... it diffuses the experience of responsible decision
throughout the population."[11] Consequently, "real law" in modern
society was "neither the accumulated precedents of tradition nor a set
of commands originating on high which are imposed like orders in an
army upon the rank and file below"; instead, "the real law in the
modern state is the multitude of little decisions made daily by millions
of men."[12] Certain modernist literary forms, such as free verse and the
"collective novel," as I have discussed, were imagined as well-fitted to
registering these simultaneously political and technological developments. Conversely, the postwar regional novel would often take exactly
the idea that political agency was quotidian, decentralized, enacted in a
diffused and multiple "experience of responsible decision," as central to
a vision of citizenship that often resisted more top-down and univocal
forms of political and cultural discourse. Of course, it is hard to imagine
Lippmann writing such a sentence in 1917 or 1933, when "set[s]
of commands from on high" had very much the feeling of "real law."
But his idea that the experience of citizenship would be inseparable from
"the multitude of little decisions made daily by millions of men" would
obtain even in the coercive and centralized nature of US political governance in 1917–1919, and would be embedded in the American literature
stamped by the experience of that time.

To recognize this is not merely to replace the idea that "writers and
intellectuals of the twenties opted to leave history behind in order to
focus on the inner workings of the human psyche and purified aesthetics" with the notion that the Progressive project continued to be

powerfully influential in the 1920s, a claim long accepted by intellectual historians (and more belatedly by literary ones).[13] It is to see the very nature of the political in American society as transformed in the decade. The convulsive debates over, and changes to, the nature of American citizenship that roiled the war years left an indelible cultural stamp. And as the federal state expanded throughout American society in highly diffused but also highly palpable forms of technological mediation, authors strove to both represent its new features and powers and understand the new forms of political relation and identity it bequeathed. This was not merely a process of acculturation and acquiescence. The American literature of World War One registered the terrifying and iniquitous outcomes of expanded federal power – its insistence on a nationwide ideological homogeneity that often brutally suppressed dissent or even debate; the readiness with which it not only pandered to and fueled nativist and racist elements in American life but codified these ideas into American governance in deeply harmful and enduring ways; and its permanent expansion of a shadowy surveillance apparatus that would so often undermine the rights established in the constitution to some of the century's most important radical movements. Yet, again and again, authors showed the state as permeable, malleable, and formed in the processes of quotidian life – and as deeply interwoven with modern experiences of both pleasure and intimacy. In so doing, they often challenged characterizations of the state as solely an externalized and domineering force dictating from afar, and also queried any possibility of individualistic separation from it. For its openness to demotic agency was the corollary to its inescapable structuring of everyday life.

In closing, it is worth returning to the ruminations, in *Plumes*, on the value of what Stallings' character Gary calls "real government" – what a federal bureau of education might accomplish, for example, or how the expertise of the Department of Agriculture means "life for thousands of farmer folk."[14] Written by a man who had endured years of agonizing pain from fighting a war that so badly disabused the lofty goals articulated by American political leaders to help bring the United States into the fight, this continued faith in progressive governance is salutary. Perhaps especially so for a contemporary moment when the democratic welfare state is under attack from both right and left – where "government is not the solution to our problem, government is the problem" in neoliberal orthodoxy, and where one of America's leading left intellectuals can pronounce that "social democracy is in our time irretrievably bankrupt," so much so that "all states are failed states, very much including … the United States."[15] World War One laid bare the perils of an empowered federal state in many ways hitherto unparalleled in American historical experience. Yet the belief of so many authors covered here that the state was open to the agency of ordinary people, and continued to be the best vehicle for collectively addressing the "purposes of humanity," is worth heeding.

Notes

Introduction

1. See, for example, his poetry cycle in the July 1919 edition of the *Liberator*, which includes poems such as "The Little Peoples," "A Roman Holiday," and "If We Must Die" (vol. 2, no. 7: 20–21); and his novel *Home to Harlem* (1928), which deals with an African American serviceman who goes AWOL in protest at his demeaning treatment in the Services of Supply in Europe.
2. Christopher Capozzola, *Uncle Sam Wants You: World War I and the Making of the American Citizen* (Oxford: Oxford University Press, 2008), pp. 46–48.
3. Claude McKay, *A Long Way from Home* (1937) (London: Pluto Press, 1985), p. 9.
4. Capozzola, *Uncle Sam Wants You*, p. 48.
5. McKay, *A Long Way from Home*, pp. 5–6.
6. Herbert Croly, *The Promise of American Life* (New York: Macmillan, 1912), p. 117.
7. W.E.B. Du Bois, *Darkwater* (1920) (New York: Dover, 1999), p. 38. As Robert H. Zeiger notes, Wilson's order in December 1917, creating the United States Railroad Administration headed by William McAdoo, "consolidated terminal facilities, coordinated traffic and routing, dipped into the federal treasury to improve rolling stock and equipment, and satisfied the restless railroad unions with generous wage settlements" (p. 71). This consolidation successfully eased the 1917/18 winter crisis in the transportation of fuel and materiel in the United States. See Zeiger, *America's Great War: World War I and the American Experience* (Lanham, MD: Rowman and Littlefield, 2000).
8. The scholarship on this relationship is huge; but important studies include Paul Fussell's *The Great War and Modern Memory* (Oxford: Oxford University Press, 1975); Eric Leed, *No-Man's Land: Combat and Identity in World War I* (Cambridge: Cambridge University Press, 1979); Trudi Tate, *Modernism, History and the First World War* (Manchester: Manchester University Press, 1998); Santanu Das, *Touch and Intimacy in First World War Literature* (Cambridge: Cambridge University Press, 2006); Margot Norris, *Writing War in the Twentieth Century* (Charlottesville: University Press of Virginia, 2000).

9. See Stanley Cooperman, *World War I and the American Novel* (Baltimore: Johns Hopkins University Press, 1967), p. 33. See also James Dawes, *The Language of War: Literature and Culture in the U.S. from the Civil War Through World War II* (Cambridge, MA: Harvard University Press, 2002), pp. 75–106. Pearl James's *The New Death: American Modernism and World War I* (Charlottesville: University Press of Virginia, 2013) offers a more recent take on this approach, seeing "modern, mechanized mass death as one of the signal preoccupations and structuring contexts of canonical American modernist writing" (p. 2). However, as Keith Gandal has recently discussed, many of the "lost generation" authors did not serve in military roles because they could not pass newly meritocratic procedures of physical assessment necessary for obtaining commissions adopted by the US Army in World War One, procedures that enabled many immigrant men to obtain commissions in a way unthinkable in the more patronage-driven army of earlier eras. This rendered these authors more of a "lost out generation," as Gandal terms it, motivated to write their war novels "not so much, as the usual story goes, by their experiences of the horrors of World War One but rather by their inability in fact to have those experiences" (p. 3). See Keith Gandal, *The Gun and the Pen: Hemingway, Fitzgerald, Faulkner, and the Fiction of Mobilization* (New York: Oxford University Press, 2008).

10. The AEF suffered 50,402 battlefield deaths and 63,114 noncombat deaths; many of the latter occurred in the influenza pandemic of 1918–1919. 204,002 servicemen received non-mortal wounds. See www.dmdc.osd.mil/dcas/pages/report_principal_wars.xhtml. In contrast, the French suffered 1,384,000 war dead; the British 743,000; and the Germans 1,800,000. These figures do not count civilian casualties, which in some nations were huge; around 750,000 German civilians died of starvation as a result of the Allied blockade of shipping. These figures are also minimum estimates. See Martin Gilbert, *The First World War: A Complete History* (New York: Henry Holt, 1994), p. 541.

11. A provocative exaggeration on the dust jacket of Christopher Capozzola's *Uncle Sam Wants You.*

12. Sean McCann, "The Presidency: Woodrow Wilson and the Reinvention of Executive Power," in Mark Van Wienen (ed.), *American Literature in Transition, 1910–1920* (Cambridge: Cambridge University Press, 2018), pp. 341–353, 346.

13. See Marc Allen Eisner, *From Warfare State to Welfare State: World War I, Compensatory State Building, and the Limits of Modern Order* (University Park: University of Pennsylvania Press, 2000), p. 13; and Gary Mead, *The Doughboys: America and the First World War* (London: Penguin, 2000), p. 358.

14. Mead, *The Doughboys*, p. 13.
15. Jennifer Keene, *Doughboys, the Great War, and the Remaking of America* (Baltimore: Johns Hopkins University Press, 2001), p. 2.
16. David M. Kennedy, *Over Here: The First World War and American Society* (New York: Oxford University Press, 2004), p. 118.
17. Jonathan Vincent, *The Health of the State: Modern U.S. War Narrative and the American Political Imagination, 1890–1964* (New York: Oxford University Press, 2017), p. 51.
18. Mead, *The Doughboys*, p. 358.
19. Michael Szalay, *New Deal Modernism: American Literature and the Invention of the Welfare State* (Durham, NC: Duke University Press, 2000), pp. 2–3.
20. John Dos Passos, "The Backwash of Our First Crusade," in *The Theme Is Freedom* (New York: Dodd, Mead, 1956), pp. 1–37, 1.
21. Patricia Chu, *Race, Nationalism and the State in British and American Modernism* (Cambridge: Cambridge University Press, 2006), p. 2.
22. Bruce Robbins argues the necessity of "rescuing Foucault from his admirers," who too often rely on an "easy or populist antistatism"; instead, he urges us to recognize him as a "sometimes reluctant but always valuable ally in the 'reformist' project of defending and extending the welfare state." *Upward Mobility and the Common Good: Toward a Literary History of the Welfare State* (Princeton: Princeton University Press, 2011), p. 92.
23. Matthew Hart and Jim Hansen, "Contemporary Literature and the State," *Contemporary Literature*, 49.4 (2008), 491–513, p. 493.
24. Keene, *Doughboys, the Great War, and the Remaking of America*, pp. 3–7; for the role World War One veterans played in the drafting and passage of the GI Bill, see pp. 205–214.
25. Kimberly Jensen, *Mobilizing Minerva: American Women and the First World War* (Urbana: University of Illinois Press, 2008), pp. 165–166.
26. Chad Williams, *Torchbearers of Democracy: African American Soldiers in the World War I Era* (Chapel Hill: University of North Carolina Press, 2010), p. 7. See also Adrienne Lentz-Smith, *Freedom Struggles: African American Soldiers and World War I* (Cambridge, MA: Harvard University Press, 2011).
27. See Steven Trout, *On the Battlefield of Memory: The First World War and American Remembrance 1919–1941* (Tuscaloosa: University of Alabama Press, 2010).
28. See Capozzola, *Uncle Sam Wants You.*
29. Gerald Gunther, *Learned Hand: The Man and the Judge* (New York: Knopf, 1994), p. 156.
30. Capozzola, *Uncle Sam Wants You*, p. 8.
31. See Szalay, *New Deal Modernism*; Michael Szalay and Sean McCann, "Do You Believe in Magic? Literary Thinking after the New Left," *The Yale*

Journal of Criticism, 18.2 (2005), 435–468; Robbins, *Upward Mobility*; Lisi Schoenbach, *Pragmatic Modernism* (New York: Oxford University Press, 2012); Jason Puskar, *Accident Society: Fiction, Collectivity, and the Production of Chance* (Stanford: Stanford University Press, 2012); Vincent, *The Health of the State*.

32. Vincent, *The Health of the State*, p. 16.
33. Ibid., p. 84.
34. Patrick Joyce, *The State of Freedom: A Social History of the British State Since 1800* (Cambridge: Cambridge University Press, 2013), p. 30.
35. Ibid.
36. Edmund Wilson, *A Prelude: Landscapes, Characters and Conversations from the Earlier Years of My Life* (New York: Farrar, Strauss, Giroux, 1967), p. 278.
37. Ibid., p. 277.
38. For an account of this tradition, see Nathaniel Cadle, *The Mediating Nation: Late American Realism, Globalization, and the Progressive State* (Chapel Hill: University of North Carolina Press, 2014), p. 5.
39. Accounts of some of the diversity of Progressivism – and the consequent difficulties in delimiting it as a political movement – can be found in the introductions to Alan Dawley's *Changing the World: American Progressives in War and Revolution* (Princeton: Princeton University Press, 2003); Kristofer Allerfeldt's edited collection *The Progressive Era in the USA: 1890–1921* (Aldershot: Ashgate, 2007); and in Michael McGerr's *A Fierce Discontent: The Rise and Fall of the Progressive Movement, 1880–1920* (Oxford: Oxford University Press, 2003).
40. John A. Thompson, *Reformers and War: American Progressive Publicists and the First World War* (Cambridge: Cambridge University Press, 1987), pp. 43–56.
41. Qtd. in Richard Rorty, *Achieving Our Country* (Cambridge, MA: Harvard University Press, 1998), p. 18.
42. Croly, *The Promise of American Life*, p. 202.
43. Ibid., pp. 200, 207.
44. John Timberman Newcomb, *How Did Poetry Survive? The Making of Modern American Verse* (Urbana: University of Illinois Press, 2013).
45. Ibid., p. 55.
46. Walter Lippmann, *A Preface to Politics* (1913) (Amherst, NY: Prometheus Books, 2005), pp. 214–215, 216.
47. Ibid., p. 214.
48. Ibid., p. 165.
49. Ibid., p. 252.
50. Ibid., p. 101.

51. Ibid., p. 99. As I go on to outline, Randolph Bourne was an important early voice in this critique. It assumed an influential Cold War turn in the work of Lionel Trilling, who expounded a critique of liberalism's hospitality to technocracy in *The Liberal Imagination* (1950) (New York: New York Review Books, 2008). For a summary of this characteristic approach to the state in much modernist work, see also Michael Whitworth's introduction to *Modernism*, ed. Michael Whitworth (Oxford: Blackwell, 2007), p. 4.

52. Walter Lippmann, "The White Passion," the *New Republic* (October 21, 1916), 293–295, p. 294.

53. Ibid.

54. Schoenbach, *Pragmatic Modernism*, pp. 3, 13.

55. Lippmann, *A Preface to Politics*, p. 41.

56. Lippmann and the *New Republic*, flush with the access it had to the Wilson administration, became a key vehicle for securing broader Progressive support for the US war effort. As Ronald Schaffer notes, from the winter of 1916 onward Lippmann and Croly met weekly with Colonel House, one of Wilson's key advisors; House characterized these meetings as an important way to maintain broader Progressive acquiescence to the drift toward war. *America in the Great War: The Rise of the War Welfare State* (Oxford: Oxford University Press, 1994), p. 114.

57. Walter Lippmann, "The World Conflict in Its Relation to American Democracy," *Annals of the American Academy of Political and Social Science*, 72 (July 1917), 1–10, pp. 7–8.

58. Ibid., p. 8.

59. Ibid., p. 10.

60. Edgar Lee Masters, "Mars Has Descended," *Poetry*, 10 (May 1917), 88–92, pp. 90–91.

61. Willa Cather, "Nebraska: The End of the First Cycle" (1923), in Virginia Faulkner (ed.), *Roundup: A Nebraska Reader* (Lincoln: University of Nebraska Press, 1957), pp. 1–8, 8.

62. Temple Bailey, *The Tin Soldier* (New York: Grossett and Dunlap, 1919), p. 289.

63. Arthur Train, *The Earthquake* (New York: Scribner's, 1918), pp. 286, 111.

64. *Mrs. Redding Sees It Through* ran from the September 1917 to the July 1918 issues of the *Ladies' Home Journal*.

65. Martha Bensley Bruére, "Mildred Carver, USA," *Ladies' Home Journal* (June 1918), 14–15, 56, 58; Isaac F. Marcosson, "The After-The War Woman," *Ladies' Home Journal* (June 1918), 13, 90, 92.

66. T.J. Jackson Lears, *Rebirth of a Nation: The Making of Modern America, 1877–1920* (New York: Harper, 2010), p. 341.

67. See "Twilight of Idols," *The Seven Arts* (October 1917), rpt. in Olaf Hansen (ed.), *Randolph Bourne: The Radical Will, Selected Writings 1911–1918* (Berkeley: University of California Press, 1977), pp. 336–347, 342.

68. Ibid., pp. 342–343.

69. Ibid., p. 340.

70. Ibid., p. 337. James Livingston observes that Bourne's "arguments of 1917–18 inform every subsequent critique of pragmatism, from Van Wyck Brooks, Lewis Mumford, Harold Stearns, Waldo Frank, C. Wright Mills, and Christopher Lasch to Casey Blake, Robert Westbrook, John Diggins, Jackson Lears, Wilfred McClay, Peter Osborne, and Brian Lloyd" (p. 440). See his "War and the Intellectuals: Bourne, Dewey, and the Fate of Pragmatism," *Journal of the Gilded Age and Progressive Era*, 2.4 (2003), 431–450. See also the chapter "The War and the Intellectuals," in Casey Nelson Blake's *Beloved Community: The Cultural Criticism of Randolph Bourne, Van Wyck Brooks, Waldo Frank and Lewis Mumford* (Chapel Hill: University of North Carolina Press, 1990), pp. 157–180.

71. Bourne, "Twilight of Idols," pp. 345–346.

72. Ibid., p. 346.

73. Ibid., p. 346; Vincent, *The Health of the State*, p. 50.

74. Dawes, *The Language of War*, p. 77.

75. H.L. Mencken, "The Coolidge Mystery" (1933), rpt. in *The Impossible H. L. Mencken* (New York: Anchor Books, 1991), pp. 414–418, 418.

76. John Dewey, "What America Will Fight for," the *New Republic*, 12.6 (August 18, 1917), 68–69, p. 69; John Dos Passos, *U.S.A.*, ed. Daniel Aaron and Townsend Ludington (New York: Library of America, 1996), p. 449.

77. Hazel Hutchison, *The War That Used up Words: American Writers and the First World War* (New Haven, CT: Yale University Press 2015), p. 237.

78. See Schaffer, *America in the Great War*, pp. 112, 117.

79. *The Selected Letters of Willa Cather*, ed. Andrew Jewell and Janis Stout (New York: Knopf, 2013), p. 327.

80. H.L. Mencken, "Portrait of the American Citizen," *Smart Set*, 69.2 (October 1922), 138–144, pp. 141–142.

81. Dawes, *The Language of War*, p. 77.

82. See Mark Van Wienen, *Partisans and Poets: The Political Work of American Poetry in the Great War* (Cambridge: Cambridge University Press, 1997), especially chs. 2 and 5; and Theodore Kornweibel, *Seeing Red: Federal Campaigns Against Black Militancy 1919–1925* (Indianapolis: Indiana University Press, 1998).

83. As Althusser defines, "in Marxist theory, the State Apparatus (SA) contains: the Government, the Administration, the Army, the Police, the Courts, the Prisons, etc., which constitute what I shall in future call the Repressive State Apparatus. Repressive suggests that the State Apparatus in question 'functions by violence' – at least ultimately (since repression, e.g. administrative

repression, may take non-physical forms)." This is in contrast to institutions within the Ideological State Apparatus, such as schools, the media, religion, culture, the family, and so on. See "Ideology and Ideological State Apparatuses," in *Lenin and Philosophy and Other Essays* (1971), trans. Ben Brewster. Accessed at Marxists.org, July 3, 2017.

84. Mark Van Wienen, *American Socialist Triptych: The Literary-Political Work of Charlotte Perkins Gilman, Upton Sinclair, and W.E.B. Du Bois* (Ann Arbor: University of Michigan Press, 2012), p. 214.

85. Leon Harris, *Upton Sinclair: American Rebel* (New York: Crowell, 1975), p. 159; Karsten H. Piep, "War as Proletarian Bildungsroman in Upton Sinclair's *Jimmie Higgins*," *War, Literature & the Arts: An International Journal of the Humanities*, 17.1/2 (2005), 199–226, p. 210.

86. See "Wanted: A Campaign of Education," *The Outlook*, 102 (December 21, 1912), 837–839.

87. Lippmann, *A Preface to Politics*, pp. 33–35.

88. Randolph Bourne, "The State," in Hansen (ed.), *Randolph Bourne: The Radical Will*, pp. 355–395, 358–359.

89. In 1916, a terrorist bombing of a Preparedness Day Parade in San Francisco killed ten people and injured forty others. Mooney, a prominent California labor leader and socialist, was arrested on suspicion of perpetrating this attack, convicted, and sentenced to death, a sentence commuted to life imprisonment in 1918. Within a year, credible evidence of perjured testimony in the trial led to worldwide protests against his conviction. A report on the Mooney–Billings case in 1931 by the National Commission on Law Observance and Enforcement was highly skeptical of the evidence introduced by the prosecution to secure Mooney's conviction, but he was not pardoned until 1939. See Jeffrey A. Johnson, *The 1916 Preparedness Day Bombing: Anarchy and Terrorism in Progressive Era America* (London: Routledge, 2017).

90. See William H. Thomas Jr.'s *Unsafe for Democracy: World War I and the U.S. Justice Department's Covert Campaign to Suppress Dissent* (Madison: University of Wisconsin Press, 2008), pp. 3–4.

91. Van Wienen, *Socialist Triptych*, p. 229; Upton Sinclair, *Jimmie Higgins* (1919) (Los Angeles: Aegypan Press, 2008), p. 240.

92. Upton Sinclair, *100%: The Story of a Patriot* (Pasadena: Upton Sinclair, 1920), p. 203. Frank Little was an IWW organizer who, in 1917, had been involved in organizing workers in the Anaconda Copper company in Butte, Montana. On August 1, 1917, he was dragged from his hotel room by masked men and lynched under a railroad trestle with the sign "first and last warning" pinned to his body. See Patrick Renshaw, *The Wobblies: The Story of the IWW and Socialism in the United States* (Chicago: Ivan Dee, 1999), pp. 162–163.

93. Ibid., p. 165.

94. Capozzola, *Uncle Sam Wants You*, p. 143.

95. Sinclair, *100%*, p. 305.

96. As Capozzola notes, the events of World War One laid the "foundations of twentieth-century political surveillance" in the United States. *Uncle Sam Wants You*, p. 201. See also William J. Maxwell's *F.B. Eyes: How J. Edgar Hoover's Ghostreaders Framed African American Literature* (Princeton: Princeton University Press, 2015), which examines how the FBI policed African American literature over a period of five decades, a surveillance that had an important effect on how African American writers shaped their work and imagined the scope of their readership.

97. Harris, *American Rebel*, p. 173.

98. Lippmann's *Public Opinion* (New York: Harcourt, Brace, 1922), was key to that shift; and he was Bernays' intellectual hero. For consideration of the change in Lippmann's outlook during these years on this issue, especially his evolving skepticism about the existence of a rational public at the heart of political decision-making, and his concomitant promotion of technocratic information bureaus to help shape public discourse, see Brett Gary, *The Nervous Liberals: Propaganda Anxieties from World War I to the Cold War* (New York: Columbia University Press, 1999), ch. 1; John A. Thompson, *Reformers and War*, pp. 280–281; Jonathan Auerbach, *Weapons of Democracy: Propaganda, Progressivism, and American Public Opinion* (Baltimore: Johns Hopkins University Press, 2015); and Stephen Vaughn, *Holding Fast the Inner Lines: Democracy, Nationalism, and the Committee on Public Information* (Chapel Hill: University of North Carolina Press, 1980), p. 235. A revisionist piece on Lippmann's thinking about the balance between technocratic expertise and popular sovereignty in democratic governance in the early 1920s is offered by Tom Arnold-Foster; see his "Democracy and Expertise in the Lippmann-Terman Debate," *Modern Intellectual History* (2017), 1–32.

99. All quotations from Edward Bernays, *Propaganda* (1928) (New York: IG Publishing, 2008), pp. 54–55.

100. Ibid., p. 39.

101. Auerbach, *Weapons of Democracy*, p. 68; Vaughn, *Holding Fast the Inner Lines*, p. 2.

102. James R. Mock and Cedric Larson, *Words That Won the War: The Committee on Public Information, 1917–1919* (Princeton: Princeton University Press, 1939), p. 4.

103. See Zeiger, *America's Great War*, pp. 75–77.

104. Kennedy, *Over Here*, p. 47.

105. Newton Baker's foreword to George Creel, *How We Advertised America: The First Telling of the Amazing Story* (New York: Harper, 1920), pp. xi–xviii, xiii.

106. Vaughn, *Holding Fast the Inner Lines*, p. 103.
107. Ibid., pp. 116–117.
108. Mock and Larson, *Words That Won the War*, pp. 66–74. See also Mark Whalan, *American Culture in the 1910s* (Edinburgh: Edinburgh University Press, 2010), pp. 158–165.
109. Auerbach, *Weapons of Democracy*, p. 75.
110. Vaughn, *Holding Fast the Inner Lines*, p. 30.
111. See Van Wienen, *Partisans and Poets*, pp. 154–157; and Mock and Larson, *Words That Won the War*, p. 110. Van Wienen discusses the work of the Vigilantes in promoting the voluntary rationing policies promoted by Herbert Hoover's Food Administration, a voluntarist approach that met with tremendous success, p. 155.
112. See www.english.uiuc.edu/maps/poets/s_z/sandburg/war.htm; also Phillip R. Yanella, *The Other Carl Sandburg* (Jackson: University Press of Mississippi, 1996). Sandburg was also briefly incarcerated and questioned by US Military Intelligence for carrying Bolshevik leaflets back into the United States in 1919; the *International Socialist Review* had its mailing privileges revoked by Burleson in 1917.
113. Katherine Anne Porter, "Pale Horse, Pale Rider," in *Katherine Anne Porter: The Collected Stories* (London: Virago, 1985), pp. 299–350, 302, 304.
114. Ibid., p. 323.
115. Matthew Stratton, *The Politics of Irony in American Modernism* (New York: Fordham University Press, 2013), p. 118.
116. Ibid., p. 123.
117. John Dos Passos, *The Big Money* (1936), in *U.S.A.*, p. 1157.
118. E.E. Cummings, *100 Selected Poems* (New York: Grove Press, 1954), p. 31.
119. Auerbach, *Weapons of Democracy*, pp. 52–53.
120. Vaughn, *Holding Fast the Inner Lines*, p. 120.
121. Ibid., p. 122. As Robert Zeiger points out, "The Four-Minute Men presentational template bent the overly universalist message of Wilsonialism into a class- and ethnic-freighted medium" (p. 81). This medium appropriated notions of patriotism and Americanism – notions that were highly contested across class, racial, and ethnic lines in the 1910s – into a specific language of corporate boosterism that "both inflated their emotive importance and threatened to trivialize their content" (p. 81). See his *America's Great War*, p. 81, and also Auerbach's account of the program, *Weapons of Democracy*, pp. 85–90.
122. E.E. Cummings, *The Enormous Room* (1922) (New York: Boni and Liveright, 1934), p. 3.

123. The CPI produced two pamphlets of his annotated speeches, which together had a circulation of over nine million. Vaughn, *Holding Fast the Inner Lines*, p. 43.

124. See "Wilson by Radio Calls Our Attitude Ignoble, Cowardly," *New York Times* (November 11, 1923), pp. 1, 3. See also John M. Kinder, *Paying With Their Bodies: American War and the Problem of the Disabled Veteran* (Chicago: University of Chicago Press, 2015), p. 206.

125. McCann, "The Presidency," p. 343.

126. Ibid., p. 344.

127. Ibid., p. 344.

128. See, for example, Ann Douglas, *Terrible Honesty: Mongrel Manhattan in the 1920s* (New York: Farrar, Strauss, Giroux, 1996), pp. 162–165.

129. McCann, "The Presidency," p. 352.

130. H.L. Mencken, "The Style of Woodrow" (1921), in William H. Nolte (ed.), *H. L. Mencken's Smart Set Criticism* (Washington, DC: Regenery Publishing, 1987), pp. 119–121, 120.

131. H.L. Mencken and George Jean Nathan, "Clinical Notes," *The American Mercury*, 2.8 (August 1924), 451–456, p. 452.

132. Laurence Stallings, *Plumes* (1924) (Columbia: University of South Carolina Press, 2006), p. 221.

133. John Dos Passos, *1919* (1932), in *U.S.A.*, p. 567.

134. See Lippmann, *Public Opinion*, p. 248.

135. See Mark Whalan, *The Great War and the Culture of the New Negro* (Gainesville: University Press of Florida, 2008).

136. Harriet Monroe, "The Armistice," *Poetry*, 33.11 (November 1928), 88–90, p. 90.

137. Ibid.

138. Ibid., pp. 89–90.

139. Ibid., p. 90.

140. Eisner, *From Warfare State to Welfare State*, p. 12.

141. Zeiger, *America's Great War*, p. 72; Kennedy, *Over Here*, p. 141.

142. Anthony Rotundo, *American Manhood: Transformations in Masculinity from the Revolution to the Modern Era* (New York: Basic Books, 1993), pp. 5–6.

143. Douglas Mao and Rebecca L. Walkowitz, "The New Modernist Studies," *PMLA*, 123.3 (2008), 737–748, p. 745.

144. See Joyce, *The State of Freedom*, p. 40.

1 Freeloading in Hobohemia

1. See David M. Kennedy, *Over Here: The First World War and American Society* (New York: Oxford University Press, 2004), p. 33.

2. Joyce Kilmer, interview with Josephine Preston Peabody, "Free Verse Hampers Poets and Is Undemocratic," *New York Times* (January 23, 1916), SM14.

3. James Oppenheim, "Democracy in Verse and Art," *New York Times* (January 30, 1916), p. xxi.

4. This omission is noted by some of the best recent critics of these magazines; see, for example, John Timberman Newcomb's recent discussion of *Poetry* in *How Did Poetry Survive? The Making of Modern American Verse* (Urbana: University of Illinois Press, 2012), p. 52.

5. The *Tribune* had a regular line in both ridiculing and following the modernist avant-garde. For a fuller discussion of the widespread prewar interest in modernist experiment in the mainstream American press, see Karen Leick's *Gertrude Stein and the Making of an American Celebrity* (London: Routledge, 2009).

6. Wallace Irwin, "Patrioteers: The Red War and the Pink," *Saturday Evening Post* (March 16, 1918), 16, 47, 49: pp. 16, 47.

7. Ibid., p. 49.

8. Ibid., p. 16.

9. Jan Cohn, *Creating America: George Horace Lorimer and the Saturday Evening Post* (Pittsburgh: University of Pittsburgh Press, 1989), pp. 5, 61.

10. Ibid., p. 62.

11. Ibid., p. 86.

12. Charles F. McGovern, *Sold American: Consumption and Citizenship, 1890–1945* (Chapel Hill: University of North Carolina Press, 2006), p. 148.

13. Kathryn V. Lindberg, "Mass Circulation versus *The Masses*: Covering the Modern Magazine Scene," *Boundary 2*, 20.2 (1993), 51–83.

14. Cohn, *Creating America*, p. 9.

15. McGovern, *Sold American*, p. 3.

16. Ibid., pp. 104, 81.

17. Sinclair Lewis, "Hobohemia," *Saturday Evening Post* (April 7, 1917), 3–6, 121–122, 125–126, 129–130, 133: p. 4.

18. Ibid., p. 5.

19. Ibid., p. 121.

20. Ibid., p. 5.

21. Thomas Crow, "Modernism and Mass Culture in the Visual Arts," *Modern Art in the Common Culture* (New Haven, CT: Yale University Press, 1998), pp. 3–38, 35. Lewis's formulation also turns on its head Marjorie Perloff's later complaint that "Imagist doctrine," based in the Poundian principles of "Exact treatment of the thing, accuracy of presentation, precise definition," was "transferred to the realm of copywriting" at this time. Timothy Materer unpacks the debate about the relation of imagist poetry to advertising copy

in his "Make It Sell! Ezra Pound Advertises Modernism," in Kevin J.H. Dettmar and Stephen Watt (eds.), *Marketing Modernisms: Self-Promotion, Canonization, Rereading* (Ann Arbor: University of Michigan Press, 1996), pp. 17–36, 27. Jesse Matz outlines some of the most influential accounts of the co-optation of modernism by the culture industry, including those by Leslie Fiedler, Irving Howe, Clement Greenberg, Fredric Jameson, and Terry Eagleton; see "Cultures of Impression," in Douglas Mao and Rebecca Walkowitz (eds.), *Bad Modernisms* (Durham, NC: Duke University Press, 2006), pp. 298–330, 298–299.

22. Janet Lyon, "Sociability in the Metropole: Modernism's Bohemian Salons," *ELH*, 76.3 (2009), 687–711, p. 698.
23. Lewis, "Hobohemia," p. 4.
24. Ibid., p. 121.
25. Irvin S. Cobb, "'Twixt the Bluff and the Sound: Improbable People of an Impossible Land," *Saturday Evening Post* (July 28, 1917), 14–15, 58: p. 14.
26. Ibid., p. 14.
27. Cohn, *Creating America*, pp. 104–106.
28. See, for example, Albert W. Atwood's "Spending or Skimping?" *Saturday Evening Post* (August 4, 1917), 9, 45, 48. For an excellent account of the Food Administration, the US food industry, and how these forces (sometimes uneasily) combined in wartime programs of publicity and advertising, see Celia Malone Kingsbury, *For Home and Country: World War I Propaganda on the Home Front* (Lincoln: University of Nebraska Press, 2010), pp. 27–65. Curtis Publishing's two major publications were the *Ladies' Home Journal* and the *Saturday Evening Post*.
29. See, respectively, the *Saturday Evening Post* for July 13, 1918, p. 32; July 13, 1918, p. 76; and December 15, 1917, pp. 44–45.
30. Discussed in McGovern, *Sold American*, p. 136.
31. Janet Lyon and Carolyn Burke have both discussed this link in the popular mind between free verse and free love; see Lyon's *Manifestoes: Provocations of the Modern* (Ithaca, NY: Cornell University Press, 1999), p. 148.
32. Following the passage of the Espionage Act in June 1917, *The Masses'* August issue was banned from the mails by the postmaster of New York, Thomas Patten, for criticizing the Selective Service Act. Seven contributors of *The Masses*, including both its editors (Max Eastman and Floyd Dell), were subsequently arrested for publishing material designed to obstruct conscription. The magazine folded after its December 1917 issue; see Christopher Capozzola, *Uncle Sam Wants You: World War I and the Making of the Modern American Citizen* (New York: Oxford University Press, 2008), pp. 154–155. *The Seven Arts* folded because its patron, Annette

Rankine, withdrew her support for the magazine in late 1917, largely due to its decision to run antiwar essays by Randolph Bourne and John Reed.

33. Newcomb, *How Did Poetry Survive?*, p. 1.
34. Harriet Monroe, "The Motive of the Magazine," *Poetry*, 1.1 (October 1912), 26–28, p. 26.
35. See David Ben-Merre and Robert Scholes, "War Poems from 1914," *PMLA*, 124.5 (2009), p. 1747.
36. Harriet Monroe, "The Poetry of War," *Poetry*, 4.6 (September 1914), 237–239, p. 239.
37. Alice Corbin Henderson, "Poetry and War," *Poetry*, 5.2 (November 1914), 82–84, p. 83.
38. Allesandria Polizzi, "'The Huge Gun with Its One Blind Eye': Scale and the War Poetry and Writings of Harriet Monroe," in Patrick J. Quinn and Steven Trout (eds.), *The Literature of the Great War Reconsidered: Beyond Modern Memory* (New York: Palgrave, 2001), pp. 77–89.
39. Harriet Monroe, "The New Era," *Poetry*, 9.4 (January 1917), 195–197, p. 195.
40. Harriet Monroe, "What War May Do," *Poetry*, 10.3 (June 1917), 142–145, pp. 144–145.
41. Polizzi, "The Huge Gun," p. 80.
42. Robert Wiebe, *The Search for Order, 1877–1920* (New York: Hill and Wang, 1966).
43. Randolph Bourne, "The State," in Olaf Hansen (ed.), *Randolph Bourne: The Radical Will, Selected Writings 1911–1918* (Berkeley: University of California Press, 1977), pp. 355–395, 358–359.
44. Michael Walzer, "On the Role of Symbolism in Political Thought," *Political Science Quarterly*, 82.2 (1967), 191–204, p. 194.
45. See Ben-Merre and Scholes, "War Poems from 1914," p. 1748.
46. Alice Corbin Henderson and Harriet Monroe, "Wanted: A Song for America," *Poetry*, 10.3 (June 1917), 165–166.
47. Ibid.
48. See Alice Corbin Henderson, "The Vigilantes," *Poetry*, 10.4 (July 1917), 218–219, p. 219; and Mark Van Wienen, *Partisans and Poets: The Political Work of American Poetry in the Great War* (Cambridge: Cambridge University Press, 1997), p. 167.
49. Harriet Monroe, "Will Art Happen?" *Poetry*, 10.4 (July 1917), 203–205, p. 204.
50. Ibid., p. 205.
51. Harriet Monroe, "The War and the Artist," *Poetry*, 11.6 (March 1918), 320–322, pp. 320–321.
52. Ibid., pp. 321–322.
53. See "Notes," *Poetry*, 13.1 (October 1918), 56–58.

54. Alice Corbin Henderson, "Send American Poets," *Poetry*, 12.1 (April 1918), 37–38.
55. Harriet Monroe, "Poetry an Essential Industry," *Poetry*, 13.2 (November 1918), 96.
56. Jane Heap, "War Art," *Little Review* (August 1917), 25.
57. See Jayne E. Marek, *Women Editing Modernism: "Little" Magazines and Literary History* (Lexington: University of Kentucky Press, 1995), p. 73; Paul Vanderham, *James Joyce and Censorship: The Trials of Ulysses* (New York: New York University Press, 1998), p. 6. For Anderson's uptake of Goldman, and her ultimate divergence from Goldman's faith in a collective politics in the name of aesthetic individualism, see David Weir's *Anarchy and Culture: The Aesthetic Politics of Modernism* (Amherst: University of Massachusetts Press, 1997), pp. 150–157.
58. Mark Morrison, *The Public Face of Modernism: Little Magazines, Audiences, and Reception 1905–1920* (Madison: University of Wisconsin Press, 2001), p. 149.
59. Lyon, *Manifestoes: Provocations of the Modern*, p. 135.
60. Ibid., p. 124.
61. Margaret Anderson, "Art and the War," *Little Review* (October 1917), 40–41, p. 41.
62. Gerald Gunther, *Learned Hand: The Man and the Judge* (New York: Knopf, 1994), pp. 333–340. Augustus Hand was also influential in relaxing the prohibition on the mailing of contraceptive material in the 1936 case *United States v. One Package of Japanese Pessaries*, which was covered under the same section of the Criminal Code as the publication of "obscene" matter. See Carole R. McCann, *Birth Control Policies in the United States 1919–1945* (Ithaca, NY: Cornell University Press, 1999), pp. 74–75.
63. Margaret Anderson, "Judicial Opinion: Our Suppressed October Issue," *Little Review* (December 1917), 46–49, pp. 47–48. See also Gunther, *Learned Hand*.
64. Anderson, "Judicial Opinion: Our Suppressed October Issue," p. 48.
65. Learned Hand's biographer classes this decision as "extraordinarily free-speech protective," and although it was quickly overturned by the circuit court of appeals, his opinion was influential in the standards adopted by the Supreme Court in the 1960s. Gunther, *Learned Hand*, p. 128.
66. Capozzola, *Uncle Sam Wants You*, p. 145.
67. As Anderson fumed, the *Little Review* "would have no function or reason for being if it did not continually conflict" with "the prevalent art values in America": "Judicial Opinion: Our Suppressed October Issue," p. 48.

68. Ezra Pound, in Thomas L. Scott, Melvin J. Friedman, and Jackson R. Bryer (eds.), *Pound/The Little Review: The Letters of Ezra Pound to Margaret Anderson: The Little Review Correspondence* (New York: New Directions, 1989), p. 174.

69. Ezra Pound, "The Classics Escape," *Little Review* (March 1918), 32–34, p. 34.

70. Ibid., p. 34.

71. Ezra Pound, "Cantico del Sole," in *Ezra Pound: New Selected Poems and Translations*, 2nd edn. ed. Richard Sieburth (New York: New Directions, 2010), p. 81. Paul Vanderham has uncovered evidence that although the story was ostensibly suppressed because it was obscene, the Post Office had actually suppressed it under the recently passed Espionage Act, which was designed to target seditious publications. See *James Joyce and Censorship*, p. 18.

72. See, for example, "Advertising Men to Aid War Work," *New York Times* (March 26, 1917), p. 2 ; "No Advertising Needed," *New York Times* (April 20, 1917), p. 12; "Advertising as War Force," *New York Times* (April 26, 1917), p. 4.

73. George Creel, *How We Advertised America* (New York: Harper's, 1920), pp. 156–157.

74. Ibid., p. 159.

75. Ibid., p. 163.

76. Ibid., p. 4.

77. Capozzola, *Uncle Sam Wants You.*

78. Margaret Anderson, "Because of the War," *Little Review* (April 1916), 26.

79. Morrison, *The Public Face of Modernism*, p. 148.

80. "A Mother's Sacrifice," *Little Review* (April 1917), 23.

81. Anita Helle, "'Blase Sorrow': Ultramodernity's Mourning at the *Little Review*, 1917–1920," in Patricia Rae (ed.), *Modernism and Mourning* (Lewisburg, PA: Bucknell University Press, 2008), pp. 118–136, 124.

82. See Kimberly Jensen, *Mobilizing Minerva: American Women and the First World War* (Urbana: University of Illinois Press, 2008), pp. 19–20.

83. Van Wienen, *Partisans and Poets*, pp. 5–6.

84. Rachel Blau DuPlessis, *Genders, Races, and Religious Cultures in Modern American Poetry, 1908–1934* (Cambridge: Cambridge University Press, 2001), p. 40.

85. Monroe, "What War May Do," pp. 143–144.

2 Letters from a Soldier

1. "'Mother's Letter' Plan Gives Every Man in A.E.F. Special Opportunity for Observing Mother's Day," *Stars and Stripes* (May 3, 1918), 1.

2. Ibid. See also "Americans All Give One Day to Mother," *New York Times* (May 13, 1918), p. 7.

3. Ibid. See also "Big Mail from Our Army," *New York Times* (June 1, 1918), p. 3.

4. See https://postalmuseum.si.edu/collections/object-spotlight/special-pass port.html.

5. Winifred Gallagher, *How the Post Office Created America* (New York: Penguin, 2016), pp. 223–228.

6. See, in particular, David M. Henkin, *The Postal Age: The Emergence of Modern Communications in Nineteenth-Century America* (Chicago: University of Chicago Press, 2006), pp. 93–118.

7. Fredric Jameson, *An American Utopia: Dual Power and the Universal Army* (London: Verso, 2016), p. 15.

8. Mark Meigs, *Optimism at Armageddon: Voices of American Participants in the First World War* (New York: New York University Press, 1997), p. 124.

9. Christopher Capozzola, *Uncle Sam Wants You: World War One and the Making of the American Citizen* (New York: Oxford University Press, 2008): dust jacket.

10. Upton Sinclair, *100%: The Story of a Patriot* (Pasadena: Upton Sinclair, 1920), p. 53.

11. See Patrick Joyce, *The State of Freedom: A Social History of the British State Since 1800* (Cambridge: Cambridge University Press, 2013), p. 55.

12. See Gallagher, *How the Post Office Created America*, p. 208.

13. Ibid., pp. 190, 204–207.

14. All quotations from Henry A. Castle, "The Post Office and Socialism," *North American Review*, 202.716 (July 1915), 68–75, p. 75.

15. "Speeding up the Mails for American Soldiers," *New York Times* (November 19, 1917), SM 5–11, p. 11; James H. Bruns, "Letters at War: The Post Office Department in World War I," *The United States Specialist*, 662 (1985), 159–166, p. 164.

16. Ibid. See also, for example, "Flood of Protests over Troops' Mail," *New York Times* (April 28, 1918), p. 17; "Military Red Tape and Delay of Soldiers' Mail," *New York Times* (May 12, 1918), p. 76.

17. "What You Can Do for Us: By an American Soldier at the Front," *Woman's Home Companion* (January 1918), p. 2.

18. See Edward G. Lengel's *World War I Memories: An Annotated Bibliography of Personal Accounts Published in English since 1919* (Lanham, MD: Scarecrow Press, 2004).

19. See "Alan Seeger's Prose Record of the Great War," *New York Times Magazine* (May 20, 1917), pp. 3–4.

20. See George Pattullo's "Tips to His Bunkie Back Home" series, which appeared periodically in the *Saturday Evening Post* in 1917; for example, *Saturday Evening Post* (September 22, 1917), pp. 6–7, 87, 90, 93–94; Ring Lardner's Jack Keefe stories are discussed below in the section entitled "Postal Intimacies in World War One Popular Writing"; Edward Streeter published three collections of his *Dere Mable* fictional letters, beginning with *Dere Mable: Love Letters of a Rookie* (New York: Frederick A. Stokes, 1918); see also the fictional war letters in Willa Cather, *One of Ours* (New York: Knopf, 1922); the letters in *A Son at the Front*, by Edith Wharton, discussed below in the section entitled "Edith Wharton's 'Writing a War Letter,' Modernism, and Charity"; Temple Bailey's *The Tin Solider* (New York: Gross and Dunlap, 1918); Edna Ferber, "Long Distance," *Carry On*, 1.4 (October–November 1918), 2–6; Ellen Glasgow, *The Builders* (New York: Doubleday, Page, 1919); and F. Scott Fitzgerald, *This Side of Paradise* (New York: Scribner's, 1920).

21. William March, *Company K* (1933) (Tuscaloosa: University of Alabama Press, 1989), p. 28.

22. John Allen Wyeth, *This Man's Army: A War in Fifty-Odd Sonnets* (1928) (Columbia: University of South Carolina Press, 2008), p. 27.

23. Ferber, "Long Distance," p. 3.

24. See Joyce, *The State of Freedom*, pp. 125–127.

25. Susan Schweik, *A Gulf So Deeply Cut: American Woman Poets and the Second World War* (Madison: University of Wisconsin Press, 1992), p. 93.

26. E.E. Cummings, *100 Selected Poems* (New York: Grove Press, 1954), p. 32.

27. Ibid.

28. Capozzola, *Uncle Sam Wants You*, pp. 151–152.

29. See Joyce, *The State of Freedom*, pp. 139–140.

30. Paul Fussell, *The Great War and Modern Memory* (New York: Oxford University Press, 1975), p. 183. See also Margaretta Jolly, "Myths of Unity: Remembering the Second World War through Letters and Their Editing," in Alex Vernon (ed.), *Arms and the Self: War, the Military, and Autobiographical Writing* (Kent, OH: Kent State University Press, 2005), pp. 144–170.

31. Santanu Das, *Touch and Intimacy in World War One Literature* (Cambridge: Cambridge University Press, 2006), p. 15.

32. Cary Nelson, "'Only Death Can Part Us': Messages on Wartime Cards," in Heidi M. Bean and Mike Chasar (eds.), *Poetry after Cultural Studies* (Iowa City: University of Iowa Press, 2011), pp. 115–141, 133.

33. Meigs, *Optimism at Armageddon*, p. 32.

34. Capozzola, *Uncle Sam Wants You*, p. 8.

35. "Free Advice for Lovelorn Lads," *Stars and Stripes* (March 29, 1918), 5.

36. "His Morning Mail Is 8,000 Letters," *Stars and Stripes* (February 8, 1918), 2.

37. Joyce, *The State of Freedom*, p. 39.

38. Susan Edmunds, *Grotesque Relations: Modernist Domestic Fiction and the U.S. Welfare State* (New York: Oxford University Press, 2008), p. 12.

39. Joyce, *The State of Freedom*, p. 50.

40. "Mobilizing the Country's Resources," *Postal Record*, 30.6 (June 1917), 160.

41. See Lauren Berlant and Michael Warner, "Sex in Public," *Critical Inquiry*, 24.2 (1998), 547–566, p. 553.

42. Michael Herzfeld, *Cultural Intimacy: Social Poetics in the Nation-State* (New York: Routledge, 1997), pp. 4, 2.

43. See Jonathan Yardley, *Ring: A Biography of Ring Lardner* (New York: Rowman and Littlefield, 2001), pp. 163–165.

44. See Todd Avery, "'The Girls in Europe Is Nuts over Ball Players': Ring Lardner and Virginia Woolf," *NINE: A Journal of Baseball History and Culture*, 13.2 (2005), 31–53.

45. See, for example, the letter from a father to his son in "Tom: The Letter He Got When He Left His Mother for 'Somewhere in France,'" *Ladies' Home Journal* (October 1917), 1; "His Christmas Letter to His Mother: The Letter of a Nineteen Year-Old Ambulance Driver 'Somewhere in France,'" *Ladies' Home Journal* (December 1917), 12, 98; and "From Him: A Letter to a Father from a Son 'Somewhere in France,'" *Ladies' Home Journal* (May 1918), 20.

46. "His Letter to His Sister: The Man Who Was Drafted Tells Her Some Home Truths," *Ladies' Home Journal* (February 1918), 1.

47. See "Introduction," in Jeff Silverman (ed.), *Lardner on War* (Guilford, CT: Lyons Press, 2003), p. xi.

48. See Capozzola, *Uncle Sam Wants You*, p. 83.

49. Ibid., p. 85.

50. Ibid.

51. Ring Lardner, *Treat 'Em Rough: Letters from Jack the Kaiser Killer* (New York: Bobbs-Merrill, 1918), p. 107.

52. Ibid., pp. 153, 157.

53. See Jennifer Haytock, *At Home, at War: Domesticity and World War One in American Literature* (Columbus: Ohio State University Press, 2003).

54. See James Longenbach, *Wallace Stevens: The Plain Sense of Things* (New York: Oxford University Press, 1991), pp. 44–45.

55. Ibid., p. 59.

56. Wallace Stevens, "The Irrational Element in Poetry," in Frank Kermode and Joan Richardson (eds.), *Collected Poems and Prose* (New York: Library of America, 1997), pp. 781–792, 788. Hereafter abbreviated to *CPP*.

57. Schweik, *A Gulf So Deeply Cut*, p. 101.
58. See *The Contemplated Spouse: The Letters of Wallace Stevens to Elsie*, ed. J. Donald Blount (Columbia: University of South Carolina Press, 2006), p. 368.
59. Harriet Monroe and Alice Corbin Henderson, "Wanted: A Song for America," *Poetry*, 10.3 (June 1917), 165–166. See also Mark Van Wienen, *I Have a Rendezvous with Death: American Poems of the Great War* (Urbana: University of Illinois Press, 2002), p. 325.
60. A. Walton Litz, *Introspective Voyager: The Poetic Development of Wallace Stevens* (New York: Oxford University Press, 1972); Wallace Stevens, *Opus Posthumous*, ed. Milton J. Bates (New York: Knopf, 1989).
61. See Schweik, *A Gulf So Deeply Cut*, p. 101; Stevens to Monroe, September 1, 1917, in Holly Stevens (ed.), *Letters of Wallace Stevens* (London: Faber and Faber, 1966), p. 202.
62. Longenbach, *The Plain Sense of Things*, pp. 47–51.
63. *Letters of Wallace Stevens*, p. 206.
64. Sandra M. Gilbert, "'Rats' Alley': The Great War, Modernism, and the (anti) Pastoral Elegy," *NLH*, 30.1 (1999), 179–201, p. 182. Gilbert, too, muses on how Stevens faced the issue of "combat gnosticism," p. 190.
65. See *The Contemplated Spouse*, ed. Blount, 335–336, p. 338; also Longenbach, *The Plain Sense of Things*, p. 47.
66. *Letters of Wallace Stevens*, p. 185.
67. See H.G. Wells, "Ideals of Organization," the *New Republic* (July 24, 1915), 301–303; Walter E. Weyl, Review of *The Dynastic State: Imperial Germany and the Industrial Revolution*, by Thorsten Veblen, the *New Republic* (July 24, 1915), 317; Norman Angell, "A New Kind of War," the *New Republic* (July 31, 1915), 327–329.
68. Fussell, *The Great War and Modern Memory*, pp. 8, 21.
69. Vincent Sherry, *The Great War and the Language of Modernism* (Cambridge: Cambridge University Press, 2004), p. 9.
70. *Letters of Wallace Stevens*, p. 209.
71. Jahan Ramazani, *Poetry of Mourning: The Modern Elegy from Hardy to Heaney* (Chicago: University of Chicago Press, 1996), p. 117.
72. Hans P. Vought, *The Bully Pulpit and the Melting Pot: American Presidents and the Immigrant, 1897–1933* (Macon, GA: Mercer University Press, 2004), p. 112.
73. Lauren Berlant, *The Queen of America Goes to Washington City: Essays on Sex and Citizenship* (Durham, NC: Duke University Press, 1997), p. 3.
74. Haytock, *At Home, at War*, p. 32.
75. Patricia Chu, *Race, Nationalism and the State in British and American Modernism* (Cambridge: Cambridge University Press, 2006), p. 102.

76. Schweik, *A Gulf So Deeply Cut*, p. 105.
77. See Ramazani, *Poetry of Mourning*, pp. 97–100. He assesses Richard Poirier and Harold Bloom's view that the poem refuses elegiac pathos, but concludes that "in screening the pathetic fallacy via what might be called the a-pathetic fallacy, the poem raises the kind of muted elegiac lament that works best in the twentieth century," p. 100.
78. Translation taken from Eugène Lemercier, *A Soldier of France to His Mother: Letters from the Trenches on the Western Front*, trans. Theodore Stanton (Chicago: McClurg, 1917), p. 73.
79. Patricia Rae, "Bloody Battle-Flags and Cloudy Days: The Experience of Metaphor in Pound and Stevens," *Wallace Stevens Journal*, 26.2 (Fall 2002), 143–159, p. 146.
80. Rae quotes William James here, and adds her italics; "Bloody Battle-Flags," p. 151.
81. Schweik, *A Gulf So Deeply Cut*, p. 107.
82. See Julie Olin-Ammentorp, *Edith Wharton's Writings from the Great War* (Gainesville: University Press of Florida, 2004), p. 6.
83. See Hazel Hutchison, *The War That Used up Words: American Writers and the First World War* (New Haven, CT: Yale University Press, 2015), pp. 74–75.
84. Edith Wharton, *Fighting France: From Dunkerque to Belport* (New York: Scribner's, 1917), pp. 219, 238, 234.
85. Edith Wharton, *French Ways and Their Meaning* (London: Macmillan, 1919), p. 11.
86. Ibid., 80; Wharton, *A Son at the Front* (1923) (Dekalb: Northern Illinois University Press, 1995), p. 193. Hereafter abbreviated as *ASATF*.
87. Wharton, *French Ways and Their Meaning*, p. 15.
88. Alan Price, *The End of the Age of Innocence: Edith Wharton and the First World War* (New York: St. Martin's Press, 1996), p. 69. This letter was sent on December 2, 1916.
89. See Benstock, quoted in Hutchison, p. 39: Hutchison, *The War That Used up Words*, pp. 37–39. In 1915, Wharton helped found another charity, the Children of Flanders Rescue Committee. Ibid., p. 81.
90. Price, *The End of the Age of Innocence*, p. 118.
91. Ibid., p. 124.
92. Ibid., p. 128. As Hutchison notes, Wharton did retain control of her convalescent home for mothers and children at Groslay, p. 211.
93. Annette Larson Benert, "Civilized Space in Troubled Times," *Twentieth Century Literature*, 42.3 (1996), 322–343, p. 337.
94. Stanley Cooperman, *World War I and the American Novel* (Baltimore: Johns Hopkins University Press, 1967), pp. 19–20.

95. This low regard for her wartime novels is addressed by all recent critics of Wharton's war fiction. See, for example, Shari Benstock's "Introduction," in *A Son at the Front*, viii–ix; Olin-Ammentorp, *Edith Wharton's Writings from the Great War*, ch. 1; Price, *The End of the Age of Innocence*, p. xi; Robin Peel, *Apart from Modernism: Edith Wharton, Politics, and Fiction before World War I* (Madison, NJ: Fairleigh Dickinson University Press, 2005), pp. 267, 273.

96. Edith Wharton, "Writing a War Story," in Linda Wagner-Martin (ed.), *The Portable Edith Wharton* (New York: Penguin, 2003), pp. 336–349, 336.

97. Ibid., pp. 336–337.

98. Ibid., pp. 338–339.

99. Ibid., p. 342.

100. Ibid., p. 348.

101. Jean Gallagher, *The World Wars through the Female Gaze* (Carbondale: University of Southern Illinois Press, 1998), p. 13.

102. See Sharon Kim, "Edith Wharton and Epiphany," *Journal of Modern Literature*, 29.3 (Spring 2006), 150–175, p. 153.

103. Edith Wharton, *The Writing of Fiction* (New York: Scribner's, 1925), p. 15.

104. Ibid., p. 14.

105. Ibid., pp. 28–29.

106. "Tendencies in Modern Fiction" (1934), in Frederick Wegener (ed.), *Edith Wharton: Uncollected Critical Writings* (Princeton: Princeton University Press, 1996), pp. 170–174, 170.

107. Claire Tylee, "Imagining Women at War: Feminist Strategies in Edith Wharton's War Writing," *Tulsa Studies in Women's Literature*, 16.2 (1997), 327–343, p. 333.

108. Ibid., p. 335.

109. A clue to this comes from Ivy's editor at *The Man-At-Arms*, who demands a "tragedy with a happy ending," a phrase that Wharton explicates more fully in *French Ways and Their Meaning*. In a discussion with W.D. Howells about American popular theater, Howells claimed that "what the American public wants is a *tragedy with a happy ending*." Wharton continues that this is "true of the whole American attitude toward life … [but] Things are not always and everywhere well with the world, and each man has to find it out as he grows up. It is the finding out that makes him grow, and until he has faced the fact and digested the lesson he is not grown up – he is still in the nursery." *French Ways and Their Meaning*, pp. 65–66 (emphasis in original).

110. June Howard, "What Is Sentimentality?" *ALH*, 11.1 (1999), 63–81, pp. 66, 76.

111. Wharton admitted to similar personal sentiments in reflections on her wartime service in her autobiography *A Backward Glance*; as she confessed, "though individual cases of distress appeal to me strongly I am conscious of

lukewarmness in regard to organized beneficence." *A Backward Glance* (1934), in Cynthia Griffin Wolff (ed.), *Edith Wharton: Novellas and Other Writings* (New York: Library of America, 1990), pp. 767–1064, 1046.

112. William M. Morgan, *Questionable Charity: Gender, Humanitarianism, and Complicity in U.S. Literary Realism* (Hanover, NH: University Press of New England, 2004), p. 148.

113. Qtd. in Michael Szalay, *New Deal Modernism: American Literature and the Invention of the Welfare State* (Durham, NC: Duke University Press, 2000), p. 167.

114. Julie Olin-Ammentorp argues that the Red Cross is also the target of Wharton's critique in *A Son at the Front*'s portrayal of the transfer of control of the Friends of French Art charity from competent and hardworking volunteers to the boorish and vain American Harvey Mayhew; see *Edith Wharton's Writings from the Great War*, p. 127.

115. Bruce Robbins, "The Smell of Infrastructure: Notes toward an Archive," *Boundary 2*, 34.1 (2007), 25–33, p. 26.

116. Hutchison, *The War That Used up Words*, p. 221.

117. Lionel Trilling, *The Liberal Imagination* (1951) (New York: New York Review of Books, 2008), pp. xix–xx.

118. See Mike Konczal, "The Voluntarism Fantasy," *Democracy*, 32 (2014). Web. Accessed August 25, 2016.

119. Ibid.

120. N.W. Peterson, "The Postal System," *Postal Record*, 30.6 (June 1917), 150.

3 The Regional Novel and the Wartime State

1. "Universal Service as Education," the *New Republic*, 6.77 (April 22, 1916), 309–310. See also Jonathan M. Hansen, *The Lost Promise of Patriotism: Debating American Identity, 1890–1920* (Chicago: University of Chicago Press, 2010), pp. 127–128.

2. "Americanism and Localism," *The Dial*, 68 (1920), 684–688. Rpt. in Jo Ann Boydston (ed.), *John Dewey, the Middle Works, 1899–1924, vol. 12: 1920* (Carbondale: Southern Illinois University Press, 1982), pp. 12–16, 12.

3. Ibid., p. 13.

4. Ibid.

5. Dewey, *The Public and Its Problems* (1927), qtd. in Philip Joseph, *American Literary Regionalism in a Global Age* (Baton Rouge: Louisiana State University Press, 2013), p. 2.

6. Dewey, "Americanism and Localism," p. 14.

7. Classic accounts in this debate include Amy Kaplan, "Nation, Region, and Empire," in Emory Elliott (ed.), *Columbia History of the American Novel* (New York: Columbia University Press, 1991), pp. 250–256; Richard Brodhead, *Cultures of Letters: Scenes of Reading and Writing in Nineteenth-Century America* (Chicago: University of Chicago Press, 1993); Carrie Tirado Bramen's *The Uses of Variety: Modern Americanism and the Quest for National Distinctiveness* (Cambridge, MA: Harvard University Press, 2000), ch. 4; Judith Fetterley and Marjorie Pryse, *Writing Out of Place: Regionalism, Women, and American Literary Culture* (Urbana: University of Illinois Press, 2003); Stephanie Foote, *Regional Fictions: Culture and Identity in Nineteenth-Century American Literature* (Madison: University of Wisconsin Press, 2001); Scott Herring, "Regional Modernism: A Reintroduction," *Modern Fiction Studies*, 55.1 (2009), 1–10; and Ryan Poll's *Main Street and Empire: The Fictional Small Town in the Age of Globalization* (New Brunswick, NJ: Rutgers University Press, 2012).

8. Robert Dorman, *The Revolt of the Provinces: The Regionalist Movement in America, 1920–1945* (Chapel Hill: University of North Carolina Press, 1993), p. xii.

9. Mark Storey, *Rural Fictions, Urban Realities: A Geography of Gilded Age American Literature* (New York: Oxford University Press, 2013).

10. "Local Color and After," *The Nation*, 109.2830 (September 27, 1919), 426–427, p. 426. See also Tom Lutz's account of this piece in his *Cosmopolitan Vistas: American Regionalism and Literary Value* (Ithaca, NY: Cornell University Press, 2004), pp. 99–100.

11. "Local Color and After," p. 427.

12. Ibid., p. 426.

13. Ibid., p. 427.

14. "Is Local-Color Fiction Passing?" *Literary Digest* (August 9, 1919), 29.

15. Carl Van Doren, "The Revolt from the Village: 1920," *The Nation* (October 12, 1921), 407–411, p. 410.

16. Leigh Ann Duck, *The Nation's Region: Southern Modernism, Segregation, and US Nationalism* (Athens: University of Georgia Press, 2006), p. 19.

17. Ibid., p. 28.

18. Walter Lippmann, "Integrated America," the *New Republic* (February 19, 1916), 62–67, p. 65.

19. Jeanette M. Keith, *Rich Man's War, Poor Man's Fight: Race, Class, and Power in the South in the First World War* (Chapel Hill: University of North Carolina Press, 2004), p. 6.

20. Willa Cather, "Roll Call on the Prairies," *Red Cross Magazine*, 14 (July 1919), 27–31, p. 27.

21. Philo M. Buck, Jr., "Pacifism in the Middle West," *The Nation* (May 17, 1917), 595–597.

22. Emile Cammaerts, "Patriotism and Poetry," *Collier's* (October 13, 1917), 11.

23. "A.E.F. Must Grow Lingo of Its Own," *Stars and Stripes*, 1.10 (April 12, 1918), 7.

24. "Army Verse," *Stars and Stripes*, 2.1 (February 7, 1919), 5.

25. Vachel Lindsay, "Review of *Yanks*," *Poetry*, 13.6 (March 1919), 329–335, p. 329.

26. Bramen, *The Uses of Variety*, p. 122.

27. Lindsay, "Review of *Yanks*," p. 329.

28. Florence Kelley, "The Menace of Localism," *Yale Review*, 9 (1920), 879–898.

29. Just one example is William Carlos Williams' famous use of Dewey's maxim in "Americanism and Localism" that "locality is the only universal" in *Contact* later in 1920, a phrase he went on to use as a long-standing basis for his "localist modernism [of] a limitation of interests based on the attachments, or affiliations, generated by a specific locus," in the words of Eric White. See White's "In the American Grain: *Contact* (1920–3, 1932) and *Pagany: A Native Quarterly* (1930–3)," in Peter Brooker and Andrew Thacker (eds.), *The Oxford Critical and Cultural History of Modernist Magazines*, 3 vols. (Oxford: Oxford University Press, 2012), vol. 2, pp. 249–27, 251.

30. Dorman, *Revolt of the Provinces*, pp. 24–25.

31. Ibid., p. 25.

32. Ibid., p. 35.

33. See Casey Nelson Blake, *Beloved Community: The Cultural Criticism of Randolph Bourne, Van Wyck Brooks, Waldo Frank, and Lewis Mumford* (Chapel Hill: University of North Carolina Press, 1990), p. 202.

34. Lewis Mumford, "Wardom and the State," *The Dial*, 67.800 (October 4, 1919), 303–305, p. 305.

35. "Patriotism and Its Consequences," *The Dial*, 66.708 (April 19, 1919), 406–407, p. 406; "The Status of the State," *The Dial*, 67.795 (July 26, 1919), 59–61.

36. See Mark Luccarelli, *Lewis Mumford and the Ecological Region: The Politics of Planning* (New York: Guilford Press, 1995), p. 23.

37. Ibid., p. 24.

38. Samuel G. Blythe, "The People," *Saturday Evening Post* (November 10, 1917), 8–9, 105–106, p. 8.

39. Ibid., p. 9.

40. Poll, *Main Street and Empire*, p. 3.

41. Ibid.

42. Mark Van Wienen, *Partisans and Poets: The Political Work of American Poetry in the Great War* (Cambridge: Cambridge University Press, 1997), p. 155.

43. Ibid., p. 156. See also Lutz, *Cosmopolitan Vistas*, pp. 101–102.

44. Hamlin Garland to Theodore Roosevelt, May 8, 1918, in Keith Newlin and Joseph B. McCullough (eds.), *Selected Letters of Hamlin Garland* (Lincoln: University of Nebraska Press, 1998), p. 256.

45. Booth Tarkington, "The Separating Hyphen: A Ringing Message for Americans and German-Americans," *Collier's* (October 1917), 29, 52, p. 29.

46. Peter Buitenhuis, *The Great War of Words: British, American and Canadian Propaganda and Fiction, 1914–1933* (Vancouver: University of British Columbia Press, 1987), p. 75.

47. Booth Tarkington, *Ramsey Milholland* (New York: Doubleday, 1919), p. 197.

48. See Rogers Smith, *Civic Ideals: Conflicting Visions of American Citizenship in U.S. History* (New Haven, CT: Yale University Press, 1999).

49. Carrie Tirado Bramen paraphrases the argument of Dainotto here. Bramen, *The Uses of Diversity*, p. 124. Richard Brodhead argues a similar position to Dainotto, contending that regionalism "could be considered as an exclusion mechanism or social eraser, an agency for purging the world of immigrants to restore homogeneous community." *Cultures of Letters*, p. 136.

50. See, for example, Guy Reynolds, *Willa Cather in Context: Progress, Race, Empire* (London: Macmillan, 1996), pp. 73–98. However, it is true that there are no German-Americans in the heavily autobiographical *My Ántonia*, despite Cather's Webster County, Nebraska, being home to a large population of German-American families, many of whom sent men to the war.

51. The fullest exploration of the impact of war on the techniques and preoccupations of Southern literary regionalism is David A. Davis's *World War I and Southern Modernism* (Jackson: University of Mississippi Press, 2017).

52. Qtd. in Mark A. Graves, "Regional Insularity and Aesthetic Isolationism: Ellen Glasgow's *The Builders* and the First World War," *Southern Literary Journal*, 44.2 (2012), 24.

53. Ellen Glasgow, *The Builders* (Garden City, NY: Doubleday, 1919), p. 350.

54. Ibid., pp. 109, 354.

55. Review of *The Builders*, *Knickerbocker Press* (November 16, 1919), n.p. In Dorothy M. Scura (ed.), *Ellen Glasgow: The Contemporary Reviews* (Cambridge: Cambridge University Press, 1992), p. 199.

56. Malcom Cowley, the *New Republic*, 21 (February 18, 1920), 364, 366; James Sibley Watson, Jr., *The Dial*, 67 (November 29, 1919), 498; both in *Ellen Glasgow: The Contemporary Reviews*, pp. 204, 202.

57. Mark A. Graves' recent assessment often echoes the judgments of early reviews of *The Builders*; see "Regional Insularity," p. 20.

58. "Willa Cather Raps Language Law and Antles' Boxing Regulations" (1921), in L. Brent Bohlke (ed.), *Willa Cather in Person: Interviews, Speeches, and Letters* (Lincoln: University of Nebraska Press, 1986), pp. 146–147. For more on the Siman Act see Christopher Capozzola, *Uncle Sam Wants You: World War One and the Making of the American Citizen* (New York: Oxford University Press, 2008), pp. 194–197.

59. Capozzola, *Uncle Sam Wants You*, p. 196.

60. "State Laws Are Cramping" (1921), in *Willa Cather in Person: Interviews, Speeches, and Letters*, pp. 147–148, 148. Sarah Wilson considers this speech alongside Cather's views on melting-pot ideas of ethnic assimilation; see her *Melting Pot Modernism* (Ithaca, NY: Cornell University Press, 2010), pp. 128–130.

61. "Willa Cather Raps Language Law," pp. 146–147.

62. Fetterley and Pryse, *Writing Out of Place*, p. 239.

63. Cather, "Roll Call on the Prairies," p. 28.

64. Ibid., p. 27.

65. Ibid., p. 30.

66. Willa Cather, *One of Ours* (1922) (London: Virago, 1997), p. 101. Hereafter abbreviated to *OOO*.

67. Cather, "Roll Call on the Prairies," p. 30.

68. Duck, *The Nation's Region*, pp. 32–33.

69. Walter Lippmann, "A Clue," the *New Republic* (April 14, 1917), 316–317, p. 317. Lippmann refers to Laski's *Studies in the Problem of Sovereignty* (New Haven, CT: Yale University Press, 1917) in the article.

70. Steven Trout, *Memorial Fictions: Willa Cather and the First World War* (Lincoln: University of Nebraska Press, 2002), p. 3.

71. Ibid., p. 105.

72. H.L. Mencken, "Portrait of an American Citizen," *Smart Set*, 69.2 (October 1922), 138–144, p. 140.

73. Reynolds, *Willa Cather in Context*, p. 111, p. 107.

74. Ibid., p. 123.

75. Andrew Jewell and Janis Stout (eds.), *The Selected Letters of Willa Cather* (New York: Knopf, 2013), p. 305.

76. See Robert Dorman's account of Mumford's *The Golden Day* in *Revolt of the Provinces*, p. 6; Stearns qtd. in Blake, *Beloved Community*, p. 205.

77. See, in particular, Susan Rosowski, *The Voyage Perilous: Willa Cather's Romanticism* (Lincoln: University of Nebraska Press, 1986).

78. Bramen, *The Uses of Diversity*, p. 126.

79. See also Rosowski, *The Voyage Perilous*, p. 104.

80. Marc Allen Eisner, *From Warfare State to Welfare State: World War I, Compensatory State Building, and the Limits of the Modern Order* (University Park: Penn State University Press, 2000), p. 75.

81. See, for example, "The Shipping Board Scandal," *New York Times* (November 13, 1920), p. 10; "Charge Shipping Board Graft Was Stupendous," *Los Angeles Times* (November 10, 1920), p. 1; "Piez Denies Graft in Shipping Board," *New York Times* (January 23, 1921), p. 3; "Lasker Finds Fleet Squandering Money in Morass of Debt," *New York Times* (July 19, 1921), p. 1; "A Record of Failure," *Los Angeles Times* (August 17, 1921), p. 114.

82. Lauren Berlant, *The Anatomy of National Fantasy: Hawthorne, Utopia, and Everyday Life* (Chicago: University of Chicago Press, 1991), p. 193.

83. Cather, "Roll Call on the Prairies," p. 30.

84. Rosowski, *The Voyage Perilous*, p. 97.

85. Stanley Cooperman, *World War One and the American Novel* (Baltimore: Johns Hopkins University Press, 1967), p. 129.

86. As Steven Trout summarizes, this critical tradition hinges "on the assumption that throughout the text Claude serves as an ironic center of consciousness, one whose misjudgments and romantic excesses are simply passed along to the reader, without explicit judgment or commentary, by the limited third-person narrator." Trout, *Memorial Fictions*, pp. 5–6.

87. Important here is Joseph Urgo's reading of *One of Ours*, which sees it as Cather's "most political" novel in tracking the development of twentieth-century US imperialism, an imperialism grounded in a military-industrial complex (p. 144). As he notes, *One of Ours* describes a situation where "winning wars through unprecedented rates of industrial production and sustaining universal influence through ideological salesmanship [means] the vacuous spirit of enterprise is transformed into the century's new order" (p. 146). Urgo, *Willa Cather and the Myth of American Migration* (Urbana: University of Illinois Press, 1995).

88. See also Reynolds, *Willa Cather in Context*, p. 110.

89. Nathaniel Cadle, *The Mediating Nation: Late American Realism, Globalization, and the Progressive State* (Chapel Hill: University of North Carolina Press, 2014), p. 62. See also Brad Evans, *Before Cultures: The Ethnographic Imagination in American Literature, 1865–1920* (Chicago: University of Chicago Press, 2005).

90. Cadle, *The Mediating Nation*, p. 7.

91. Willa Cather, "Nebraska: The End of the First Cycle," *The Nation*, 117 (September 5, 1923), 236–238, p. 238.

92. Ibid.

93. Amanda Claybaugh, "Washington Novels and the Machinery of Government," in Gregory Downs and Kate Masur (eds.), *The World the Civil War Made* (Chapel Hill: University of North Carolina Press, 2015), pp. 206–225.

94. See Christopher Capozzola, www.politico.com/magazine/story/2014/08/washington-dc-world-war-one-109822#ixzz48TsbKH4g. Accessed May 12, 2016.

95. Zane Grey, *30,000 on the Hoof* (New York: Grossett and Dunlap, 1940), p. 278.

96. Carlton Jackson, *Zane Grey*, rev. edn. (Boston: G.K. Hall, 1989), p. 55.

97. Ibid., p. x; Candace C. Kant (ed.), *Dolly and Zane Grey: Letters from a Marriage* (Reno: University of Nevada Press, 2008), p. 155.

98. These novels include *The Day of the Beast* (1922), *The Call of the Canyon* (1924), *Rogue River Feud* (1948; this was serialized as *Rustlers of Silver River* in *The Country Gentleman* in 1929–30); *The Shepherd of Guadeloupe* (1930); and *30,000 on the Hoof* (1940).

99. Jackson, *Zane Grey*, p. 33.

100. Zane Grey, *The Day of the Beast* (New York: Harper and Brothers, 1922), p. 183.

101. As Lee Clark Mitchell notes, Grey's main achievement was the development of a new narrative form that achieved a "triumph ... in [its] responsiveness to anxieties about standards of female behavior ... at once reinforcing and undercutting an emergent discourse on women's independence." See *Westerns: Making the Man in Fiction and Film* (Chicago: University of Chicago Press, 1996), pp. 123–124.

102. "Latest Works of Fiction," *New York Times Book Review and Magazine* (August 27, 1922), 11, 17, 19, 28: p. 17.

103. See Richard Slotkin's *Gunfighter Nation: The Myth of the Frontier in Twentieth-Century America* (Norman: University of Oklahoma Press, 1993); and Christine Bold, *The Frontier Club: Popular Westerns and Cultural Power, 1880–1924* (New York: Oxford University Press, 2013).

104. As Susan Kollin notes, "in dominant national discourse, the American West has been imagined and celebrated largely for its status as 'pre' – for its position as a pre-lapsarian, pre-social, and pre-modern space," p. xiii. "Introduction: Postwestern Studies, Dead or Alive," in Susan Kollin (ed.), *Postwestern Cultures: Literature, Theory, Space* (Lincoln: University of Nebraska Press, 2007), pp. ix–xix.

105. As Mitchell notes, Grey's novels "can be described as a series of 'convalescence narratives,' with plots that concentrate on scenes of rehabilitation in which true manhood or womanhood is at last discovered," a formula Grey began with *The Heritage of the West* in 1910.

See *Westerns: Making the Man in Fiction and Film*, p. 177. For more on Roosevelt's singular role in shaping cultural perceptions of the American West, especially with regard to gender identity, see Gail Bederman, *Manliness and Civilization: A Cultural History of Gender and Race in the United States, 1880–1917* (Chicago: University of Chicago Press, 1996), ch. 5; and Steven McVeigh, *The American Western* (Edinburgh: Edinburgh University Press, 2007), pp. 13–21.

106. Slotkin, *Gunfighter Nation*, p. 213.
107. Zane Grey, *The Desert of Wheat* (New York: Grosset and Dunlap, 1919). Hereafter abbreviated as *DOW*.
108. *Dolly and Zane Grey: Letters from a Marriage*, p. 159.
109. Slotkin, *Gunfighter Nation*, p. 212.
110. As Sarah Chinn notes, "the very invisibility of blood made it a potent symbol: race was not what was on the outside, but rather what was constituted in the most basic unit of human life, the blood itself. So when white courts and legislatures were establishing the language to talk about and prohibit miscegenation, or establish segregation, they abandoned racial categories based on skin and took up a discourse of genealogy, that is, blood." *Technology and the Logic of American Racism* (London: Continuum, 2000), p. 96.
111. Weber, "Politics as Vocation," http://anthropos-lab.net/wp/wp-content/u ploads/2011/12/Weber-Politics-as-a-Vocation.pdf. Accessed May 23, 2016 (emphasis in original). See also Patricia Chu, *Race, Nationalism, and the State in British and American Modernism* (Cambridge: Cambridge University Press, 2009), pp. 28–29.
112. Michael Cohen, "'The Ku Klux Government': Vigilantism, Lynching, and the Repression of the IWW," *Journal for the Study of Radicalism*, 1.1 (2006) 31–56, p. 33.
113. H. Jon Rosenbaum and Peter C. Sederburg, "Vigilantism: An Analysis of Establishment Violence," in H. Jon Rosenbaum and Peter C. Sederburg (eds.), *Vigilante Politics* (Philadelphia: University of Pennsylvania Press, 1976), pp. 3–29.
114. As Michael Cohen notes, "The history of nineteenth century vigilantism – particularly in the western states ... romantically imagines vigilantism as a temporary embodiment of popular sovereignty, a body of citizens compelled to preserve local order on the frontier in the absence of legitimate law enforcement." "The Ku Klux Government," pp. 34–35.
115. Grey's fictional events closely followed the historical record of Western vigilante action against the IWW in World War One. He conflates two episodes: one was the infamous Bisbee deportations of June 1917 in Arizona, when over 1,000 men, many of them IWW members and striking mineworkers who were disrupting copper mining in the town, were rounded up and loaded onto filthy boxcars by 2,000 members of a

vigilante "Citizens' Protective League" and transported out of the state to be dumped in the desert in New Mexico. There were unsubstantiated rumors that the IWW in Bisbee had been infiltrated by Germans, and were planning armed resistance. See Patrick Renshaw, *The Wobblies: The Story of the IWW and Syndicalism in the United States*, rev. edn. (Chicago: Ivan R. Dee, 1999), pp. 187–188; and Cohen, "The Ku Klux Government," p. 40. The second incident Grey shadows was the lynching of Frank Little, an IWW leader, in Butte, Montana, in August 1917. Little had been effective in helping striking workers organize against the Anaconda Copper Company in Butte, and gave several antiwar speeches. On August 1, he was abducted from his lodging, beaten, dragged behind a car, and lynched from a railway bridge with a sign reading "3-7-77" and containing the initials of other local IWW leaders pinned to his clothing. No police or federal investigation was ever conducted, and no arrests were made. See Cohen, "The Ku Klux Government," p. 41; Renshaw, *The Wobblies*, pp. 162–163.

116. Sean McCann, *Gumshoe America: Hard-Boiled Crime Fiction and the Rise and Fall of New Deal Liberalism* (Durham, NC: Duke University Press, 2000), p. 77.

117. Wilson was responding, in particular, to the lynching of German-American Robert Prager in Illinois in April 1918. His antilynching proclamation was made on July 26, 1918. Capozzola, *Uncle Sam Wants You*, p. 117; see also www.amistadresource.org/documents/document_07_06_030_wilson.pdf.

118. "The Industrial Workers of the World," *The Outlook* (August 15, 1917), 572.

119. Schwantes first outlined this concept in his "The Concept of the Wageworker's Frontier: A Framework for Future Research," *Western Historical Quarterly*, 18.1 (1987), 39–55. He also discusses the disjunction between the "frontier or classic West" that so oriented the majority of Grey's fiction and the actuality of a "wageworker's frontier" on p. 41.

120. See William H. Thomas, "Bureau of Investigation," in *1914–1918-online: International Encyclopedia of the First World War*, ed. by Ute Daniel, Peter Gatrell, Oliver Janz, Heather Jones, Jennifer Keene, Alan Kramer, and Bill Nasson, issued by Freie Universität Berlin, Berlin. See also William H. Thomas, *Unsafe for Democracy: World War I and the U.S. Justice Department's Covert Campaign to Suppress Dissent* (Madison: University of Wisconsin Press, 2008).

121. Sarah Cole, *At the Violet Hour: Modernism and Violence in England and Ireland* (New York: Oxford University Press, 2012), p. 22.

122. Daniel Worden, *Masculine Style: The American West and Literary Modernism* (London: Palgrave Macmillan, 2011), p. 10.

123. Cole, *At the Violet Hour*, p. 43.
124. Ibid., pp. 44, 65.
125. Margot Norris, *Writing War in the Twentieth Century* (Charlottesville: University Press of Virginia, 2000), pp. 17–18.
126. Ibid., p. 18.
127. Grey wrote these letters and diary entries in mid-February 1918. See Jackson, *Zane Grey*, pp. 70–71.
128. Malcolm Cowley, *Exile's Return: A Literary Saga of the Nineteen Twenties* (New York: Viking Press, 1951), pp. 4–5.
129. Cohen, "The Ku Klux Government," pp. 34–35.
130. See Bramen, *The Uses of Diversity*, p. 125; Jason Arthur, *Violet America: Regional Cosmopolitanism in U.S. Fiction since the Great Depression* (Iowa City: University of Iowa Press, 2013), p. xii; and Lutz, *Cosmopolitan Vistas*, pp. 14–15.
131. Berlant, *The Anatomy of National Fantasy*, pp. 215–216.

4 U.S.A., World War One, and the Petromodern State

1. John Dos Passos, "England under a Labor Government: 1947," *Occasions and Protests* (New York: Henry Regnery, 1964), pp. 216–242, 242.
2. See Alastair J. Reid and Henry Pelling, *A Short History of the Labour Party*, 12th edn. (London: Palgrave, 2005), p. 84.
3. William D. Rubenstein, *Twentieth-Century Britain: A Political History* (London: Palgrave, 2003), p. 232; see also Tony Judt, *Ill Fares the Land* (New York: Penguin, 2010), pp. 42–80.
4. John Dos Passos, "England under a Labor Government," p. 217.
5. Ibid., p. 238.
6. Ibid., pp. 234–235.
7. In the 1920s, Dos Passos expressed enthusiasm for the Soviet Union, and in the early 1930s, became a fellow-traveler with the Communist Party; although he never joined, he endorsed their presidential and vice-presidential candidates in the 1932 election. He became severely disillusioned by the Soviet Union and its influence on international communism by the mid-1930s, triggered by the Communist Party's disruption of a socialist gathering at Madison Square Garden in 1934, and exacerbated by Stalin's purges and Soviet actions in the Spanish Civil War. As John Trombold observes, by "the early 1950s Dos Passos was more of a 'willing aide' to the U.S. Federal Bureau of Investigation's inquiries into possible revolutionary subversion than he was an object of those federal inquiries," and by the late 1950s and 1960s, he was writing the foreword to William F. Buckley Jr.'s *Up from Liberalism* and publishing articles in support of Barry Goldwater's 1964 presidential

candidacy. For accounts of this political trajectory, see John Trombold, "From the Future to the Past: The Disillusionment of John Dos Passos," *Studies in American Fiction*, 26.2 (Fall 1998), 237–256; Virginia Spencer Carr's *John Dos Passos: A Life* (Evanston, IL: Northwestern University Press, 2004); and Steven Koch, *The Breaking Point: Hemingway, Dos Passos, and the Murder of José Robles* (Berkeley, CA: Counterpoint, 2005). Seth Moglen details the reasons behind his break with the Communist Party in the mid-1930s in *Mourning Modernity, Literary Modernism and the Injuries of American Capitalism* (Stanford, CA: Stanford University Press, 2007), pp. 113–116.

8. "Looking Back on *U.S.A.*," in Donald Pizer (ed.), *John Dos Passos: The Major Nonfictional Prose* (Detroit, MI: Wayne State University Press, 1988), pp. 235–237, 237. See also Dos Passos's "Interview with David Sanders," in ibid., pp. 241–252, 246.

9. Donald Pizer, "Introduction," in *John Dos Passos: The Major Nonfictional Prose*, pp. 12–16, 15.

10. Dos Passos, "Interview with David Sanders," p. 244.

11. Alfred Kazin, "John Dos Passos and His Invention of America," *The Wilson Quarterly*, 9.1 (1985), 154–166, p. 159. Other critics dispute such judgments, and challenge Dos Passos's later, revisionary account of his own political biography; see, for example, Trombold's "From the Future to the Past." Others have aligned Dos Passos's politics as essentially anarchist; Matthew Stratton, for example, finds *U.S.A.* "controversial at least in part because its politics – roughly and revisionally anarchist – fall outside the discursive bounds delineated by communism, liberalism, republicanism, and progressivism." See "Start Spreading the News: Irony, Public Opinion, and the Aesthetic Politics of *U.S.A.*," *Twentieth-Century Literature*, 54.4 (2008), 419–447, p. 441.

12. See "There Is Only One Freedom," in *John Dos Passos: The Major Nonfictional Prose*, pp. 209–213, 211.

13. See John Dos Passos, *Mr. Wilson's War: From the Assassination of McKinley to the Defeat of the League of Nations* (New York: Doubleday, 1962), pp. 185–291.

14. John Dos Passos, "The Backwash of Our First Crusade," in *The Theme Is Freedom* (New York: Dodd, Mead, 1956), pp. 1–37, 1.

15. Dos Passos, "Interview with David Sanders," p. 250.

16. As Marc Allen Eisner notes, in 1901, the federal government had only 239,476 civilian employees, 136,192 of whom worked for the post office, while 44,524 worked for the War and Navy departments. See his *From Warfare State to Welfare State: World War I, Compensatory State Building, and the Limits of Modern Order* (University Park: University of Pennsylvania Press, 2000), p. 22. And "between 1880 and 1910, the US federal government devoted over a quarter of its expenditures to pensions" distributed to Civil War veterans. See

Theresa Skocpol, *Protecting Soldiers and Mothers: The Political Origins of Social Policy in the United States* (Cambridge, MA: Harvard-Belknap, 1995), p. 37.

17. Eisner, *From Warfare State to Welfare State*, p. 12.

18. As Leo Marx notes, the large-scale technical system was characterized by a "blurring of the borderlines between their constituent elements, notably the boundary separating the artefactual equipment (the machinery or hardware) and all the rest: the reservoir of technical – scientific – knowledge; the specially trained workforce; the financial apparatus; and the means of acquiring raw materials." Qtd. in Patrick Joyce, *The State of Freedom: A Social History of the British State Since 1800* (Cambridge: Cambridge University Press, 2013), p. 40.

19. Ibid., p. 41.

20. US corporations controlled 60 percent of Mexico's oil production in 1912; nationalist anger at foreign resource extraction in Mexico had helped precipitate the 1910 Mexican revolution that ultimately toppled the government of Porfirio Diaz. See Nell Irving Painter, *Standing at Armageddon: A Grassroots History of the Progressive Era, 1877–1919* (New York: Norton, 2008), pp. 283–292.

21. Joshua Schuster, *The Ecology of Modernism: American Environments and Avant-Garde Poetics* (Tuscaloosa: University of Alabama Press, 2013), p. 162.

22. John Dos Passos, *U.S.A.* (1938), ed. Townsend Ludington and David Aaron (New York: Library of America, 1996), p. 844. Hereafter parenthetically abbreviated as *USA*.

23. For example, Michael K. Walonen's fine essay "The Black and Cruel Demon and Its Transformations of Space: Toward a Comparative Study of the World Literature of Oil and Place," *Interdisciplinary Literary Studies*, 14.1 (2012), 56–78, on the genre of the world oil novel, nowhere mentions Dos Passos's epic – despite mentioning important early examples of this genre, including Upton Sinclair's *Oil!* (1927) and B. Traven's *The White Rose* (1929).

24. Stephanie LeMenager, *Living Oil: Petroleum Culture in the American Century* (New York: Oxford University Press, 2014), p. 11.

25. On how the ubiquity of oil, paradoxically, often causes it to pass from notice, see also Michael G. Ziser, "Home Again: Peak Oil, Climate Change, and the Aesthetics of Transition," in Stephanie LeMenager, Teresa Shewry, and Ken Hiltner (eds.), *Environmental Criticism for the Twenty-First Century* (London: Routledge, 2011), pp. 181–195.

26. Frederick Buell, "A Short History of Oil Cultures: Or, the Marriage of Catastrophe and Exuberance," *Journal of American Studies*, 46.2 (2012), 273–293, pp. 277–280. As Timothy Mitchell notes, the geographies of a coal-based economy assisted organized labor's extension of political power;

for as "great volumes of energy now flowed along narrow, purpose-built channels," "between the 1880s and the interwar decades, workers in the industrialised countries of Europe and North America used their new powers over [these] energy flows to acquire or extend the right to vote and, more importantly, the right to form labour unions, to create political organisations, and to take collective action including strikes. In most cases, these changes enabled mass-based parties to win power for the first time" (p. 26). Oil – which needed less manual labor to extract and transport, was a more thoroughly internationalized industry, and was moved along more dispersed and flexible networks – gave labor much less power to halt or disrupt energy flows as a means of securing political agency. Timothy Mitchell, *Carbon Democracy: Political Power in the Age of Oil* (London: Verso, 2011).

27. Bruce Robbins, "The Smell of Infrastructure: Notes Toward an Archive," *Boundary 2*, 34.1 (2007), 25–33, p. 31.

28. See Cotten Seiler, *Republic of Drivers: A Cultural History of Automobility in America* (Chicago: University of Chicago Press, 2008); and also Sarah Frohardt-Lane, "Essential Driving and Vital Cars: American Automobile Culture in World War II," in Ross Barrett and Daniel Worden (eds.), *Oil Culture* (Minneapolis: University of Minnesota Press, 2014), pp. 91–108.

29. LeMenager defines "petromodernity" as "modern life based in the cheap energy systems long made possible by oil." LeMenager, *Living Oil*, p. 67. She argues that at its apex – an apex beginning in the United States in the 1920s – petromodernity is experienced by the human bodyâs existence as a "natureculture," to use Bruno Latour's term, an "inevitable intermixture of the self-generating (organic) and the made" (p. 69).

30. David Sanders, "Interview with John Dos Passos," in Donald Pizer (ed.), *John Dos Passos: The Major Nonfictional Prose* (Detroit, MI: Wayne State University Press, 1988), pp. 241–252, 242; Alfred Kazin, "John Dos Passos and His Invention of America," *The Wilson Quarterly*, 9.1 (1985), 154–166, p. 158.

31. See *The Fourteenth Chronicle: Letters and Diaries of John Dos Passos*, ed. Townsend Ludington (Boston: Gambit, 1973), pp. 79–85. See also Melvin Landsberg, *Dos Passos' Path to U.S.A.: A Political Biography* (Boulder: Colorado Associated University Press, 1972), ch. 3.

32. Landsberg, *Dos Passos' Path to U.S.A.*, pp. 64–65.

33. Ibid., p. 67.

34. Norman Shannon Hall, "John Dos Passos Lies!" *Foreign Service*, 10 (November 1921), 11–12. Rpt. in Barry Maine (ed.), *Dos Passos: The Critical Heritage* (London: Routledge, 1988), pp. 47–51.

35. Steven Trout, *On the Battlefield of Memory: The First World War and American Remembrance* (Tuscaloosa: University of Alabama Press, 2010), pp. 3–4.

36. John Dos Passos, *Manhattan Transfer* (1925) (London: Penguin, 1987), p. 247.

37. Ibid., p. 327.

38. Ibid., p. 255.

39. Cecelia Tichi, *Shifting Gears: Technology, Literature, Culture in Modernist America* (Chapel Hill: University of North Carolina Press, 1987), p. 200.

40. Bernard De Voto, "John Dos Passos: Anatomist of Our Time," *Saturday Review* (August 1936). Rpt. in *Dos Passos: The Critical Heritage*, pp. 121–130, 128.

41. Georg Lukács, "Realism in the Balance," in Ronald Taylor (trans. and ed.), *Aesthetics and Politics: Theodor Adorno, Walter Benjamin, Ernst Bloch, Bertolt Brecht, Georg Lukács* (London: Verso, 1997), pp. 28–59, 32.

42. Mike Gold, "The Education of John Dos Passos," *The English Journal*, 22.2 (1933), 87–97, p. 95.

43. Matthew Josephson, "A Marxist Epic" (1932). Rpt. in *Dos Passos: The Critical Heritage*, pp. 106–109, 106–107.

44. Barbara Foley, *Radical Representations: Politics and Form in U.S. Proletarian Fiction, 1929–1941* (Durham, NC: Duke University Press, 1993), p. 436. Major examples of international collective novels included Klaus Neukrantz's *Berlin Barricades* in Germany; Valentin Kataev's *Time, Forward!* and Alexsandr Fadeyev's *The Nineteen* in the Soviet Union, all of which were translated into English, p. 398. Foley also examines other US collective novels such as Josephine Herbst's *Rope of Gold* (1939), John Steinbeck's *The Grapes of Wrath* (1939), Mary Heaton Vorse's *Strike!* (1930), and Arnold Armstrong's *Parched Earth* (1934).

45. Fredric Jameson, "Cognitive Mapping," in Carey Nelson and Lawrence Grossberg (eds.), *Marxism and the Interpretation of Culture* (Urbana and Champaign: University of Illinois Press, 1988), pp. 347–360, 348–349.

46. John Dos Passos, "Contemporary Chronicles," in *John Dos Passos: The Major Nonfictional Prose*, pp. 238–240, 240.

47. Foley, *Radical Representations*, pp. 400–401.

48. Michael North, *Camera Work: Photography and the Twentieth Century Word* (New York: Oxford University Press, 2005), pp. 155–156.

49. Ibid., p. 162.

50. Sanders, "Interview," p. 247.

51. Daniel Yergin, *The Prize: The Epic Quest for Oil, Money, and Power* (New York: Simon and Schuster, 1991), p. 183.

52. Ibid., pp. 154–157, 173.

53. David S. Painter, "Oil and the American Century," *Journal of American History*, 99.1 (2012), 24–39, pp. 24–25.

54. Yergin, *The Prize*, p. 178; Painter, "American Century," p. 25.

55. Painter, "American Century," p. 25.

56. The Minnesota Legislature also supported nationalizing the US oil industry at this time. See Roger M. Olien and Diana Davids Olien, *Oil and Ideology: The Cultural Creation of American Petroleum* (Chapel Hill: University of North Carolina Press, 2000), p. 161; and Mitchell, *Carbon Democracy*, p. 31.

57. Eisner, *From Warfare State to Welfare State*, p. 12.

58. For example, the US government spent $85 million – twice the cost of the Panama Canal – to build "Old Hickory," a huge munitions plant completed in 1918 and run by the specially established DuPont Engineering Corporation. By the war's end, DuPont had delivered $141 million in dividends to its shareholders from total war revenues of $1.05 billion. Gary Mead, *Doughboys: America and the First World War* (London: Penguin, 2000), pp. 360–361.

59. Gerald D. Nash, *United States Oil Policy 1890–1964: Business and Government in Twentieth Century America* (Pittsburgh: Pittsburgh University Press, 1968), pp. 35–36.

60. Yergin, *The Prize*, pp. 189–190.

61. Olien and Olien, *Oil and Ideology*, p. 138.

62. Yergin, *The Prize*, p. 199.

63. Nash, *United States Oil Policy*, pp. 49–71.

64. Painter, "American Century"; Mitchell, *Carbon Democracy*, pp. 95–97.

65. Yergin, *The Prize*, pp. 208–209.

66. Ibid., p. 209.

67. See www.eisenhower.archives.gov/research/online_documents/1919_convoy.html. Accessed July 17, 2014.

68. See Carlos Arnaldo Schwantes, *Going Places: Transportation Redefines the Twentieth Century American West* (Bloomington: Indiana University Press, 2003), pp. 152–153.

69. Christopher W. Wells, "Fueling the Boom: Gasoline Taxes, Invisibility, and the Growth of the American Highway Infrastructure, 1919–1956," *Journal of American History*, 99.1 (2012), 72–81, p. 73.

70. LeMenager, *Living Oil*, p. 14.

71. See Winifred Gallagher, *How the Post Office Created America* (New York: Penguin, 2017), pp. 226–228.

72. LeMenager, *Living Oil*, p. 80.

73. Moglen, *Mourning Modernity*, p. 203.

74. Donald Pizer, *Dos Passos' U.S.A.* (Charlottesville: University of Virginia Press, 1988), p. 124.

75. North, *Camera Work*, p. 162.

76. Robbins, "The Smell of Infrastructure," p. 31.

77. Buell, "A Short History of Oil Cultures," p. 280.

78. See Caren Irr's "'All Right We Are Two Nations': Speed and the Stratification of Culture in *U.S.A.*," in *The Suburb of Dissent: Cultural Politics in the United States and Canada During the 1930s* (Durham, NC: Duke University Press, 1998), pp. 45–67, 61–62.

79. Enda Duffy, *The Speed Handbook: Velocity, Pleasure, Modernism* (Durham, NC: Duke University Press, 2009), pp. 3–4.

80. Ibid., p. 114.

81. See also Irr's "All Right We Are Two Nations."

82. John Dos Passos, "The Writer as Technician," in *John Dos Passos: The Major Nonfictional Prose*, pp. 169–172, 169.

83. Ibid., pp. 169–170.

84. Ibid., p. 171.

85. Enda Duffy also observes that the car was an unusual commodity in that it "challenges and contests the model of a largely passive consuming subject"; through delivering the "new thrill of independent speed" (p. 115), cars functioned as a "commodity [that] promised that commodification would be overcome" (p. 134). *Speed Handbook.*

86. Seiler, *Republic of Drivers*, pp. 62–63 (emphasis in original).

87. Ibid., p. 144.

88. Charles Taylor, *The Ethics of Authenticity* (Cambridge, MA: Harvard University Press, 1992), p. 4.

89. Matthew T. Huber, "Refined Politics: Petroleum Products, Neoliberalism, and the Ecology of Entrepreneurial Life," in Barrett and Worden (eds.), *Oil Culture*, pp. 226–243, 234.

90. Critics have begun to analyze *U.S.A.* in light of contemporary network theory; see Wesley Beal's "Network Narration in John Dos Passos's *U.S.A.* Trilogy," *Digital Humanities Quarterly*, 5.2 (2011). Accessed May 18, 2014.

5 Fictions of Rehabilitation

1. Perley Poore Sheehan and Robert H. Davis, "Efficiency: A Play in One Act," *McClure's*, 49 (August 1917), 33, 56–58, p. 33.

2. Ibid.

3. Ibid., p. 57.

4. Ibid., p. 56.

5. Ibid., p. 57.

6. Ibid.

7. Theodore Roosevelt, "'Efficiency': Appreciation by Theodore Roosevelt," in Perley Poore Sheehan and Robert H. Davis (eds.), *Efficiency* (New York: Doran, 1917), pp. v–vii, vi.

8. John M. Kinder, *Paying with Their Bodies: American War and the Problem of the Disabled Veteran* (Chicago: University of Chicago Press, 2015), p. 117.
9. Beth Linker, *War's Waste: Rehabilitation in World War One America* (Chicago: University of Chicago Press, 2011), p. 2.
10. Catherine Belling, "Introduction: From Bioethics and Humanities to Biohumanities?" *Literature and Medicine*, 34.1 (2016), 1–6, p. 1.
11. Kinder, *Paying with Their Bodies*, pp. 118–119.
12. Ibid., p. 5.
13. Linker, *War's Waste*, p. 12.
14. Ibid.
15. Ibid., p. 20.
16. Kinder, *Paying with Their Bodies*, p. 117.
17. Linker, *War's Waste*, p. 80.
18. Ibid., p. 166.
19. Ibid., p. 180.
20. Alice Duer Miller, "How Can a Woman Best Help?" *Carry On* (June 1918), 17–18, p. 18.
21. Linker, *War's Waste*, p. 30.
22. See Paul Starr, *The Social Transformation of American Medicine: The Rise of a Sovereign Profession and the Making of a Vast Industry* (New York: Basic Books, 1982), pp. 235–266.
23. Linker, *War's Waste*, p. 9.
24. Col. Frank Billings, "A Message to the Fathers, Mothers, Wives, Sisters and Brothers of Disabled Soldiers," *Carry On*, 1.8 (May 1919), 3–4, p. 4.
25. See David Lubin, *Grand Illusions: American Art and the First World War* (New York: Oxford University Press, 2016), p. 227.
26. Timothy Barnard, "'The Whole Art of a Wooden Leg': King Vidor's Picturization of Laurence Stallings's 'Great Story,'" in Sally Chivers and Nicole Markotíc (eds.), *The Problem Body: Projecting Disability on Film* (Columbus: Ohio State University Press, 2010), pp. 23–41, 24.
27. Kinder, *Paying with Their Bodies*, p. 139.
28. David M. Kennedy, *Over Here: The First World War and American Society* (New York: Oxford University Press, 2004), p. 47.
29. Qtd. in Beth Linker, "Shooting Disabled Soldiers: Medicine and Photography in World War I America," *Journal of the History of Medicine and Allied Sciences*, 66.3 (2011), 313–346, p. 316.
30. "Creed of the Disabled," anon., *Carry On* (March 1919), i.
31. Herman Hagedorn, "The Man Who Overcame," *Carry On* (March 1919), 2–4, p. 3.
32. "From His Neck up, a Man May Be Worth $100,000 a Year," anon., *Carry On* (June 1918), 23.

33. Herbert Kaufman, "The Only Hopeless Cripple," *Carry On* (October–November 1918), 22.
34. Arthur H. Samuels, "Reconstructing the Public," *Carry On* (June 1918), 15–16, p. 15.
35. Ibid.
36. Julie Goldsmith Gilbert, *Ferber: Edna Ferber and Her Circle, A Biography* (New York: Applause, 1999), p. 412.
37. Edna Ferber, "Long Distance," *Carry On* (October–November 1918), 2–6, p. 5.
38. Ibid.
39. Ibid., p. 6.
40. Ibid., p. 3.
41. "For Further Service: A Plan to Refit the Disabled Soldier into the Army or Back to Civilian Life," anon., *Carry On* (September 1918), 30–32, p. 30; Eleanor Rowland Wembridge, "How the Reconstruction Aides Have Proved What They Are For," *Carry On* (April 1919), 10–11.
42. Harry E. Mock, "Curative Work," *Carry On* (June 1919), 12–15.
43. Alice Duer Miller, "How Can a Woman Best Help?" *Carry On* (June 1918), 17–18, p. 18.
44. Ibid.
45. June Howard, "What Is Sentimentality?" *American Literary History*, 11.1 (1999), 63–81, p. 76.
46. Linker, *War's Waste*, p. 31.
47. Ibid., p. 62. As Linker explores, physiotherapy was a "new, undefined field in the United States," and although government programs of physical therapy employed a largely female force this work nonetheless pushed at the limits of acceptable morality (p. 62). In order to distance themselves from the illicit implications of massage, and assume the respectable mantle of non-sexual professionalism, female physical therapists in particular were trained in antisentimental bedside manners, and taught that their massage techniques should be physically uncomfortable for their patients to avoid any implication of impropriety. See *War's Waste*, pp. 73–75.
48. Linker, *War's Waste*, p. 62.
49. Trevor Dodman notes that Ward's "avowed complicity with the wartime propaganda machine, her steadfast patriotism throughout the conflict, and her unwavering defense of the anti-Suffragist platform" has made her an unpalatable subject for feminist reclamation (p. 30). Moreover, her "linear, resolving, romantic, and comfortable plots" (p. 28) distanced her from a generation of women modernist writers; Virginia Woolf caustically remarked of Ward's books that "we never wish to open them again" (p.

30). *Shell Shock, Memory, and the Novel in the Wake of World War I* (Cambridge: Cambridge University Press, 2015).

50. Kinder, *Paying with Their Bodies*, pp. 106–107.

51. Zane Grey, *The Day of the Beast* (New York: Grosset and Dunlap, 1922), p. 111.

52. Ibid., p. 136.

53. A similar pastoral therapy is operative in Ernest Hemingway's two-part story "Big Two-Hearted River," wherein Nick Adams finds recuperative solace from his mental and physical war injuries in the solitary experience of fishing in backwoods Michigan. The efficacy of this contrasts to the limited value of the rehabilitative medical treatments Nick receives in a clinic in Milan in the story "In Another Country."

54. Sinclair Lewis, "Things" (1919), in Sally E. Parry (ed.), *Go East, Young Man: Sinclair Lewis on Class in America* (New York: Signet, 2005), pp. 25–63, 52.

55. Ibid.

56. Celia Malone Kingsbury, *For Home and Country: World War Propaganda on the Home Front* (Lincoln: University of Nebraska Press, 2010), p. 113.

57. Bruce Robbins, *Upward Mobility and the Common Good: Toward a Literary History of the Welfare State* (Princeton: Princeton University Press, 2009), p. xiv.

58. Carlos Baker, *Ernest Hemingway* (Harmondsworth: Penguin, 1969), pp. 66–69.

59. Ernest Hemingway, "In Another Country," in *Ernest Hemingway: The Short Stories* (New York: Scribner, 2003), pp. 267–272, 267.

60. Ibid., p. 271.

61. Ibid., p. 268.

62. Ibid.

63. Philip D. Beidler, "Introduction," in William March, *Company K* (Tuscaloosa: University of Alabama Press, 1989), pp. vii–xxvi, x.

64. William March, *Company K* (1933) (Tuscaloosa: University of Alabama Press, 1989), p. 227.

65. Ibid., p. 231.

66. Beidler, "Introduction," pp. xi–xii.

67. March, *Company K*, p. 239.

68. Ibid.

69. Ibid.

70. Linker, "Shooting Disabled Soldiers," p. 47.

71. Elaine Scarry, *The Body in Pain: The Making and Unmaking of the World* (New York: Oxford University Press, 1985), pp. 54–55.

72. Santanu Das, *Touch and Intimacy in First World War Literature* (Cambridge: Cambridge University Press, 2005), p. 224.

73. March, *Company K*, p. 239.
74. Alyson Patsavas, "Recovering a Cripistemology of Pain: Leaky Bodies, Connective Tissue, and Feeling Discourse," *Journal of Literary and Cultural Disability Studies*, 8.2 (2014), 203–218, p. 203.
75. Joan T. Brittain, *Laurence Stallings* (Boston: Twayne, 1975), p. 20.
76. Steven Trout, "Afterword," in Laurence Stallings, *Plumes* (1924) (Columbia: University of South Carolina Press, 2006), pp. 349–353, 350.
77. See Timothy Barnard's "The Whole Art of a Wooden Leg." As Barnard notes, the movie "grossed the highest box-office receipts of the silent era," established MGM as a major studio player, and greatly boosted the careers of its male lead, John Gilbert, studio bosses Irving Thalberg and Louis B. Mayer, and director Vidor.
78. For example, *The First World War* sparked a high-profile exchange of open letters between Archibald MacLeish and Malcolm Cowley in the *New Republic* in 1933, an exchange discussed in the Conclusion.
79. Laurence Stallings (ed.), *The First World War: A Photographic History* (New York: Simon and Schuster, 1933), n.p.
80. Laurence Stallings, *Plumes* (1924) (Columbia: University of South Carolina Press, 2006), p. 3. Hereafter abbreviated as *PL*.
81. Sanders Marble, *Rehabilitating the Wounded: Historical Perspective on Army Policy* (Falls Church, VA: Office of Medical History, Office of the Surgeon General, 2008), p. 12. Accessed online.
82. Vivian Sobchack, "A Leg to Stand on: Prosthetics, Metaphor, and Materiality," in *The Prosthetic Impulse: From A Posthuman Present to a Biocultural Future* (Cambridge, MA: MIT Press, 2006), pp. 17–41, 19.
83. Tim Armstrong, *Modernism, Technology, and the Body: A Cultural Study* (Cambridge: Cambridge University Press, 1998), pp. 19–21.
84. Laurence Stallings, "The Whole Art of a Wooden Leg," *Smart Set*, 70 (March 1923), 107–111, p. 107.
85. As Patsavas notes, "With particular attention to the power dynamics inherent in processes of knowledge production, standpoint epistemology privileges experience as a source of knowledge and grants that marginalized positionalities offer unique vantage points from which to expose systems of oppression." "Cripistemology of Pain," p. 205.
86. Lauren Berlant, "The Theory of Infantile Citizenship," *Public Culture*, 5.3 (1993), 395–410, p. 395.
87. Nancy J. Hirschmann and Beth Linker, "Introduction," in Nancy J. Hirschmann and Beth Linker (eds.), *Civil Disabilities: Citizenship, Membership, and Belonging* (Philadelphia: University of Pennsylvania Press, 2015), pp. 1–21, 5; see also Rosemarie Garland-Thomson,

Extraordinary Bodies: Figuring Disability in American Culture and Literature (New York: Columbia University Press, 1997), p. 8.

88. Jonathan Vincent, *The Health of the State: Modern US War Narrative and the American Political Imagination, 1890–1964* (New York: Oxford University Press, 2016), p. 107.

89. John C. Farrar, "Editor Recommends," *Bookman* (October 1924), 219–220, p. 219.

90. Kimberly Jensen, *Mobilizing Minerva: American Women in the First World War* (Urbana: University of Illinois Press, 2008), p. 15.

91. I discussed segregation in the military extensively in my *The Great War and the Culture of the New Negro* (Gainesville: University Press of Florida, 2008). See also Chad Williams, *Torchbearers of Democracy: African American Soldiers in the World War I Era* (Chapel Hill: University of North Carolina Press, 2010); and Adrienne Lentz-Smith, *Freedom Struggles: African Americans and World War I* (Cambridge, MA: Harvard University Press, 2011). As Beth Linker notes, although rehabilitation hospitals were initially nonsegregated, that did not prevent frequent incidents of racist hostility within these hospitals, and also institutional recalcitrance in providing wounded black veterans access to all the benefits and financial support owed to them through the WRIA. Once the OSG transferred control of many rehabilitation hospitals to the Public Health Service and local volunteer hospitals, many – especially in the South – reinstituted racial segregation, against the directives of the Medical Department. When the federal government established its new program of Veterans' hospitals in 1923, racial segregation was reestablished. See Linker, *War's Waste*, pp. 135–139.

92. Rogers M. Smith, *Civic Ideals: Conflicting Visions of Citizenship in U.S. History* (New Haven, CT: Yale University Press, 1997), p. 3.

93. Hirschmann and Linker, "Introduction," p. 9.

94. Stallings, "Whole Art," p. 107.

95. Ibid.

96. Ibid., p. 111.

97. Emily Russell, *Reading Embodied Citizenship: Disability, Narrative, and the Body Politic* (New Brunswick, NJ: Rutgers University Press, 2011), p. 15.

98. Garland-Thomson, *Extraordinary Bodies*, p. 46.

99. Qtd. in Kinder, *Paying with Their Bodies*, p. 79.

100. M.A. De Wolfe Howe, "The Known Soldier," in *The Known Soldier and Other Reminders of the War Decade* (Boston: McGrath-Sherrill Press, 1924), p. 7.

101. Sean McCann, *A Pinnacle of Feeling: American Literature and Presidential Government* (Princeton: Princeton University Press, 2008), p. 13.

102. Of course, this was incorrect. Wilson was far from silent after 1921, and his opinions continued to have considerable impact on national policy; this was especially true of his famous Armistice Day radio address in 1923, which berated American isolationism and was – at the time – the most listened-to radio broadcast in history. See "Wilson Calls Our Attitude Ignoble, Cowardly," *New York Times* (November 11, 1923), 1, 3; www.cnn.com/inter active/2015/10/politics/woodrow-wilson-house-history/. Accessed March 8, 2017. It is inconceivable Stallings would have missed this; the paper he wrote for at the time – the *New York World* – was passionately pro-Wilson, and covered the speech extensively.

103. McCann, *A Pinnacle of Feeling*, p. 6.

104. The idea of burying one soldier whose remains could not be identified as a way of memorializing all soldiers who suffered this fate was pioneered in Britain in World War One, and became a memorial form duplicated across most of the belligerent nations. The American unknown was interred on Armistice Day in 1921, and stood in for the 4,500 American fatalities whose bodies were still unaccounted for on the French battlefields. See Steven Trout, *On the Battlefield of Memory: The First World War and American Remembrance, 1919–1941* (Tuscaloosa: University of Alabama Press, 2010), p. 130. Owing to its reliance on figurative representation, and because it hosted some of the most elaborate and complex national memorial services in the postwar period – which blended grief, national self-fashioning, and fructive possibilities for counternarratives to official versions of remembrance – the US Tomb of the Unknown Solider became a key location used by American authors to consider the legacy of the war. Work by John Dos Passos, William March, James Weldon Johnson, and Carl Sandburg, among others, treated this subject. See Trout, *On the Battlefield of Memory*, pp. 124–156; Benedict Anderson, *Imagined Communities: Reflections on the Origin and Spread of Nationalism*, rev. edn. (London: Verso, 1991); Marc Redfield, "Imagi-nation: The Imagined Community and the Aesthetics of Mourning," *Diacritics*, 29 (December 1999), 58–83, and my own work on how the unknown soldier became an important figure in African American literary memorializations of the conflict in *The Great War and the Culture of the New Negro*, pp. 191–213.

105. Trout, *On the Battlefield of Memory*, p. 136.

106. Kinder, *Paying with Their Bodies*, p. 195.

107. Ibid., p. 208.

108. "Belated Beginning," anon., *American Legion Weekly*, 4.16 (April 21, 1922), 10. Archive.legion.org. Accessed February 9, 2017.

109. Edward A. Hayes, "Address of Edward A. Hayes, National Commander, the American Legion, at the Service at the Tomb of the Unknown Soldier,

Arlington National Cemetery, Washington D.C., 11am, November 11, 1933." Archive.legion.org, accessed February 9, 2017.

110. Billy Rose, "The Unknown Soldier," in Hazel Felleman and Edward Frank Allen (eds.), *The Best-Loved Poems of the American People* (New York: Doubleday, 1936), pp. 428–429.

111. See, for example, the contemporary review in *The Outlook*, which opined that "In the end, it turned out not to be the 'war to end war' – nobody but these intellectuals thought it was – and so they have been writing articles, novels, and stories ever since to tell how 'disillusioned' they are now. *Plumes* is another of these novels." "The New Books: Fiction," *The Outlook*, 139.1 (1925), 35–37, p. 37.

112. Vincent, *The Health of the State*, p. 109.

113. Harold J. Laski, "Books and Things," the *New Republic*, 17.217 (December 28, 1918), 254.

114. "The Meaning of American Citizenship." Reprinted from *This Constitution: A Bicentennial Chronicle*, Fall 1985, published by Project '87 of the American Political Science Association and American Historical Association. Accessed at Academia.edu on March 2, 2017.

115. Stallings, "Whole Art," pp. 107–108.

116. Hirschmann and Linker, "Introduction," p. 10.

117. Lauren Berlant, *The Queen of America Goes to Washington City: Essays on Sex and Citizenship* (Durham, NC: Duke University Press, 1997), p. 27.

118. Citing Berlant, Emily Russell has proposed the more critical position of the "savvy citizen" as available to disabled veterans. Applying this to the disabled Vietnam War veteran Ron Kovic, Russell sees the savvy citizen as someone "who can identify naïveté and provide political critique." *Reading Embodied Citizenship*, p. 122.

119. *American Journal of Physical Medicine and Rehabilitation*, 49 (October 1925), 405; "Laurence Stallings," *Medical Journal and Record*, 121 (1925), 380.

Conclusion

1. Archibald MacLeish and Malcolm Cowley, "Lines for an Interment," the *New Republic*, 76 (September 20, 1933), 159–161, p. 159.

2. Ibid., p. 161.

3. Ibid.

4. Archibald MacLeish and Malcolm Cowley, "A Communication," the *New Republic*, 76 (October 4, 1933), 214–216, p. 216.

5. Ibid., p. 215.

6. Kenneth Burke, "War, Response, and Contradiction," in *The Philosophy of Literary Form: Studies in Symbolic Action* (Baton Rouge: Louisiana State University Press, 1941), pp. 234–257, 239.

7. Ibid., p. 240.

8. Ibid., p. 245.

9. Perry Anderson, "Modernity and Revolution," *New Left Review*, 1.144 (March–April 1984), 96–113, p. 105.

10. See Michael Rubenstein, Bruce Robbins, and Sophia Beal, "Infrastructuralism: An Introduction," *Modern Fiction Studies*, 61.4 (2015), 575–586.

11. Walter Lippmann, *A Preface to Morals* (New York: Macmillan, 1929), pp. 274–275.

12. Ibid., p. 275.

13. Chip Rhodes, *Structures of the Jazz Age: Mass Culture, Progressive Education, and Racial Disclosures in American Modernism* (London: Verso, 1998), p. 11. Rhodes' introduction well summarizes the history of the idea that the 1920s was an apolitical moment, but also surveys the considerable amount of scholarship in political and intellectual history that stresses the persistence of Progressive traditions in the decade.

14. Laurence Stallings, *Plumes* (1924) (Columbia: University of South Carolina Press, 2006), p. 156.

15. Ronald Reagan, "Inaugural Address," January 20, 1981. Online by Gerhard Peters and John T. Woolley, *The American Presidency Project*. Fredric Jameson, *An American Utopia: Dual Power and the Universal Army* (London: Verso, 2016), pp. 3, 25.

Index